CASES OF TEACHERS' DATA USE

Cases of Teachers' Data Use addresses applications of student data beyond theoretical, school-, and district-level examinations by presenting case studies of teachers' data use in practice. Within the context of data-driven education reform policies, the authors examine the effective and ineffective ways that teachers make use of student data in instruction, evaluation, and planning. Promising practices, based on the empirical research presented, offer strategies and routines for sound data use that can be applied in schools. Chapters written by scholars from diverse methodological perspectives offer readers multiple lenses to use in considering issues of data use such that current theoretical assumptions may be challenged and the field advanced. This uniquely focused yet comprehensive work is an indispensable resource for researchers and students interested in classroom assessment and for professionals looking to support teachers' use of student performance data for adaptive instruction.

Nicole Barnes is Associate Professor of Educational Foundations in the College of Education and Human Services at Montclair State University, USA.

Helenrose Fives is Professor of Educational Foundations in the College of Education and Human Services at Montclair State University, USA.

CASES OF TEACHERS' DATA USE

Edited by Nicole Barnes and Helenrose Fives

NEW YORK AND LONDON

First published 2018
by Routledge
711 Third Avenue, New York, NY 10017

and by Routledge
2 Park Square, Milton Park, Abingdon, Oxon, OX14 4RN

Routledge is an imprint of the Taylor & Francis Group, an informa business

© 2018 Taylor & Francis

The right of Nicole Barnes and Helenrose Fives to be identified as the authors of the editorial material, and of the authors for their individual chapters, has been asserted in accordance with sections 77 and 78 of the Copyright, Designs, and Patents Act of 1988.

All rights reserved. No part of this book may be reprinted or reproduced or utilized in any form or by any electronic, mechanical, or other means, now known or hereafter invented, including photocopying and recording, or in any information storage or retrieval system, without permission in writing from the publishers.

Trademark notice: product or corporate names may be trademarks or registered trademarks, and are used only for identification and explanation without intent to infringe.

Library of Congress Cataloging-in-Publication Data
A catalog record for this title has been requested

ISBN: 978-1-138-05639-8 (hbk)
ISBN: 978-1-138-05640-4 (pbk)
ISBN: 978-1-315-16537-0 (ebk)

Typeset in Bembo
by Apex CoVantage, LLC

CONTENTS

List of Contributors   *vii*
Foreword   *x*
Preface   *xiv*

1 Context for Data Use and the Emergence of Promising Practices   1
  Andrea Conklin Bueschel

2 Teachers' Practice-Based Data Use Strategies   15
  Helenrose Fives and Nicole Barnes

3 Following the Path of Greatest Persistence: Sensemaking, Data Use, and the Everyday Practice of Teaching   30
  Carolyn J. Riehl, Hester Earle, Pavithra Nagarajan, Tara E. Schwitzman, and Laura Vernikoff

4 Using a Learning Trajectory to Make Sense of Student Work for Instruction   44
  Caroline B. Ebby

5	From Focusing on Grades to Exploring Student Thinking: A Case Study of Change in Assessment Practice *Stephanie Rafanelli, Hilda Borko, Matthew Kloser, and Matthew Wilsey*	63
6	Using Data Meaningfully to Teach for Understanding in Middle-School Science *Melissa Braaten, Chris Bradford, Sadie Fox Barocas, and Kathryn L. Kirchgasler*	80
7	Using Standardized-Test Data as a Starting Point for Inquiry: A Case of Thoughtful Compliance *Brette Garner and Ilana Horn*	96
8	Beyond Matchmaking: Considering Aims for Teacher Data Use *Margaret Evans, Priya LaLonde, Nora Gannon-Slater, Hope Crenshaw, Rebecca Teasdale, Jennifer Green, and Thomas Schwandt*	112
9	Moving Beyond Academic Achievement: Using Nonacademic Data to Identify and Support Struggling Students *Tammy Kolbe, Katharine G. Shepherd, and Jonathan Sessions*	128
10	"Everyone's Responsibility": Effective Team Collaboration and Data Use *Amanda Datnow, Vicki Park, and Bailey Choi*	145
11	Adjustment in Practice: A Critical Response to Data-Driven Instruction *Nora M. Isacoff, Dana Karin, and Joseph P. McDonald*	162
12	Promising Practices of Data Use for Literacy and Language Development of Kindergarten Students *Tonya R. Moon, Catherine M. Brighton, Jordan M. Buckrop, Kerrigan Mahoney, and Marcia A. Invernizzi*	176
Index		*193*

CONTRIBUTORS

Nicole Barnes
Montclair State University
Educational Foundations

Sadie Fox Barocas
University of Wisconsin Madison
Curriculum and Instruction

Hilda Borko
Stanford University
Graduate School of Education

Melissa Braaten
University of Colorado Boulder
School of Education

Chris Bradford
University of Wisconsin Madison
Curriculum and Instruction

Catherine M. Brighton
University of Virginia
Curriculum, Instruction, and Special Education

Jordan M. Buckrop
University of Virginia
Educational Leadership, Policy, and Foundations

Andrea Conklin Bueschel
Northwestern University
Office of the Provost

Bailey Choi
University of California, San Diego
Education Studies

Hope Crenshaw
Teen Health Mississippi

Amanda Datnow
University of California, San Diego
Education Studies

Hester Earle
Teachers College, Columbia University
Education Policy and Social Analysis

Contributors

Caroline B. Ebby
University of Pennsylvania
Consortium for Policy Research in Education

Margaret Evans
Illinois Wesleyan University
Educational Studies

Helenrose Fives
Montclair State University
Educational Foundations

Nora Gannon-Slater
Breakthrough Schools
Performance and Data Analytics

Brette Garner
Vanderbilt University
Teaching and Learning

Jennifer Green
University of Illinois at Urbana-Champaign
Educational Psychology

Ilana Horn
Vanderbilt University
Teaching and Learning

Marcia A. Invernizzi
University of Virginia
Curriculum, Instruction, and Special Education

Nora M. Isacoff
New York University
Teaching and Learning

Dana Karin
New York University
Teaching and Learning

Kathryn L. Kirchgasler
The University of Kansas
Curriculum and Teaching

Matthew Kloser
University of Notre Dame
Notre Dame Center for STEM Education

Tammy Kolbe
University of Vermont
Leadership and Policy Studies

Priya LaLonde
Georgetown University
Educational Transformation

Kerrigan Mahoney
University of Virginia
Leadership, Foundations, and Policy

Joseph P. McDonald
New York University
Teaching and Learning

Tonya R. Moon
University of Virginia
Educational Leadership, Policy, and Foundations

Pavithra Nagarajan
Teachers College, Columbia University
Education Policy and Social Analysis

Vicki Park
San Jose State University
Educational Leadership

Stephanie Rafanelli
Stanford University
Graduate School of Education

Carolyn J. Riehl
Teachers College, Columbia University
Education Policy and Social Analysis

Thomas Schwandt
University of Illinois at Urbana-Champaign
Educational Psychology; Educational Policy, Organization, and Leadership

Tara E. Schwitzman
Teachers College, Columbia University
Curriculum and Teaching

Jonathan Sessions
University of Vermont
Educational Leadership and Policy Studies

Katharine G. Shepherd
University of Vermont
Education

James Spillane
Northwestern University
Human Development and Social Policy; Learning Sciences

Rebecca Teasdale
University of Illinois at Urbana-Champaign
Educational Psychology

Laura Vernikoff
Teachers College, Columbia University
Curriculum and Teaching

Matthew Wilsey
University of Notre Dame
Center for STEM Education

FOREWORD

Data use and data-based decision-making have become all the rage over the past decade or more, in the education sector. Whether used as a popular refrain for rallying the school-reform troops or advanced as yet another remedy to cure all that ails our nation's schools, data use and data-based decision-making have gained considerable traction among philanthropists, policymakers, practitioners, and even the public. The trendiness of data is not unique to the education sector; data use and data-based decision-making have become fashionable (requirements) in several other nonprofit and for-profit sectors, popularized and sometimes incentivized by social reformers. Though lionized by some, while censured by others, data use in and of itself is of course neither good nor bad, though such a dispassionate position is increasingly difficult to maintain among academics hungry for the media spotlight and where positioning oneself either "for" or "against" is often the price of media "airtime" (Henig, 2008). Keeping an open mind on data use can also be difficult in an academy where usefulness is often confused with taking a position (whether on the right or left of the political spectrum, or in the center) and then doing research to advance that position. The authors of the chapters in this volume eschew such simplistic and problematic scholarship and, in so doing, offer rich empirical insights into data use and data-based decision-making on the ground—the micro-processes of decision-making about teaching and learning, and the role of data and other sorts of information therein.

The chapters that follow examine data use in situ—*in practice* inside schools and classrooms. Focusing on whether and how teachers use data in their everyday practice is critical in understanding the data-based decision-making trend. Considering data use from the perspective of practice in schools and classrooms, the book offers interesting empirical insights into how data and other types of information get noticed, taken up, and used (or not) and to what purpose by practitioners on the ground. In examining data use from the perspective of practice, the authors underscore that data don't speak for themselves! What is critical is how teachers notice what data (and other types of information) and how they understand what they notice in their everyday work practice. In this way, the book challenges the "policy" folklore, that the data say which of any competing options might be optimal. Instead, the chapters capture the complexity of making decisions about instruction *with* data (and other information) in everyday practice.

The book also attends nicely to the "collective" nature of practice, foregrounding in several chapters how teachers make decisions with data *in interaction* with colleagues (and school and system leaders, either directly or indirectly). This is important because it challenges accounts that equate practice with individual behavior and, in so doing, gets us away from thinking about improving the practice of instructional decision-making purely in terms of incentivizing individuals or building their individual capability. The challenge of transforming practice is rather different when it is conceptualized in terms of interactions, rather than individual actions (Spillane, 2012). Some chapters also highlight how teachers do not interact with one another in a vacuum, but, rather, within a social structure that both enables and constrains their interactions—how they negotiate what data to notice and value, and the meanings of these data for teaching and learning. Aspects of the social structure of classrooms, schools, and school systems, including (but not limited to): rules/regulations/policies (e.g., mandates of various sorts), formal positions (e.g., facilitators), organizational routines (e.g., data teams, grade-level teams), various tools (e.g., standardized-test data), and so on are important in that they influence how teachers interact with one another about instruction and the value of different sorts of data therein. In making instructional decisions, school staff interact with one another using these aspects of their social structure—what my colleagues and I refer to as "educational infrastructure" (Cohen, Spillane, & Peurach, under review; Hopkins & Spillane, 2015). A school and school system's educational infrastructure both enables and constrains teacher interactions about teaching (Spillane, Hopkins, & Sweet, 2017) and, as some of these chapters capture, whether, how, and what sorts of data are used in these interactions.

Attending carefully to practice, the authors identify various ways in which teachers use data in their everyday decision-making about teaching and learning, identifying approaches or strategies that contribute to the interpretation and use of data for instructional decision-making, such as curriculum-embedded assessments, using tracking systems and learning trajectories, contextualizing, jointly examining student data with colleagues, and deliberating together on various beliefs, practices, and the use of data (among other topics). In doing so, the chapters offer important practical knowledge for teachers, as well as school and system leaders struggling to improve decision-making in general and working to encourage decision-making about instruction that is informed by data. Further, the book offers insights into how schools and school systems, mandated to engage in data-based decision-making about instruction, might minimize the pitfalls and maximize the benefits of using data in making decisions about instruction. Another contribution here is suggesting that data use in instructional decision-making will also depend, in important measure, on educational infrastructure and its redesign; simply mandating that teachers use data or participate in data teams is insufficient, if the goal of school reformers is to get teachers to use data so that they make better instructional decisions.

Reflecting on this manuscript and some other recent writings on data use (Prøitz, Mausethagen, & Skedsmo, 2017), including some of my own work, I have found it helpful to consider my own use of data in everyday decision-making. For those of us interested in data use and data-based decision-making, "pressing the pause button" and reflecting just briefly on our own everyday experiences with using data is instructive. Consider how we all, even the most critical of scholars among us, have taken rather effortlessly and easily to using data in our own everyday decision-making. Yes, of course, as academics, we consider data of all sorts in making decisions about student admissions, tenure and hiring, and the appeal of a new job offer—GPAs, GREs, h-index, *U.S. News & World Report* rankings of various programs, and so on (Sauder & Espeland, 2009). But let's dwell on the more mundane decisions for a moment. Recall the last time you were considering where to have dinner when traveling out of town. Most us very likely consulted TripAdvisor or Google (or perhaps some other more fashionable rating system) for deciding where to eat, pondering the pros of a 4.1 over a 3.8 rating. I suspect most of us used some sort of data in making our decision about where to dine. Yes, if you are a qualitative data nerd like me, you likely also sometimes read the written reviews, especially if a decision is difficult based on the metrics alone, but that often contributes to an even more difficult decision.

Data seduce us all, and data are especially seductive when they come in forms that enable us to easily consume and compare similar entities using the "same" rating scale: it easily and effortlessly pervades our everyday decision-making, even when no one mandates us to use particular data in our decision-making. Of course, these (data-based) metrics hide a multitude, simplifying much and masking important complexity (Espeland & Sauder, 2007). The lessons I take from this everyday example are two. First, we have easily and effortlessly become avid consumers of data in our own everyday decision-making as data metrics have become ubiquitous. Second, these metrics have, in many respects, become institutionalized, in that no one tells us or even has to remind us, let alone require us, to use them. We have all become, relatively easily, complicit in the data-use and data-based decision-making rage—whether for good or bad, or out of indifference.

James P. Spillane
Spencer T. & Ann W. Olin
Professor of Learning & Organizational Change
Northwestern University
Chicago, IL, September 2017

References

Cohen, D., Spillane, J. P., & Peurach, D. (under review). Educational reform as system building. *Educational Researcher.*

Espeland, W. N., & Sauder, M. (2007). Rankings and reactivity: How public measures recreate social worlds. *American Journal of Sociology, 113*(1), 1–40.

Henig, J. R. (2008). *Spin cycle: How research gets used in policy debates: The case of charter schools.* New York, NY: Russell Sage Foundation.

Hopkins, M., & Spillane, J. P. (2015). Conceptualizing relations between instructional guidance infrastructure (IGI) and teachers' beliefs about mathematics instruction: Regulative, normative, and cultural-cognitive considerations. *Journal of Educational Change, 16*(4), 421–450.

Prøitz, T. S., Mausethagen, S., & Skedsmo, G. (2017). Data use in education: Alluring attributes and productive processes. *Nordic Journal of Studies in Education Policy, 3*(1), 1–5.

Sauder, M., & Espeland, W. N. (2009). The discipline of rankings: Tight coupling and organizational change. *American Sociological Review, 74*(20), 63–82.

Spillane, J. P. (2012). Data in practice: Conceptualizing the data-based decision-making phenomena. *American Journal of Education, 118*(2), 113–141.

Spillane, J. P., Hopkins, M., & Sweet, T. (2015). Intra-and interschool interactions about instruction: Exploring the conditions for social capital development. *American Journal of Education, 122*(1), 71–110.

Spillane, J. P., Hopkins, M., & Sweet, T. (In press). School district educational infrastructure and change at scale: Teacher peer interactions and their beliefs about mathematics instruction. *American Educational Research Journal.*

PREFACE

In spring 2014, we (Helenrose Fives and Nicole Barnes) learned that we were the recipients of a grant from the Spencer Foundation for their special call, titled *Evidence for the Classroom (EFC): Investigating Whether, When, and How Student Performance Data Inform Instruction*. The evolution of this grant program and its administration are detailed in Chapter 1 of this book, however, of note for this edited volume, Spencer organized annual meetings for all the grant recipients. The purpose of these meetings was to discuss progress on our grants, common findings, and obstacles we faced studying data use in schools. As a cohort and in small groups, we helped each other problem solve challenges and pushed one another to define and refine our conceptualizations and theories. It was a community of scholars. By our second yearly meeting, we were all knee deep in our particular research projects. The projects varied by grade level, subject areas, and state contexts. Despite such differences, some trends started to emerge. Inspired to find some commonalities, we approached Andrea Bueschel, the Senior Program Director and meeting facilitator for the Spencer Foundation, with an idea to organize an edited volume on the research funded by the EFC. Supportive of the idea, Andrea challenged us to think about how we might structure such a book, and what the particular focus might be. We spent the next year continuing our own work, learning more about our fellow grantees' work, and thinking about the common threads across the projects. What became clear by our third annual meeting was that, amid the complex and expansive findings about classroom-level data use, some of which were disheartening, there were glimmers of *promising practices*. We had it!

We started with the premise that teachers are *expected* to engage in data use to make instructional decisions and that this process should improve teaching and student learning (Data Quality Campaign, 2009; US DOE, 2009). Far from groundbreaking, this expectation has been articulated in national reform initiatives (e.g., No Child Left Behind; U.S. DOE, 2002) and state and national teaching standards (e.g., American Federation of Teachers, National Council on Measurement in Education, & National Education Association, 1990; Council of Chief State School Officers, 2012; National Council for the Accreditation of Teacher Education, 2010). Less known is how this expectation manifests in real classrooms. Namely, *how* teachers understand and use data in authentic contexts, including what practices those individuals use that might help others interested in pursuing or already engaged in data use efforts. To understand this, each chapter depicts a case of a teacher or group of teachers as they use student data for a variety of practice activities, including instruction, evaluation, and planning (both long and short term). Moreover, the authors offer recommendations and strategies, all derived empirically from their research projects. The case studies described in each chapter can serve as examples for those in teacher preparation and teacher development, or as a starting point for current or new scholars to better examine teachers' data use practices in ways that will allow for the identification of avenues for future research.

In the first chapter, Bueschel explains how the initiation of this grant program was situated in the recognition that the field was experiencing key policy and research shifts. The chapters that follow are empirical studies generated by scholars funded through this program. Authors offer detailed descriptions of teachers' data use strategies that emerged from classroom practice (Fives & Barnes, Chapter 1; Riehl, Earle, Nagarrajan, Schwitzman, & Vernikoff, Chapter 3) as well as teachers' responses to interventions intended to facilitate data use (Ebby, Chapter 4; Rafanelli, Borko, Kloser, & Wilsey, Chapter 5). These chapters provide insight into what teachers, who are on the front line of data use, do to gather, organize, analyze, and, ultimately, use data in their daily practice.

The next four chapters provide insight into data use by teacher teams. Middle-level content-area teams were explored in science (Bratten, Bradford, Kirchgasler, & Barocas, Chapter 6) and mathematics (Horn, Garner, Kane, Applegate, Wilson, & Brasel, Chapter 7). These chapters describe how teachers collaboratively developed strategies for data use and analysis, and made shared decisions about data use in relation to larger goals, such as overall math or science instruction. Alternatively, some teams spanned grade levels and content areas (Evans et al., Chapter 8; Kolbe, Shepherd, & Salembier, Chapter 9; Datnow & Parc, Chapter 10). In these chapters, the authors explain the challenge and potential for collaboration among teachers, related to student data.

The final chapters focus on the data use interactions of teachers with district- and school-level administrators (Isacoff, Karin, & McDonald, Chapter 11; Moon, Brighton, Invernizzi, Buckrop, & Mahoney, Chapter 12). The cases described in these final chapters provide insight into the ways that district-level policy initiatives for data use get instantiated in classroom practice.

The chapters of this book provide a complex picture of data use that is contextualized by school, district, state, and national policy expectations. Moreover, data are used by individual teachers or groups of teachers in a variety of effective and ineffective ways. These authors do not present data use as a panacea for educational interventions, but they do provide specific examples of strategies and practices used by teachers and teacher groups that can lead to adaptive educational actions for all learners.

Nicole Barnes and Helenrose Fives
Montclair State University

Note

We contributed equally to the editing of this book. We rotate order of authorship in our scholarship.

1

CONTEXT FOR DATA USE AND THE EMERGENCE OF PROMISING PRACTICES

Andrea Conklin Bueschel

> Is this data deluge making a difference?
>
> —Melissa Roderick (2012, p. 5)

It was not that long ago that the word dashboard was associated primarily with cars. In the short time since then, dashboards have become one way among many to display data. In recent years, educators have encountered data dashboards, data walls, data reports color-coded by student performance, data tables, data growth timelines, and assessments of all flavors—benchmark, interim, formative, summative. There are as many ways to communicate data as there are data. Measuring student performance is not new. So, what changed? There is no single explanation for the proliferation of education data, or any other data for that matter, though the ability to collect, aggregate, and distribute it got much easier and much faster with technological advances. And growing trends for greater accountability in schools, from No Child Left Behind to district mandates, meant there was an outlet for the data that were being generated. Data—whatever that meant for whoever chose to use them—became self-justifying. If we have data, then of course we should use data. Even if "use" meant a lot of different things to a lot of different people. Educational data are out there—in classrooms, schools, district offices, state departments, and the federal government. So what? Depending on who you ask, they are either the solution to all of our problems or the bane of our existence. Can both these things be true?

Given the strong opinions that have formed around educational data and their possible use, it is worth seeking out research that might speak to the benefits and pitfalls of using educational data. About a decade ago, several of us did just that. We worked at the Spencer Foundation, a research organization, and decided to dig into this then-emerging phenomenon around data and education, exploring whether there might be an opportunity to learn. We were not the only ones trying to understand more, of course; we were not even the only foundation venturing into these waters. There was a range of foundations that had a range of goals in engaging the topic. Although most funders would say that improving outcomes for students was a goal, they differed in how they thought they could foster that improvement. As a research foundation, our contribution was likely to be in funding high-quality, peer-reviewed research projects that could provide a knowledge base to inform policy, practice, and additional research, and that was our focus.

This opening chapter has a different tone from the rest of the volume, reflecting the opportunity to address an interesting moment in educational improvement efforts and how different actors have tried to influence that improvement. My goal in writing this chapter is to help frame the thinking around research-based efforts, to understand how data of different types get used in educational settings, for better and worse. There are lots of approaches to this topic, and my vantage point is that of a former foundation officer who had the privilege of witnessing the inception of a new effort, which is why I use the first person. In recounting some of the early thinking, the hope is that you, the reader, can see how this work has evolved, culminating in the excellent studies featured in later chapters of this volume. The efforts described in this chapter represent input from a wide range of colleagues and friends; it has been a collaborative effort from the beginning. In this chapter, I share some background and rationale for the foundation research initiatives (there were two phases of funding in this area), frame the important concepts that have shaped it, and offer some thoughts about how the work might continue into the future.

Background and Rationale[1]

At a research foundation, any new initiative or project should be informed by research. As stewards of an endowment, foundation staff have the responsibility of trying to place good bets, recognizing there is risk in any investment. Our process included a great deal of reading, interviewing, and convening of talented scholars. We also contracted with an expert faculty member who partnered with us in that early work. The process of exploration and development was most greatly informed by a group of 15 scholars whom we commissioned to write background papers and whom we convened three times over the course of a year.[2] We cast the net quite wide at the beginning, trying to get a sense of where there was an existing research base that could be built upon and where there was opportunity to seed some entirely new work. Some of our early thinking addressed broad questions about what might constitute data and data use, what settings it happened in, and who might be the user in any given situation. These might be considered the "what" questions; we did not even know what was known or even knowable. Just as important, we did not have preset notions about what any of it should be. We were agnostic, but eager to learn more.

As we learned more and began to appreciate the complexity of the issues, we became motivated by more probing "how" and "why" questions: What kind of educational improvement can the use of data achieve? How? Under what conditions? Why might change be happening? How are those efforts aided or hindered? It was clear to us that there was something there to pursue, and we began to develop the outline of a funding initiative. Addressing these questions in a more formal way necessitated a framework that could provide greater clarity about different concepts and account for important organizational factors that affect improvement processes.

If the goal is improving student learning, one's conception of better schooling is a powerful force for shaping the conditions under which certain data might be used toward that end. For example, if one's idea of better schooling is an integrated curriculum and pedagogy supplemented by regular, aligned formative assessments, the type of data (low stakes and diagnostic) and how they are used (to improve student understanding of a topic) will be quite different from a vision that favors an external policy lever of a test-based accountability system that equates better schooling with improved student test results on high-stakes, summative assessments. Both examples may share the same goal—improved student outcomes—but the approaches to improvement, and which data are used in what way, are quite different. We wanted to delve more deeply into those different kinds of uses to better understand what motivates the process of data use, what conditions facilitate or constrain that use, how the process is enacted, and what effects there are on the improvement goal.

We found many important reasons to study data use. In the past decade, data use, in various forms, has become one of the dominant strategies for educational improvement—promoted by federal and state policies, funded by multiple foundations, and supported by a raft of external organizations and consultants. These practice and policy initiatives have gotten far ahead of the research, and these activities alone justified support of high-quality research in this area.

More compelling, however, was the fact that using data was already a fundamental part of the work of educators at multiple levels of the educational system, and there was and still is much to be learned from existing practices and efforts at improving educational outcomes. Not only is data use touted as a part of those practices and efforts, it is also part and parcel of the daily work of people at every level in educational settings. Teachers are constantly checking for understanding, using formative assessments from various sources, discussing test scores, and drawing on a wide range of information to individually and collectively decide upon next steps. School leaders observe classrooms, look at test performance, and evaluate teachers based on formal metrics as they make decisions about teacher placement, student placement, and improvement initiatives. District leaders draw on evidence from schools—a range of process and outcome measures, and information from the environment—as they design professional development, make curriculum decisions, develop improvement initiatives, and respond to and implement state and federal policies. Even higher education has engaged in more standardized assessments than a generation ago, and clicker technology in college classrooms is no longer a novelty. As these examples highlight, there is a full spectrum of data, uses, and users, and we wanted to be open to all of them as we launched our work in this area.

We often think of data as being formalized and part of a specific program, or the use of data as a separate and discrete process. But it is actually a deep and interwoven part of the day-to-day work of people throughout the system. Educators are constantly making attributions about the nature of the problem, discerning potential solutions, and acting on these interpretations. These meaning making processes can be more or less systematic, more or less collective, more or less expert, and more or less helpful in improving one's practice and student learning. Regardless, our thinking at the time was: if we better understand these processes, if we better understand how people engage with data and make meaning of it, if we understand how that fits into overall patterns or action, and how that is shaped by tools, routines, and organizational conditions, we can better understand how to help people meet the goals of educational improvement. Data use was already happening in all kinds of formal and informal ways, and we thought a focused effort to study it—using a conceptual framework that keeps the focus on the many factors influencing it—would strengthen those efforts and recommend other and perhaps better ways to do so. It seemed possible that many educational problems could benefit from a deliberate and effective use of data, and we thought an initiative like this would have the potential to inform some of those problems and possible solutions.

Concepts

As we dug into existing research and engaged with scholars and practitioners in a range of settings, it was clear that there was inconsistency surrounding various concepts. Like a Rorschach ink blot, people saw what was meaningful for them. It was helpful for us to wrestle with and try to articulate what we meant, for the purposes of this program, thinking a lot about the key concepts that might inform the research funded in the initiative. We did not want to be overly prescriptive in this initial phase of funding, but we also wanted to signal the general scope of how we thought about the work. Initially, we focused on data, data use, educational improvement, and the overall framework for this first initiative, all of which evolved over the course of the program.

Data

At the time, we conceived of data broadly, thinking they must be considered in terms of context and the background of those engaging with them, for them to have meaning. Data, as a term, is often interchanged with information, evidence, and even knowledge, though we did not treat those as equivalents. Data might be thought of most simply as representations of information. Evidence might best be thought of as data marshaled for a position or argument.

Data Use

The focus on data *use* was an attempt to draw attention to what happens when educators actually encounter or engage with data of various kinds. In many cases, attention, funding, and the limited research at the time focused on the production of data, often with an advocacy stance that supported increased production and some (often implicit) version of use that may or may not have aligned with existing practices and organizational functions. The most attention-getting version of data use in early stages of educational-data movements was a unidirectional flow of data (usually standardized-assessment results) from an external entity (most often state or district offices) to teachers or administrators at the school site. Those individuals were supposed to—somehow—"use" those data in ways that led to change, most often in student achievement outcomes. In fact, however, we knew very little about what happens at this stage. How do practitioners make sense of the data? What capacities allow them to better understand and apply them? In what ways do basic practices—especially teaching and learning—change? These are all very important questions, especially in light of the various pressures to increase production and use. We conceived of data use as a process best understood as embedded in organizational structures, cultures, norms, and routines. This process is affected not only by those organizational factors but also by the knowledge, background, and expertise of those engaging in it.

Educational Improvement

There are so many ways to conceive of educational improvement, from increased student-achievement scores to improved retention of teachers to reduced school violence to getting vendors paid in a timely fashion. Each of these areas is worthy of attention and resources, and can be a source of improvement. For our purposes, we limited our concept of educational improvement to improvements in schooling or, more specifically, improvements in teaching and learning. Although there were still lots of directions to go, even within teaching and learning, this choice provided some boundaries that gave us a better chance to learn, even with our relatively limited resources to devote to these issues.

Framework for the Initiative

This initiative had its roots in the foundation's work in organizational learning, which informed our thinking about how data might be used for educational improvement. In the most generic version of organizational learning, the use of information is often stressed, especially for decision-making that leads to change and, ideally, improvement. Although we did not frame data use simply as decision-making (or, in the current parlance, data-driven decision-making), there is an element of determining what to actually do with data in educational settings, how to apply what might be learned from data to one's practice. Continuous improvement is, as the name suggests, an ongoing process that incorporates data that can inform actions and decisions. Those actions and decisions are then assessed, adjustments are made based on that new information, and the cycle continues. This process does not map perfectly to every educational setting, but our intention was to highlight an ongoing improvement process and the role that both individuals and organizations can play in it.

Perhaps the most important way that we used the larger framework of organizational learning is that we did not consider data—in whatever form—in a vacuum. Data of any kind have no meaning without knowing the context and actors involved. An organizational learning framework keeps other key factors on the table, including organizational structure, leadership, organizational culture, and available tools and resources. For example, if someone wanted to do a social-network analysis of how new data were shared between teachers and which teachers were most likely to be sources or conduits of that information, we still expected the study to account for things like the organizational structure (i.e., what formal role each person in the network held and where they were physically located) and the culture (i.e., whether collaboration was encouraged).

We decided to call the initiative "Data Use and Educational Improvement." At the risk of being labeled too esoteric, the "and" was important to us. We deliberately chose not to use the word "for" because we were concerned it would signal that we already knew that using data led to better outcomes. When we announced the initiative, we received lots of interest, not only from potential grantees but also from other funders who had gotten into this space. Several of them had staked out an advocacy position, funding projects and programs to increase the collection and distribution of data to educators. Although we chose a different approach, understanding their perspective helped us appreciate the environment we were entering.

Early Efforts: Data Use and Educational Improvement

In one sense, the goal of the first initiative was simple, if not easy: support high-quality research that has the potential to affect policy, practice, theory, and other research. More specifically, we thought it valuable to be able to make some claims about certain conditions, interventions, or strategies that seem to help educators improve teaching and learning. These are not easy claims to make, as there are lots of factors to address, and we were not in a position to support huge, multiyear experimental trials. But figuring out what we could say, in part by selecting the right lines of research to focus on, could help us achieve that goal. In this way, the work could then inform practitioners and policy makers, who are in the position of using data, about the processes and mechanisms that might best lead to improvement.

Our hope was that a consistent focus on situating the use of specific types of data in a larger context of educational improvement could shift the focus of some of the national conversations away from an oversimplified theory of action about how educators use data (i.e., if you put data in front of them, they will "use" it in a way that leads to improvement, regardless of context). Although of course not every effort to promote data use is that simple, it is clear that, too often, the relevant contextual and individual aspects of how educators work has not been given sufficient attention. So, what happened?

We announced that we would be funding research studies informed by the concepts described previously, and we got a strong response. The initial proposals for funding ran the gamut, and we learned a great deal from them about how people thought about different forms of data and their use. We funded 16 small and large grants over a three-year period, and they focused on everything from data coaches to the citywide data system in New York City to data literacy to how data might improve outcomes in higher education. Researchers were creative, persistent, and clever, making the most of the resources we provided. Additionally, the projects were sprinkled across the landscape, which made it hard to make any claims beyond the very specific settings each studied. We were pleased with the quality and energy in these first grants. We also knew that if we were to be able to help educators and make contributions to the larger literature, we needed to tighten our focus.

Evidence for the Classroom

Having had the benefit of going through several cycles of funding on data use, more generally, we were able to return to the literature and background work with a fresh perspective and appreciation for some of the challenges. Our biggest learning was that, for us to be able to have some impact beyond the success of an individual study, we needed a tighter focus. Inevitably, it is difficult to let go of the full range of excellent ideas and projects we knew people would have. But we wanted to be strategic about investing the foundation's resources in a way that would create a body of work that could better inform this trend around data use, which had grown even larger than when we started.

Since we knew we did not have all the good ideas, we once again consulted our talented colleagues in the field—researchers and practitioners. We vetted concepts, incorporated feedback, and eventually drafted an RFP that we had reviewed by a dozen or more critical friends.[3] There were a few key shifts in our focus. First, we narrowed our definition of data to student-performance data, ideally formative-assessment data. Although we knew there were more informal and idiosyncratic versions of data that could be learned from, we thought our ability to make broader claims would hinge on data that were more widely used.[4] We also chose the word "evidence" to signal the interpretive role required to make data evidence.

We focused more tightly on the users of those data, and we chose teachers themselves. It seemed clear to us that these were the key players in any data-use effort, and as we noted in the RFP: "We want to better understand the microprocesses and stages of the data use process that occur when teachers adjust their teaching as a response to different kinds of student performance data." It seemed clear to us that what research had been done focused on early stages of data use. Also from the RFP: "Previous research on data use tells us more about the early stages of the process—how data are generated and what access teachers have to that data—than the crucial later stages in which teachers interpret, analyze, and apply data-based knowledge to ongoing practice (Marsh, 2012; Means, Padilla, & Gallagher, 2010)." Our hope was that studies we funded would really delve deeply into teachers' lived experiences with data, accounting for their background and expertise (Little, 2012).

Finally, we did not want to lose sight of what we called the organizational conditions of data use. This could be interpreted widely, but our focus was on various organizational factors—structure, infrastructure, leadership, collaboration, resources, accountability environment, and any other context that might influence how data are used or not. Earlier research suggested that organizational factors were instrumental in influencing how different types of data were used and to what end (e.g., Marsh, 2012; Spillane, 2012).

We also spent a long time deciding whether to restrict the scope, in terms of population studied. After much debate, we decided to limit the population of teachers studied to those teaching from kindergarten to eighth grade, in hopes of balancing competing needs. Our sense was that the proliferation of standardized data had been focused primarily on this population, so there would still be plenty of choice. We also hoped that narrowing the focus somewhat would aid our desire to be able to make stronger claims across this more limited population.

There were a couple of things we did not change though, and these were primarily philosophical. First, the foundation has for most of its existence, been of the mind that the best ideas come from the field. That is, we did not assume we had all the answers, and the foundation has funded an incredibly wide range of good ideas relating to education that have been wholly generated by scholars. Although we wanted to limit the scope of this initiative in ways that served our impact goals, we still very much wanted for researchers to have the latitude to act creatively in responding to the call. We knew we could not anticipate all of the ways smart people might answer the questions we were posing, so we wanted to preserve some of that field-initiated spirit.

The other thing we did not want to lose, with this new call, was our learning stance. Although we had learned plenty from our first efforts at funding in this area, we certainly did not think we had data use issues solved. One way we tried to signal our openness to any findings was with the initiative title—"Evidence for the Classroom: Investigating whether, when, and how student performance data inform instruction." The "whether, when, and how" were important to us, and we hoped those words would signal that we did not expect findings to affirm only positive outcomes of data use.

Another way we tried to signal our learning stance was by creating cohorts of grantees that we planned to convene at least once a year, for the duration of their grants. Given this relatively new research space, we thought a learning community of scholars would help foster the knowledge base. (I discuss grantee meetings later on.) We also hoped that it would signal that we did not want performances from grantees where we only heard good news. Part of our learning, and what might grow the field, was understanding what was hard about this kind of research, about the challenges scholars face in tackling these big questions. With other grants, we have been happy to trust PIs to execute their work without oversight. We did not want to micromanage the Evidence for the Classroom (EFC) grantees, but we thought there was an opportunity to learn as a group in a way not afforded by our other grants.

To get some sense of the approach and rationale for the RFP, I include some of the opening paragraphs here, starting with the overall question guiding the initiative:

> *How do K-8 teachers use student performance data for instructional decisions and how do organizational and individual factors affect that use? . . .* We think the time is right to advance a research agenda that deepens our understanding of how and under what conditions teachers use data for instructional improvement. In the current educational environment, there is much attention to gathering and analyzing student data, and considerably less to whether and how teachers can use these data. There are many people and institutions—including the federal government—that have committed significant resources to creating and maintaining systems to collect student performance data (most often summative, year-end test scores) and to generate analyses for schools and teachers across the country, usually at the K-12 level. Those who promote data use are optimistic not just about better accountability but also improved student outcomes. School districts across the country, as well as school systems outside the US, are investing in systems to create or enhance access to these sorts of data. Some are embarking on training to encourage teachers, principals, and district leaders to integrate attention to data in their ongoing practice.
>
> Despite the resources devoted to promoting the use of student data and the investments in data systems to generate and analyze that data, there is a dearth of high-quality research on how teachers use data and what effects data use can have on teaching and learning. A recent review of the research

base on the use of data explains, "In many ways, the practice of data use is out ahead of research. Policy and interventions to promote data use far outstrip research studying the process, context, and consequences of these efforts. But the fact that there is so much energy promoting data use and so many districts and schools that are embarking on data use initiatives means conditions are ripe for systematic, empirical study" (Coburn & Turner, 2011, p. 200).

Behind the movement for greater data use are some common assumptions, especially about teachers' use of data. Some are individual-level assumptions—that educators will have the right skills to interpret the data and the capacity and expertise to respond to those data in ways that improve their instructional practice and outcomes for students. Other assumptions are infrastructural—that there are tools and systems in place to ensure teachers will have access to the right kind of data, when it is most needed. Others are structural—that schools and curricula are organized in such a way as to promote the use of data and the development of capacity to use data and to foster professional learning communities that support both of these goals.

Among both educators and researchers, there is a growing awareness that we need to investigate what is behind these assumptions. We are interested both in what normally occurs in classrooms and in promising strategies for improvement in these settings, and we want to understand better the many influences that affect how data *can* be used and how they actually *are* used in the service of improving instruction. Until we gain an understanding of how such factors combine to support or undermine effective data use for the improvement of instruction and student learning, efforts promoting data use are less likely to have the positive impact they could.

In this RFP, we tried to bring together much of what we had learned up to that point. You can see our effort to maintain some impartiality while still being clear that we think there is still plenty to learn. And we learned! Next, I write about some of our early takeaways from the proposal process and early grantee meetings.

The EFC Projects and the Learning Community

Our learning took several forms and was ongoing. We got authorization to fund two rounds of the EFC initiative, and, even before we had announced the call for the second round, we were trying to learn from the first. A few insights came even then and only grew in prominence as we moved forward. It was clear that the focus on teachers was key. The best proposals were powerful in making the case for the importance of input from teachers, to ensure their voices were part of the research. Although we had originally thought mostly about individual teachers and their decisions, these proposals helped us appreciate collective efforts, formal and informal, like faculty inquiry groups and professional learning communities, structures that had existed in different ways over the years, but which might have added value in this new data world. These proposals also did not shy away from the complexity of data use and the various factors that might influence it. Very similar processes can look completely different depending on the setting and the individuals engaging in them.

One thing we looked for and found in the strongest proposals was the understanding and application of theory. These proposals used theory as a lens to understand the problem, as a framework for situating their research design, and as an analytic tool to make sense of findings. Researchers who neglected theory or applied it as an afterthought were not successful in our process. And we wanted a good rationale for the tools and measures proposed. Given the deep "how" and "why" questions we were interested in (and given that the funding limits were relatively low, at $300,000 per study), we were impressed that there was so much attention devoted to capturing the voices and experiences of teachers, often through observation and interviews. The successful P.I.s also often used their own assessments or adapted others for this new work.

And of course even the best-laid plans may not succeed. To help the researchers manage challenges that arose, we held meetings that not only allowed them to get feedback on how they might move forward but also created networks that extended beyond the meetings, at the foundation and at the annual professional conference. At these meetings we tried to go beyond typical show and tell, asking research teams to identify a specific problem they were wrestling with; by framing it that way we signaled that we expected there would be challenges that we as the funder wanted them to be honest about. We also brought in outside coaches and speakers to provide additional perspectives beyond the set of studies addressed there. And we felt strongly about informal times in the schedule, allowing researchers, some of whom were doctoral students, to get to know and learn from one another. At the risk of sounding overambitious, we were not just trying to create a research base, we were trying to create a community of scholars.

Here is the thing: it worked. As you will see in the following chapters, the studies contribute new insights, theories, and questions to the issue of how teachers engage with and use data. If you consult other publications by these scholars, you will learn that not all of what they learned was positive, and knowing what does not work or what might cause harm is really important for us to learn from. But, here, the editors have chosen to focus on promising practices, and what is exciting is that each of these teams was able to identify ways for teachers to help their students have better outcomes. It is often messy, and it is always changing, but there are a few things that seem to resonate across these studies.

The best teachers are creative, persistent, and committed. They can adapt and figure out how to learn from what is expected of them, what one team refers to as "thoughtful compliance" (Garner & Horn, Chapter 7). They can benefit from peer learning and from strong leadership. They can work with coaches and make the most of new tools. They can keep their eye on the real goal of success for their students.

But this does not happen in a vacuum. The beauty of these studies is that they elucidate in specific and thoughtful ways how the best work occurs and why it was possible in that setting at that time. Perhaps the worst thing we can do is lift these thoughtfully crafted insights and promising practices and decontextualize them. Assuming they will play out in the same way elsewhere is a recipe for disappointment at best, and for harm to students and teachers, at worst. The real gift is that these scholars have taken the time to explain the how and why, and if this initiative is to have any success, those who want to learn from this research must learn those lessons, too. There is an opportunity to improve.

Moving Forward

And there is more to do. Each of these research teams has far more to share than what is in this volume. I hope those interested will explore their other work for additional lessons learned and recommendations for how to help teachers best manage the many expectations around data use. I hope practitioners will take to heart the hard-earned knowledge in these studies, that policy makers will heed the challenges, and that other researchers will build on the foundation created by these scholars.

Funders have a role here, too. This was a small but mighty collection of talented researchers. There are plenty more researchers to support on this topic. But there are other ways to think about this work, as well. What might data use look like at different levels, like high schools or colleges? Are there applications for early childhood or out-of-school settings? Some lessons may be generalizable, but the different contexts must surely have more to teach us.

Do we have the right tools and measures to conduct this research as rigorously as we would like? Are there things that we wanted to capture, but did not have a good way to? Presumably, focusing attention and resources on useful tools for researchers might also be a profitable way for funders to contribute to our knowledge in this area.

Finally, questions of equity came up in many conversations and writings on this work. There is no question that different forms of data use have different implications for students. At the risk of oversimplifying, low-income districts and schools are more likely to be subject to strong accountability regimes. What impact does that have? When we talk about students who are underperforming on assessments, are we as careful as we could be to not reduce them to a color code or label? Several of the promising practices described in this volume require financial resources. Not all classrooms and schools are going to be able to access those, no matter how willing they are to engage in that promising practice. It seems clear that good research on this—and any intervention, really—must account for questions of equity in multiple dimensions.

The efforts of this collection of talented scholars are necessary, but not sufficient to help shift the conversation around data use. The promising practices shared here are important, even if they cannot fully support the weight of the rhetoric exhorting even more data in schools. Regardless of your role in education or your position on the continuum of data use, the studies here are a contribution, and I am thrilled that we all have a chance to learn from them.

Notes

1 The thinking and writing in this section was informed by early development work of Andrea Bueschel and Paul Goren, formerly of the Spencer Foundation; and Cynthia Coburn and Erica Turner, then of the University of California, Berkeley, after working with an advisory group for about a year.
2 Many of those commissioned papers later appeared in special issue volumes of the *American Journal of Education* (Volume 118, number 2) and *Teachers College Record* (Volume 114, number 11), edited by Cynthia Coburn and Andrea Bueschel.
3 The RFP was written by Andrea Bueschel, Colin Ong-Dean, and Neil Albert, all formerly of Spencer Foundation, and benefited from feedback from many colleagues in the field.
4 From the description in the RFP: First, by emphasizing teachers' use of student performance data in ongoing practice, we want to direct attention to data that teachers can use to adapt their instruction to what they learn about student learning and needs; as such, we are especially interested in the use of data from "formative" assessments, although data gathered from end-of-year assessments may also be of interest insofar as these can be used by teachers to modify their instructional practices. Second, we confine this Initiative to studies that help us to understand the use of data that are generated on the basis of shared or widely used tools, training, or practices. By specifying shared tools, training, and practices, our intention is to focus on forms of data, or processes for generating data, that could be, or already have been, replicated in other settings. . . . Third, we are interested in the use of recorded data—that is, data that exist in some sort of permanent and codified form. Such data are not only more likely to address concerns about generalizability, but also to support research on data use as a type of practice that can be readily distinguished from other teaching practices. Finally, we focus on student performance data, meaning that data are generated through students' efforts that demonstrate some form of academic knowledge or some type of creative or intellectual ability, or through their second-order efforts to explain or examine their own learning or performance.

References

Coburn, C. E., & Turner, E. O. (2011). Research on data use: A framework and analysis. *Measurement: Interdisciplinary Research and Perspectives*, 9(4).
Little, J. W. (2012). Understanding data use practices among teachers: The contribution of micro-process studies. *The Practice of Data Use*, a special issue for *American Journal of Education*, C. E. Coburn & A. C. Bueschel (eds.), *118*(2).
Marsh, J. A. (2012). Interventions promoting educators' use of data: Research insights and gaps. *Promoting Data Use in Education: Promises and Pitfalls*, a special issue for *Teachers College Record*, C. E. Coburn & A. C. Bueschel (eds.), *114*(11).
Means, B., Padilla, C., & Gallagher, L. (2010). *Use of education data at the local level: From accountability to instructional improvement*. Washington, DC: US Department of Education, Office of Planning, Evaluation, and Policy Development.

Roderick, M. (2012). Drowning in data but thirsty for analysis. *Promoting Data Use in Education: Promises and Pitfalls*, a special issue for *Teachers College Record*, C. E. Coburn & A. C. Bueschel (eds.), *114*(11).

Spillane, J. P. (2012). Data in practice: Conceptualizing the data-based decision-making phenomena. *The Practice of Data Use*, a special issue for *American Journal of Education*, C. E. Coburn & A. C. Bueschel (eds.), *118*(2).

2
TEACHERS' PRACTICE-BASED DATA USE STRATEGIES

Helenrose Fives and Nicole Barnes[1]

Teachers are expected to know and understand central assessment concepts (beyond technical acumen), and how to use information from assessments to make decisions related to teaching and learning (US DOE, 2009; Interstate Teacher Assessment and Support Consortium, 2011). As defined by Popham (2011), "[a]ssessment literacy consists of an individual's understandings of the fundamental assessment concepts and procedures deemed likely to influence educational decisions" (p. 267). Important to assessment literacy are teachers' knowledge and skills for data use. Data use refers to "knowing how to identify, collect, organize, analyze, summarize, and prioritize data" and how to use these data to inform classroom instructional decisions (Mandinach & Gummer, 2013, p. 30). Together, assessment literacy and data use are symbiotic constructs that are integral to teaching practice and serve to inform each other in the process of teaching.

Teachers can use data for instructional decisions, including designing lessons, assigning students to collaborative groups, and differentiating instruction (Young & Kim, 2010). Evidence suggests that engaging in data use can positively influence teachers' instructional practices (Gambell, 2004; Gearhart & Osmundson, 2009) and student learning and achievement (Young & Kim, 2010; Teddlie & Reynolds, 2000). Not surprising, then, the expectation for teachers to engage in data use is articulated in state and national teaching standards (e.g., Interstate Teacher Assessment and Support Consortium, 2011) and national reform initiatives (e.g., Every Student Succeeds; U.S. DOE, 2015). Despite the demand to develop teachers' ability to use data to inform instruction, there is little empirical evidence on *how* individual teachers understand and use data in authentic contexts that can be referenced to guide these policies and inform learning opportunities for practicing and/or preservice teachers (Mandinach, Honey, Light, & Brunner, 2008).

The systematic study of teachers with expertise in data use can be utilized to identify the data use processes embedded in classroom practices that expert teachers engage in on a daily basis. Furthermore, it can result in a repertoire of specific promising practices for data use that can be empirically confirmed in future research, and which can be used to guide policy and practice.

Theoretical Framing

The present chapter is framed by research and theory in the fields of data use and teacher expertise. We explored the assessment and data use practices of teachers recognized as having expertise in these areas. Data use includes an array of activities that can support teachers' practice and facilitate student learning. Studies of expertise can provide insight and models for best practice that can be used to inform and expand the field. Given the relatively limited evidence of teachers' classroom-level data use practices, we chose to investigate how teachers recognized for doing this well actually engage with and use data to inform their work and to highlight their promising practices.

Teachers' Data Use Practices

U.S. teachers spend up to half of their professional time on assessment-related activities and are more likely to rely largely on data from classroom assessments than standardized tests to make decisions about students (Baird, 2010; Stiggins, 1999). Investigations of preservice and practicing teachers' assessment knowledge and practices have focused on their conceptions of assessment literacy (Siegel & Wissehr, 2011), understanding of measurement principles (DiDonato-Barnes, Fives, & Krause, 2014; Gotch & French, 2013), formative assessment (Black & Wiliam, 2009), the use of varied assessment types (DeLuca, Chavez, & Cao, 2013), and grading (Brookhart et al., 2016). When teachers use data to inform their instructional decisions, such data use practices have been positively correlated with student learning and achievement (e.g., Young & Kim, 2010). In general, however, teachers lack the assessment-related knowledge and skills to use data from assessment events for planning and instruction (Beswick & Sloat, 2006; Mertler, 2004). One potential explanation is that teacher preparation on data use has primarily focused on strategies to collect or access student data, instead of the more difficult processes of analysis, interpretation, and the application of findings from these processes to make instructional decisions (Goertz, Nabors Oláh, & Riggan, 2009; Mandinach & Gummer, 2013). In response, policy makers and scholars have called for increased attention to assessment processes and practices during preservice teacher education (DeLuca et al., 2013) and supported the use of structured data use team meetings for practicing teachers (Mandinach & Gummer, 2016; U.S. DOE, 2009). However, these responses largely treat assessment as separate from teaching, which may explain why teachers continue to have a difficult time using assessment results to inform instruction (Farrell & Marsh, 2016).

Teacher Expertise

One approach to understanding teachers' classroom-level data use for instructional decisions is to look closely at the practices and conditions of those recognized as experts by members of their professional community (Palmer, Stough, Burdenski, & Gonzales, 2005). These investigations provide insight into the "complex and dynamic cognitive processing that underlies the instructional decisions made by classroom teachers" (Palmer et al., 2005, p. 13). Across domains of practice, experts are those who (1) have knowledge that is vast, deeply integrated, and that can be easily accessed, (2) are able to identify the underlying structure of problems, and (3) select and use appropriate strategies for domain tasks (Ericsson & Smith, 1991; Glaser & Chi, 1988). Experts and expert performance have been examined in many fields, including teaching, to identify learning trajectories and facilitate expert development (e.g., Bereiter & Scardamalia, 1993; Bransford & Schwartz, 1999), provide models of successful learners (e.g., Pellegrino, Chudowsky, & Glaser, 2001), and identify problem-solving and decision-making strategies that can be taught to learners in the domain (e.g., VanSledright, 2002; Harris & Graham, 1992; Clement, 1991). In this chapter, we seek to share the latter of these purposes by highlighting promising practices in classroom-level data use by teachers identified as having expertise in this area.

Method

Our investigation employed a qualitative collective-case-study methodology, which allowed us to garner an in-depth understanding and detailed descriptions of phenomena situated in context (Miles & Huberman, 1994). A collective case study (Yin, 2003) involves the compilation and analysis of research data from several individual cases, such that comparisons can be made across individual cases and to theory. Our collective cases include seven practicing fifth-grade-teachers' data use and assessment practices. We also defined our collective case study as *instrumental* because individual participants were selected to provide insight and understanding into the phenomenon of teachers' data use, as understood in conversation with the extant research and existing data use models (Stake, 1995).

Participants

We selected participants for this study using Palmer et al.'s (2005) two-gate process for identifying experts and the Model of Domain Learning (MDL). According to Palmer et al. (2005), gate one requires that teachers have a minimum of three years of experience in their present context, with requisite degree(s) and certification(s) for their present position. Gate two requires recognition from informed perspectives (e.g., principals, principal investigators) relative to salient indicators. The MDL is a developmental model of expertise that identifies knowledge, interest, and strategic processing as mechanisms that facilitate development through the stages of acclimation, competency, and proficiency/expertise (Alexander, 1997). We used the MDL to identify and articulate indicators relative to teachers' knowledge, strategic processing, and interest in classroom-level data use.

Teachers were nominated by their school principals to be considered for participation in this study. The nomination form provided to school leaders guided them to identify teachers who met our study criteria, as well as the two gates described previously that are used to identify teachers with expertise. By conference call, we interviewed teachers using open-ended questions intended to elicit information on their data use practices. In this interview, we attempted to ascertain the degree to which nominated teachers were actively engaged in data use and demonstrated knowledge, interest, and strategic processing around classroom assessment and data use practices. We used a rubric to guide our evaluation of teachers' responses during the interview and to select teachers for the study. Selected teachers indicated that they had the knowledge, interest, and strategic processing related to classroom assessment and data use to suggest expertise in data use. Participants included seven Caucasian teachers from five districts in the Northeast region of the United States. All of the teachers except one were female. They ranged in teaching experience from four to twenty-five years teaching elementary-school children.

Context

All participants taught in middle- to upper-class towns (average family household income for 2012 ranged from $63,000 to $150,000) in northern New Jersey. The ethnic/racial makeup of the residents was predominantly Caucasian. The schools enrolled anywhere from 238 to 447 students for the 2011–2012 school year, and had an average faculty-to-student ratio of 11:1. According to the publicly available school report card, the percentage of students identified as economically disadvantaged or eligible for free/reduced-price lunch ranged, by district, from 0% to 10.6%. Students were in fifth grade (ages 10–11) and class sizes ranged from 22 to 25 students.

We observed participants teaching English Language Arts (ELA), and social studies or science. We focused on these subject areas for three reasons. First, ELA is assessed as part of the state evaluation system in New Jersey and, therefore, carried high stakes for these teachers. Second, ELA teachers also provided instruction in social studies or science and we were interested in investigating potential carry-over effects from one (high stakes) content area to another (low stakes) content area. Third, the majority of our partner school districts used a scripted mathematics curriculum that had prepackaged assessments, which made it less likely that we would observe all aspects of their data use processes. In this chapter, we focused on teachers' use of data gathered from ELA assessments, as these provided richer examples of data use.

Student Performance Data

We examined teachers' use of student-performance data gathered through systematic assessment processes at the classroom level, because, in general, teachers report that these data (in contrast to state- or district-mandated assessments) are more useful to their instructional decision-making (Mandinach, 2012). In this investigation, we focused on student data that teachers gathered intentionally to discern and improve students' learning and to inform teachers' ongoing instructional practices.

Data Collection

We conducted initial interviews with all the teachers in early fall 2014. From fall 2014 through spring 2015, we engaged in data collection cycles. Data collection cycles spanned two weeks and involved two days of classroom observation, followed by intensive data use think-aloud interviews that focused on the teacher's assessment and instructional-planning-related activities. All interviews were audio recorded and transcribed. In addition, photos were taken of student work and the tools teachers used when engaging with student data. At the end of the school year, all of the teachers participated in an end-of-study interview.

Findings

Teachers used data for a variety of purposes in the context of their work. For instance, they used data to assign grades, make recommendations for student placement, and evaluate their own practice. Here, we focused on the promising practices of teachers' data use, with respect to instructional decisions. Specifically, these teachers sought to make proximal (within the week) and distal (within the month or year) decisions about instructional actions for particular students or student groups (who), related to the content or skills that needed support (what), the timing of the action (when), and methods for instruction (how). In the text that follows, we highlight three promising practices that facilitated teachers' ability to make these decisions: double dipping, tracking systems, and contextualization.

Promising Practice: Double Dipping

Teachers in our sample were able to use data collection activities and data gathered for multiple purposes, what we call *double dipping*. For example, Ms. Cooper[2] was able to use data collected from running records as an opportunity for conferencing with students about their reading. Ms. Cooper was in the first year of implementing a new reading/writing curriculum purchased by her district. At the beginning of our two-week data collection cycle with her in January, she shared that, although the information from the running records was "good," it took such a large amount of class time that she was uncertain if the benefits of the data made up for the cost, in terms of class time. When we visited her again at the end of the school year, in June, her response was quite different.

> I slowed down the running records and I started realizing that this was going to really become my opportunity to confer, because it was becoming too hard to do it any other way. So, I felt like, "While I've got you back here, let me just share with you some things that I'm observing".... So, we did this [running-record assessment], and these got to where they weren't taking us that long, but then it would be like, "Wait, let's look at what else you're doing in class," and just spending some time with them. So, I was spending, probably all in all, about 10 to 15 minutes with each child.
> (Ms. Cooper, Closing interview, 06/16/15)

Thus, as she became more familiar with the data collection task and assessment practice of using the running records, she was able to see openings for additional interactions with students. She made this one-on-one time with students into more of an interaction about their overall reading progress, rather than simply the curriculum-embedded assessment. It seems she found a way to make the cost of time with the entire class worth it, because she was able to use the individual time for more than data collection on one task.

Teachers also used a single assignment to meet multiple assessment goals. For instance, Ms. Jones used students' monthly book reports to both develop and assess their reading skills and motivation, as well as to assign a grade and evaluate their progress with regard to reading and listening standards from the Core Content Curriculum Standards. When talking about the book reports, she stated:

> Ok, so this [book-report assignment] is meant, first of all, to develop them into lifelong readers [and], second of all, to give them a good grade toward their [overall] English/language-arts grade. I'm not looking to play "gotcha." It's also looking to cover the speaking and listening standards. It is so very important, how they present.
> (Ms. Cooper, Initial Interview, 09/26/14).

Mr. Walker also used student data responses to the same assignment for multiple purposes. In particular, students were required to write weekly reading-response papers about the books they were reading. Mr. Walker evaluated these papers and then generated two scores. He used a rubric to assign a grade to the paper and to guide feedback he provided to the student. In addition, he evaluated the papers for evidence of target reading skills, such as prediction, character theory, and conflict identification. For each skill, he evaluated students' progress as beginning, developing, or secure. He maintained a weekly Skill Development Chart for the class, and used this to track changes in students' progress and to inform his own understanding of the class.

Another way Mr. Walker double dipped with student data was to identify examples of student work to use as a model for the class. When scoring a student's assignment, he stated, "I would be tempted to share this with the class, so whenever we see something that is like a perfect three [on the rubric], I put it on the board and we go over it as the standard to work toward" (Mr. Walker, Think Aloud, Day 5, 12/10/14). Thus, although the intention of the task was to evaluate and understand students' reading progress, he also recognized that student work could be used as a teaching tool for the entire class.

Promising Practice: Tracking Systems

Teachers used a variety of methods to organize and track student-performance data, and they relied on these systems to inform their instructional actions. For example, Mr. Walker recorded students' progress on the Skill Development Chart mentioned previously (SDC). He maintained the SDC as an Excel file that contained each student's name and the target skills that they were developing that week in ELA class. As Mr. Walker engaged in assessment by conferring with students and evaluating assignments or other classwork, he made note of students' progress on these target skills and recorded them on his SDC as "0" for beginning, "/" for developing, or "+" for secure. The SDC then became a new form of data Mr. Walker analyzed to make instructional decisions about who needed help regarding what skills, and how to provide that help, and to monitor student progress on these skills over time. He explained:

> And, really, the reason I like doing [this, the SDC,] is just so, for instance, if you look here, for some of the skills, I could see right away, like, if there are two 0s in a row, that's somebody I need to meet with right away. That needs to be among the first conferences . . . So, it's just a good visual reminder that, if I see more 0s than not, or if I see, like, a patch of 0s, that's something to go over.
>
> *(Mr. Walker, Initial Interview, 10/29/14)*

In the prior quote, we see Mr. Walker's analysis of the information in the SDC result as part of a decision about priority, in terms of whom to conference with first (i.e., instructional action).

Another way teachers tracked student performance over time was using packing labels to record notes about students' progress. For example, Ms. Burke used carbon-copy packing labels to keep track of her comments and annotations to students. She pasted one copy of the label on the student's work and had a carbon copy for herself. Ms. Burke explained:

> I use labels . . . their initials go here, the date, and whether we are doing reading, writing, or math, and then I just write myself a quick note if it's a skill that I want them to keep focusing on. I'll write a label for them, and, when I peel it off, I have a copy for me. I stick theirs in their notebook. So, once we're done conferencing, they remember that they should be doing these things. Then, in my binder, everybody has a page where all of their notes go, their little labels, and it is easier for me. Usually, at the end of the day, or at the end of the workshop lesson, by the time that I'm getting through the conferences that I've already done, I'm able to see if there's a small group of people . . . for example, I know tomorrow I'm gonna pull a small group of students who need to focus on including more "show not tell" in their personal narratives.
>
> *(Ms. Burke, Initial Interview, 10/15/14)*

Thus, Ms. Burke used carbon-copy packing labels as a tracking system to organize and manage information about student-performance data. These packing labels became a new form of data that Ms. Burke reviewed and analyzed to make decisions about next steps in instruction.

Promising Practice: Contextualization

Teachers in our sample were able to repeatedly contextualize their analysis and evaluations to the specifics of their students (individual, groups, and whole class), curriculum or sequencing, and school (e.g., winter concert) or community (e.g., Thanksgiving break) events. In the following sections, we elaborate on the different ways that teachers contextualized their analysis and use of student data. Although we discuss these as separate kinds of contextualization, it is important to note that teachers frequently employed multiple points of contextualization throughout any one analysis process.

Contextualizing to Students

Teachers contextualized their analyses to individual students, small groups, and the whole class. Individual-student contextualization was often framed based upon the teacher's recollections of the individual student, their current standing, and typical behaviors. Typical remarks reflecting this contextualization included "she's not that kind of student" (Mr. Walker, Think Aloud, 12/03/14) and "because when you know what level they're at" (Ms. Lang, Think Aloud, 12/05/14).

Teachers used their existing knowledge of student abilities to help frame their response to student work. Contextualizing did not necessarily change the quality of their evaluations, but teachers considered it as a secondary piece of data to confirm or question that evaluation. For example, in evaluating Stacey's assignment, Mr. Walker contextualized his evaluation of her written work, as informed by the conference he had with her earlier that day, his overall conception of her current abilities related to verbal and written explanation, and his awareness of having communicated this concern to her parents. He explained:

> Alright, so, that's something she [Stacey] and I will have to go over because it doesn't mention the things we talked about, which is a theme that comes up with her where . . . her verbal explanations are very detailed, but her written explanations don't match up. And that's something not only she and I have talked about, but, when I've conferred with her parents, we've talked about the same thing, so that's something I'm going to have to talk to her about.
>
> *(Mr. Walker, Think Aloud, 12/10/14)*

Thus, while evaluating this one small class assignment, Mr. Walker relied on other sources of information to contextualize his evaluation of this task. Since Stacey was *repeating* a common error, for her, the need to confer was prioritized as an instructional action.

Teachers also contextualized student data to the whole class or larger groups. Teachers noted and often acted when a large number of students were perceived to be struggling on some issue. Reflecting on her students' progress in reading, specifically, their skills as demonstrated in reading responses, Ms. Burke stated:

> At the beginning of the year, they [the class] weren't understanding how to make a valid prediction, so I was reading through their reading responses and, although they were predicting in grades past, I had to kind of jump into a mini-lesson on what a good prediction looks like, sounds like, and then, from there, even in terms of what was expected of the reading response.
>
> *(Ms. Burke, Think Aloud, 01/13/15)*

Thus, since Ms. Burke noticed a pattern across the class, as a whole, with respect to making predictions, she decided to implement a mini-lesson on the topic for the whole class, to address the concern. She elaborated on this further and contextualized the concern to the overall experience and work produced by the class.

> So, we had gone over it [the reading responses] a bunch of times. They had written about four for the year and just weren't doing as well as they should've been doing, so that's when I came up with the color-coded system to give them, and I kind of did a whole lesson on that and how it looks different than what they had already been writing.
>
> *(Ms. Burke, Think Aloud, 01/13/15)*

Here, we see how looking at the class, as a whole, over the course of four iterations of the assignment led Ms. Burke to further refine the task by providing them with a strategy to facilitate their success on the project.

Contextualizing to Curriculum or Sequencing

Teachers also made meaning of student work by considering it within the context of their overall curricular goals and sequencing plan. For example, when discussing her plan for how to respond to student work, Ms. Jones contextualized the student data she was reviewing by considering it in light of her curricular goals. She stated:

> So, there's reading standards for literature. The big one— I'm tending to go, like, zip through the others, like setting, characters, plot, because they do that ad nauseam in third and fourth grade. If you don't know it by now, then we are gonna probably put you in—we'll probably INRS [Intervention and Referral Services] and put you in foundational skills, because I'm not gonna really teach that, except in reading conferences. So, I started with summarizing. That was really important to me, but I did include all the other things on the Fiction Strategy Bookmark.
>
> *(Ms. Jones, Initial Interview, 11/24/14)*

Since Ms. Jones had a sound understanding of the salient skills in her class, she was able to identify this as a particularly relevant concern. Moreover, this led to a prioritizing decision, in terms of her instructional actions.

Contextualizing to School or Community Events

While considering students' work and engaging in the data use processes, we saw teachers at various times reference events and expectations from beyond their classrooms, which tempered their thinking and framed their decision-making around certain instructional actions. For instance, on the basis of his Post-it analysis, Mr. Walker determined that he needed to review character theory and predication with his whole class because all but five students had things that needed to be addressed. Once this decision was made, however, Mr. Walker needed to determine when he could do this in his current schedule. The excerpt that follows, from our Think Aloud, illustrates how he contextualized decisions on multiple levels, including: the class needs, curriculum sequencing, school events (i.e., Shakespeare resident, winter break, half days), and his personal context. He stated:

> So, the mental debate I'm going over right now is, do I do it on Friday, and address it immediately or, because it is a little bit to the side, because it was— Not tangential, that's the wrong word, but because it wasn't— Because it

was a bit to the side, can I wait and do it where it might fit in, a little bit later on down the road? The problem with that is there is no more down the road. We have next week and, like, the Shakespeare Resident, he wants to meet three days next week . . . that's no good. Then we have Thursday, Friday, I don't even know if I'll be here [Mr. Walker's wife was pregnant and due at the time] . . . then winter recess—there's nothing that I can do that's meaningful that half day. I shouldn't say it that way, but it's really not going to be something that they'll carry after the break, so I have to do it Friday, because I have to make sure they get it, and what I'll probably do is do an in-class reading response after they have it, to make sure that not only do they have the skill but that they can write about it, talk about it, and really prove it in more than one way.

(Mr. Walker, Think Aloud, 12/10/14)

We also observed teachers contextualizing their more distal planning, as connected to student data and awareness of larger contextual issues in the district, such as the upcoming standardized tests. Across these contextualizing activities, teachers relied on their prior knowledge and beliefs, along with their understanding of learning goals/target skills to guide instructional actions.

Discussion

We described three categories of promising practices for data use that emerged in the work of the teachers identified as having some expertise in this area. Our findings suggest that these teachers engaged in promising data use practices that facilitated their instructional decision-making. In particular, these practices helped teachers make decisions about who needed help, how quickly they needed it, on what topic or skill, and, upon occasion, how the help should be given. These promising practices served to expedite and focus teachers' work so that that they could attend to the learning and instructional issues that were important for their students.

The practices of double dipping, using tracking systems, and contextualizing may seem obvious in their practicality. However, issues emerged as we further analyzed the research data and identified the supports and constraints, both internal and external to the teacher, for/on their use. By engaging in double dipping, teachers were able to more efficiently use class time and student work to generate deeper understandings of student progress. Only a few of the teachers we observed did this in intentional ways, however. Most of these expert teachers gathered multiple forms of data from their students, but, typically, each assignment was used for a single purpose. It is unclear why some teachers were able to see opportunities for mining their student data to garner multiple insights about their students, while others did not.

A second challenge that emerged in our findings was the difficulty of designing and then utilizing a viable tracking system for student data. Once established, tracking systems helped teachers organize their data management and analysis procedures, allowing them more time to consider the potential implications and instructional actions that should result from the work. Getting the system rolling took a lot of time and effort, however. That said, once it became automatic and folded into daily practice, the information was seen as useful. The teacher with the most effective system developed it over years of practice, during which he was able to build rich practical knowledge of his content and the nature of the students in his classes. He used the system he developed because he tailored it to his needs for instruction. We also saw Ms. Cooper attempt to build systems, but with a great deal of trial and error.

Despite the seemingly obvious nature of these practices, we did not see them being used consistently by teachers. In particular, the practice of contextualizing seemed to occur to teachers, sometimes, as prompted by the student data they were analyzing. Although all the teachers used this strategy, the extent to which this practice was or can be systematized remains uncertain. For instance, several teachers, when scoring student work, reported that they noticed a trend in responses that warranted an instructional response from them. One teacher, however, Ms. Murphy, based her decision on her "feel" of the data (Ms. Murphy, Think Aloud, 11/18/14). She determined that she needed to "go over" a reading-comprehension question with the class, since most of the students had gotten the question wrong, but her feel was not an accurate reflection of the item that she most frequently marked incorrect. In another instance, Ms. Cooper scored a multiple-choice test for her students and got a sense that there were some common errors on a few questions. After scoring the tests, she went back through them and tallied the number of students who got each item incorrect by hand. She accurately identified the problem items on the test, but at the cost of valuable time that she could have spent more productively if there had been a simple method or system in place for her to do this kind of analysis.

Practical Considerations for Practice

The identification of promising practices, followed by rich descriptions of how teachers enact them, has several implications for practice. First, teachers need help developing and using these practices in the context of their own classrooms, schools, and curricula. This may be particularly difficult for teachers, especially novice teachers, who do not have the knowledge and experience needed to go beyond learning a promising practice, to adapting or integrating it meaningfully for/into their own context. Such a task requires a deep understanding of content, the curriculum, assessment strategies, the students, and development. Teacher educators, coaches, or school leaders can help teachers develop and use these promising practices in their classrooms. Some examples include sharing a variety of instances of the same practice being carried out in different contexts, modeling, providing feedback, allowing multiple opportunities for teachers to practice these strategies with guided assistance, and creating systems that provide time and resources for teachers to observe each other and think deeply about their own work.

Second, as suggested by the MDL, in order for teachers to develop expertise, they must develop domain-specific knowledge, strategic processing, and interest. Domain specificity in teaching is a challenge because teachers must develop expertise in their content area (ELA), as well as in the practice of data use. Without an understanding of the texts students are reading, teachers are limited in their ability to engage in deeper processing strategies that would provide them with better insights into student learning. Moreover, teachers need to be motivated to engage in data use; thus, they need to develop an interest in this aspect of practice in order to insure active and ongoing development in this area. Knowledge, strategic processing, and interest—the three components of the MDL—work in tandem to spur development. The more knowledge teachers acquire, the better they can use deep-processing strategies with ease and the more interested they become in their topic. Teacher educators who provide preservice preparation or ongoing development need to attend to the three components of the MDL, as well as to individual teachers' current levels of expertise. More sophisticated strategies, for example, may not be appropriate for teachers until they have developed requisite background knowledge.

Conclusion

In our work, we examine how teachers analyze and use data from classroom assessments to inform instructional decisions. This adds to and extends the research on data-based decision-making that has typically focused on data teams or individuals examining standardized-test data. We identified three promising practices, double dipping, tracking systems, and contextualizing, that facilitated teachers' data use and guided their instructional responses. These practices can be empirically confirmed in future research, and used to guide policy, practice, and professional development.

Acknowledgements

This work was supported by Spencer Foundation through the Evidence for the Classroom Grant Initiative. We are sincerely thankful to Spencer Foundation for supporting our work and to the teachers, principals, and research team members who deepened our understanding of teachers' data use in practice and who made this work possible.

Notes

1 We contributed equally to this chapter. We rotate order of authorship in our scholarship.
2 All names of people and places are pseudonyms

References

Alexander, P. A. (1997). Mapping the multidimensional nature of domain learning: The interplay of cognitive, motivational and strategic forces. In P. R. Pintrich & M. L. Maehr (Eds.), *Advances in motivation and achievement* (Vol. 10, pp. 213–250). Greenwich, CT: JAI Press.

Baird, J. (2010). What constitutes legitimate causal linking? *Measurement, 8*(1), 151–153. doi:10.1080/15366361003748219

Bereiter, C., & Scardamalia, M. (1993). *Surpassing ourselves: An inquiry into the nature and implications of expertise.* Chicago, IL: Open Court.

Beswick, J., & Sloat, E. (2006). Assessment expertise: A vital component of effective early literacy. *Canadian Children, 31*(1), 14–21.

Black, P., & Wiliam, D. (2009). Developing the theory of formative assessment. *Educational Assessment, Evaluation & Accountability, 21*(1), 5–31. doi:10.1007/s11092-008-9068-5

Bransford, J. D., & Schwartz, D. L. (1999). Rethinking transfer: A simple proposal with multiple implications. *Review of Research in Education, 24*, 61–100.

Brookhart, S., Guskey, T., Bowers, A., McMillan, J., Smith, J., Smith, L., Stevens, M., & Welsh, M. (2016). A century of grading research. Meaning and value in the most common educational measure. *Review of Educational Research, 86*(4), 803–848. doi:10.3102/0034654316672069

Clement, J. (1991). Nonformal reasoning in experts and in science students: The use of analogies, extreme cases, and physical intuitions. In J. F. Voss, D. N. Perkins, & J. W. Segal (Eds.), *Informal reasoning and education* (pp. 345–362). Hillsdale, NJ: Erlbaum.

DeLuca, C., Chavez, T., & Cao, C. (2013). Establishing a foundation for valid teacher judgement on student learning: The role of pre-service assessment education. *Assessment in Education: Principles, Policy & Practice, 20*(1), 107–126. doi:10.1080/0969594X.2012.668870

DiDonato-Barnes, N., Fives, H., & Krause, E. S. (2014). Using a table of specifications to improve teacher-constructed traditional tests: An experimental design. *Assessment in Education: Principles, Policy & Practice. 21*(1), 90–108. doi:10.1080/0969594X.2013.808173

Ericsson, K. A., & Smith, J. (1991). Prospects and limits of the empirical study of expertise: An introduction. In K. A. Ericsson & J. Smith (Eds.), *Toward a general theory of expertise* (pp. 1–38). Cambridge: Cambridge University Press.

Farrell, C. C., & Marsh, J. (2016). Metrics matter: How properties and perceptions of data shape teachers' instructional responses. *Educational Administration Quarterly, 52*, 423–462. doi:10.1177/0013161X16638429

Gambell, T. (2004). Teachers working around large-scale assessment: Reconstructing professionalism and professional development. *English Teaching, 3*(2), 48.

Gearhart, M., & Osmundson, E. (2009). Assessment portfolios as opportunities for teacher learning. *Educational Assessment, 14*(1), 1–24.

Glaser, R., & Chi, M. T. H. (1988). Overview. In M. T. H. Chi, R. Glaser, & M. J. Farr (Eds.), *The nature of expertise* (pp. xv–xxviii). Hillsdale, NJ: Erlbaum.

Goertz, M. E., Nabors Oláh, L., & Riggan, M. (2009). *From testing to teaching: The use of interim assessments in classroom instruction* (CPRE Research Report No. RR-65). Philadelphia, PA: Consortium for Policy Research in Education.

Gotch, C. M., & French, B. F. (2013). Elementary teachers' knowledge and self-efficacy for measurement concepts. *The Teacher Educator, 48*, 46–57. doi:10.1080/08878730.2012.740150

Harris, K. R., & Graham, S. (1992). *Helping young writers master the craft: Strategy instruction and self-regulation in the writing process.* Cambridge, MA: Brookline.

Interstate Teacher Assessment and Support Consortium. (2011). *InTASC model core teaching standards: A resource for state dialogue*. Washington, DC: Council of Chief State School Officers.

Mandinach, E. B. (2012). A perfect time for data use: Using data-driven decision making to inform practice. *Educational Psychologist, 47*(2), 71–85. doi:10.1080/00461520.2012. 667064

Mandinach, E. B., & Gummer, E. S. (2013). A systematic view of implementing data literacy in educator preparation. *Educational Researcher, 42*, 30–37.

Mandinach, E. B., & Gummer, E. (2016). What does it mean for teachers to be data literate: Laying out the skills, knowledge, and dispositions. *Teaching and Teacher Education, 60*, 366–376.

Mandinach, E. B., Honey, M., Light, D., & Brunner, C. (2008). A conceptual framework for data-driven decision making. In E. B. Mandinach & M. Honey (Eds.), *Data-driven school improvement: Linking data and learning* (pp. 13–31). New York, NY: Teachers College Press.

Mertler, C. (2004). Secondary teachers' assessment literacy: Does classroom experience make a difference? *American Secondary Education, 33*(1), 49–64. Retrieved from www.jstor.org/stable/41064623

Miles, M. B., & Huberman, A. M. (1994). *Qualitative data analysis: An expanded sourcebook*. Thousand Oaks, CA: Sage.

Palmer, D. J., Stough, L. M., Burdenski, T. K., Jr., & Gonzales, M. (2005). Identifying teacher expertise: An examination of researchers' decision making. *Educational Psychologist, 40*(1), 13 25.

Pellegrino, J., Chudowsky, N., & Glaser, R. (2001). *Knowing what students know: The science and design of educational assessment*. Washington, DC: National Academy Press. *Research in Science Teaching, 49*(6), 831–841. doi: 10.1002/tea.21032

Popham, W. J. (2011). Assessment literacy overlooked: A teacher educator's confession. *The Teacher Educator, 46*(4), 265–273.

Siegel, M. A., & Wissehr, C. (2011). Preparing for the plunge: Preservice teachers' assessment literacy. *Journal of Science Teacher Education, 22*(4), 371–391. doi:10.1007/s10972-011-9231-6

Stake, R. E. (1995). *The art of case study research*. Thousand Oaks, CA: Sage.

Stiggins, R. J. (1999). Evaluating classroom assessment training in teacher education programs. *Educational Measurement: Issues and Practice, 18*(1), 23–27. doi:10.1111/j.1745-3992.1999.tb00004.x

Teddlie, C., & Reynolds, D. (2000). *The international handbook of school effectiveness research*. London: Falmer.

U.S. Department of Education. (2009). *Race to the top executive summary*. Retrieved from www2.ed.gov/programs/racetothetop/executive-summary.pdf

U.S. Department of Education. (2015). *Every student succeeds act: A progress report on elementary and secondary education*. Retrieved from www.whitehouse.gov/ sites/whitehouse.gov/files/documents/ESSA_Progress_Report.pdf

VanSledright, B. (2002). *In search of America's past: Learning to read history in elementary school*. New York, NY: Teachers College Press.

Yin, R. K. (2003). *Case study research: Design and methods* (3rd ed.). Thousand Oaks, CA: Sage.

Young, V. M., & Kim, D. H. (2010). Using assessment for instructional improvement: A literature review. *Education Policy Analysis Archives, 18*(19), 1–40. Retrieved from http://epaa.asu.edu/ojs/article/view/809

3

FOLLOWING THE PATH OF GREATEST PERSISTENCE

Sensemaking, Data Use, and the Everyday Practice of Teaching

Carolyn J. Riehl, Hester Earle, Pavithra Nagarajan, Tara E. Schwitzman, and Laura Vernikoff

Introduction[1]

In recent years, policymakers and practitioners have sought to increase the use of data in education, and this has presented both challenges and opportunities for classroom teachers. Using new forms of information in new ways can alter, for better or worse, the way teachers see their students, the instructional decisions they make, and the learning that results. It can also change how teachers view their own teaching, and their sense of professionalism and control over their work.

The practices that constitute data use—in both their idealized and realized forms—have evolved over the past several decades. In early approaches to data-based decision-making, district and school administrators and teachers were exhorted to examine aggregate patterns of achievement, and made decisions about allocating resources to solve problems—curricula to purchase, teachers to hire and deploy, and ways to group and assign students to tracks, teachers, or supplementary services (e.g., Fickes, 1998; Flaherty, 2004; Olson, 2002; Protheroe, 2001). Data for these purposes typically were derived from standardized tests and routine administrative measurements, such as attendance records. We can think of this use of data as *data for analysis*.

Over time, emphasis has shifted to a different use of data, one inspired not so much by what administrators do to oversee classrooms and schools as by what teachers do to improve. This has led to forms of school-based action learning that include teachers examining student work together (Blythe, Allen, & Powell, 2015), formalized teacher-led inquiry teams (Talbert, 2011), whole-school models of instructional inquiry (Huffman & Kalnin, 2003), and networked improvement communities and "improvement science" (Bryk, Gomez, Grunow, & LeMahieu, 2015). With these practices, teachers (sometimes with their administrators) take a closer look at what students are producing and accomplishing as a result of their teaching. Often, teachers use structured protocols to facilitate these inquiries (e.g., McDonald, Mohr, Dichter, & McDonald, 2003). We can think of this use of data as *data for learning*. It is consistent with and supported by prior work on teacher collegiality, experimentation, and professional learning communities (e.g., Kruse, Louis, & Bryk, 1994; Little, 1982).

Using data for analysis and learning frequently have been touted as innovations of the data era (Weinstock, 2009). They are presented as new aspects of professional practice in education and systematic ways of improving teaching, learning, and leadership.

In our research, we have studied a third way in which teachers use data: *data for sensemaking*. This type of use is not new, but rather is how teachers already incorporate many different types of information about students in their everyday practice (Breiter & Light, 2006). This classroom-centered data use is a path of least resistance and greatest persistence for teachers, but it sometimes seems to have taken a back seat to the other two approaches. In this chapter, we set this form of data use in a conceptual frame of cognitive and situated sensemaking, and then bring it to light through case studies of two teachers.

What is Sensemaking?

Sensemaking is the active, ongoing making of meaning (Weick, 1969, 1995). With conceptual roots in social psychology and organization theory, sensemaking refers to how individuals, rooted in particular contexts and with their own unique identities and motivations, construct understandings and interpretations of the world they inhabit. Objects, events, and messages from the environment do not carry predetermined meanings. Instead, people perceive what is going on outside of them, filter that information through their prior experiences and knowledge, and formulate new understandings. By making meaning, persons actively shape or enact their environments and their own identities as well. Sensemaking is a process, and the results of that process are sometimes described as *accounts* we tell ourselves and others (Maitlis, 2005; Maitlis & Christianson, 2014). Creating accounts is crucial when persons encounter situations that are new, uncertain, or conflicting—situations for which they have not yet made meaning and, therefore, in which they do not have a sense of who they are or what they should do.

Weick (1995) argued there is no such thing as a singular sensemaker. Other people play a part in structuring the environments we encounter and how we make sense of them. Some of these influences are reciprocal, but often they are not socially or politically neutral. Persons in positions of authority, for example, may serve as *sense-givers* whose framings of meaning have influence over others.

Teachers are sensemakers. They construct meaning as they experience the environments of their classrooms and schools. They are influenced by and develop shared understandings with the people who surround them. School leaders may act as sense-givers for teachers, framing situations and information in ways that try to direct them toward particular interpretations and actions (Coburn, 2006; Spillane, Reiser, & Reimer, 2002).

Perhaps most importantly, teachers must construct accounts and make meaning of their classroom work with students. This classroom-based sensemaking draws from teachers' ongoing perceptions of the students they work with, the tasks they are charged with, the resources available to them, and their own identities as persons and teachers. Teachers do not simply respond to students; they cocreate the classroom with their students, who are engaged in meaning-making processes of their own (e.g., Hand, 2010). As sensemakers, teachers perceive and absorb many forms of information, and, therefore, we characterize this as a third type of data use: *data for classroom sensemaking*.

Other analysts use sensemaking as a broad construct to cover the myriad ways educators use data, including those strategies we have framed as using data for analysis and learning (e.g., Bertrand & Marsh, 2015; Park, Daly, & Guerra, 2013). We agree that sensemaking is a pervasive activity in schools, and we affirm that, when educators interact with data for analysis and learning, they are engaged in meaning making and the construction of accounts that can guide their work. Yet, we stress that teachers' most immediate, ongoing, and crucial work of sensemaking happens in their daily interactions in the classroom.

Classrooms are, at once, quite familiar and strikingly novel contexts for teachers. Framed by a durable "grammar of schooling" (Tyack & Tobin, 1994), classrooms are characterized by common tasks, scripts, routines, and patterns of interaction. It would be easy for teachers to maintain static accounts about how to do school with their classes. Yet, every year—indeed, every day—teachers are presented with ambiguity and uncertainty in the form of new students, with their personalities and needs, and their developing minds and learning trajectories.

To do their work well, teachers must resist the complacency of familiarity and engage in a process of constant calibration, incorporating new information about students into their ongoing meaning-laden accounts of the classroom. That information may come in the form of a student's test score, a reply to a teacher's question, or a behavioral outburst. It is crucial to understand how teachers see past their usual understandings through their use of data for classroom sensemaking.

Methods

We present and discuss two examples of teachers' use of information about students in their daily work of teaching. We derived these examples from a multi-year study of teachers' data use at four elementary schools in a large urban school district. Our team of researchers worked with two grade levels in each school and spent over 200 hours in the schools. We observed classroom instruction, teacher planning meetings, and professional-development sessions. We also interviewed focal teachers, principals, assistant principals, and curriculum specialists in the schools. We produced field notes and interview transcripts, which we then coded and analyzed to identify patterns of data use. We developed thematic propositions about the types of data use we saw, the factors that supported or impeded data use, and the impact on teachers' instructional practice and professional identity. In this chapter, we provide brief case studies of two second-grade teachers whom we refer to as Ms. Apple and Ms. Edwards. We chose these two teachers because, among our sample of teachers, they were examples of strong teachers working within very different contexts.

Ms. Apple taught in an arts-themed school, School A, serving a low-income (89% eligible for free or reduced-price lunch), racially diverse student population (31% black, 44% Hispanic, 20% Caucasian) on the outskirts of the city. This school was considered high performing, based on its standardized test scores, and, as a result, enjoyed more flexibility and autonomy than many other schools in the district. The principal founded this turnaround school with 11 longtime, trusted colleagues and friends, including Ms. Apple, and handpicked almost every teacher in the school (School A, Epstein interview, 07/02/15). The principal and teachers were relatively young, mostly Caucasian, and mostly female; many came from the suburb right across the city limit. In her tenth year of teaching when our research began, Ms. Apple was still highly engaged in her work, reflective, and curious about how to improve. She co-taught with another full-time teacher and valued this because it gave her somebody to "bounce ideas off of," though she sometimes missed having more autonomy (School A, Apple interview, 06/18/15).

Ms. Edwards taught at a high-needs elementary school, School B, which received Title I funding. Almost all of its students (97%) were black or Hispanic, 7% were English-Language Learners (ELLs), and 22% received special-education services. The school had received an average grade of "C" on its last three school report cards. Recently, fewer than 13% of its students demonstrated proficiency on the state mathematics exam and only 12% of its students were marked proficient on the literacy exam. As a result, the school was under considerable accountability pressure from the district, and the school administration was well aware of the need for students to demonstrate more progress. The assistant principal, who was the school's data specialist, coordinated efforts to help the school's inquiry team of teachers obtain and examine student performance data from summative standardized tests and other predictive assessments. As he described, "I provide them the data. I try to lead them [in] how to analyze the data, to see, you know, the skills that need to be targeted, and how can you map those skills, based on our pacing calendar" (School B, Esquivel interview, 10/29/14). Some teachers responded by flexibly grouping their students or building more questioning into their pedagogy, while others held to more rigid didactic teaching. Teachers were expected to bring a data binder when they met with the principal, showing how they used data to help children progress, but teachers did have flexibility in the kinds of data they could use (School B, Esquivel interview, 10/29/14). The school staff was comprised of mostly older women of color who had been at the school over 10 years, and the principal despaired of finding new teachers for the school (School B, Aldridge interview, 07/28/14). Ms. Edwards was a highly experienced teacher, with almost two decades in the classroom, at the time of our study. She prided herself on her connection to the community and talked about seeing former students out and about in the neighborhood, or when they came back to visit from college.

To bring the teachers' practice to life, we begin each case discussion that follows with a vignette constructed from direct observations we made in the teachers' classrooms over multiple visits. We then discuss how each composite vignette reflects the overall patterns of data use we observed, and how those patterns connected to the broader school context.

Ms. Apple—Vignette

In the second-grade classroom led by Ms. Apple and her co-teacher, Ms. Donner, attractive bulletin boards displayed students' math, writing, and science work. Each paper had a Post-it note attached with teacher and student comments. Hanging on the side of a cabinet in the back of the room were two clipboards, one marked "Daily Math Assessment" and the other "Daily Homework Check." Each held a paper with a grid full of names, dates, checks, and stars.

After morning meeting, students had a quick session of Karate Math, a program Ms. Apple adapted from the internet. While students paired up to practice math facts using laminated flash cards, the teachers passed out one-page tests of subtraction problems. The orange-belt students got one-digit problems; the tests for the brown-belt ninjas were more complicated. Students slipped their tests into clear, plastic sleeves and had two minutes to write their answers on the sleeves with felt markers. When time was up, the teachers visually scanned students' answers, but did not write anything down. They collected the blank tests and the students wiped their sleeves clean.

For literacy, the class divided into two groups, which the teachers reassigned heterogeneously every few weeks. In the front of the classroom, Ms. Donner told the students a story incorporating the day's vocabulary words, then sent them to their desks to use the words in their own writing. One by one, she called a few students to a kidney-shaped table to discuss their work.

Meanwhile, with the other half of the class, Ms. Apple read aloud from a nonfiction book. Then, the students worked in pairs to answer comprehension questions, writing on Post-it notes, which they placed in their reading journals. Every journal had a smattering of notes with student and teacher comments from throughout the year.

After a quick break, when students danced along with an online music video, they took their math notebooks and plopped down on the rug, facing a SMART board. Along the edges of the SMART board were prompts such as: "Can you prove your answer another way?" Ms. Apple directed their attention to the board: "There's a problem like this on the test tomorrow, I just looked." She read the multi-digit addition problem aloud and called on several students to explain how to solve it. She repeated their answers so the whole class could hear and affirmed the students' work. Ms. Apple asked if anybody stacked the numbers and then modeled the process, saying, "This is how it works for my brain . . . if you have many numbers, you can ALWAYS stack them." Together, they solved the stacking problem. She wrote another question, 25 + 17, which she worked through on the board. The students groaned when she forgot to carry a digit. "Okay, tell me what I've done wrong," she said, and various students called out.

As Ms. Apple got the class ready for lunchtime, Ms. Donner wrote some notes on a clipboard hanging on the back wall and prepared materials for the next day.

Commentary

This vignette illustrates the many ways Ms. Apple used information from and about students in her ongoing sensemaking in the classroom. Perhaps most important is the fact that co-teaching gave her many opportunities to divide the class into smaller groups and to confer with another adult about what was happening in the classroom. Although Ms. Apple was the senior teacher, little of her sensemaking developed in isolation from Ms. Donner.

Both teachers recorded and assessed a variety of individual student needs. The Karate Math quizzes gave daily feedback on students' progress in learning their basic math facts, and they were used to individualize the practice students received. Whole-group instruction sessions gave Ms. Apple the chance to query students about their mathematics understanding, which she often pursued later in individual seat work. Her frequent review of their workbooks was another source of information. Ms. Apple and her co-teacher used the formal curriculum in ways they found helpful for generating information about student performance. For example, on the daily math clipboard, the teachers made notes about student performance on math problems that the math curriculum guide suggested they monitor, to determine who needed extra help (School A, Classroom observation, 10/23/15). As Ms. Apple explained:

> After we teach the lesson, we'll go back. Often, the first two problems are "share and show." We did them together. And then problems three and four, the first on-your-own-problems, we'll have them do it at the carpet. And then we often will say, if they get them, "Okay, go back to your seat. Start working [on the next problems]." And the kids who are left on the carpet are the kids who didn't get them, for whatever reason, and we'll keep those kids. And, you know, mark an X by the name [on the clipboard] and just note that we know they didn't get it. And if we do, like, a mid-chapter checkpoint, we'll have already looked at the kids who are not getting this.
>
> *(School A, Apple interview, 06/18/15)*

For literacy, small-group instruction and time for individualized help enabled Ms. Apple to keep tabs on student progress. Both teachers used Post-it notes in numerous notebooks and folders. The frequent exchange of notes between teachers and students served as a form of ongoing conversation and documentation about what students understood and the pedagogical strategies and resources teachers decided to try next (School A, Classroom observation, 03/17/15, 04/29/15, 10/06/15, 10/23/15, 11/06/15, 11/22/15, 12/16/15).

Even when assessments were mandated by the school and/or district, Ms. Apple still used sensemaking to determine which assessments were useful. For example, she disliked the predictive math assessment in the fall. Since the school used a scripted curriculum, she reasoned, it was unlikely that students would have been exposed to second-grade math in first grade, and they have to teach the entire second grade curriculum anyway. For Ms. Apple, the fall assessment was frustrating for the students and not very helpful to the teachers (School A, Apple interview, 06/18/15).

Ms. Apple also acknowledged that information about student performance or needs does not automatically indicate new pedagogical techniques to try. When describing a student with an auditory-processing challenge, she explained:

> I feel like I should be doing more to figure it out. But, like, I don't know—sort of, throwing everything at her, working with sight words, working with chunking sounds, working with her speech teacher to talk about her ideas. I mean, she's grown—slowly, slowly over the year. But she ended last year at reading level E. She came back in reading level B. And guess where she's at now? E. Oh, great! I just corrected your summer slide! It took me 10 months to correct. And to fix that? I don't know. But I guess my point is: I'm not doing anything new or different. I'm not getting a different method of teaching her. But that is probably what I need to do. And I don't know where that's at.
>
> *(School A, Apple interview, 06/18/15)*

Recognizing these limitations of data, however, did not seem to weaken Ms. Apple's overall stance that using data is good practice. Nor did it cause her to question whether measurements of student learning might actually be the source of problems, as those who study the socially constructed (and often racially disproportionate) use of learning-disability diagnoses have pointed out (e.g., Dudley-Marling & Gurn, 2010; Ferri & Connor, 2006; Harry & Klingner, 2005; Kozleski, 2016; Sleeter, 1986).

The school context appeared to influence Ms. Apple's sensemaking with and about data. When the school first opened, there were many consultants, and the principal herself led much of the teachers' professional development. But, over time, teacher competency developed, so that "they just run with it" and have considerable autonomy in their classrooms (School A, Epstein interview, 07/02/15).

The principal did, however, expect teachers to use data. She had periodic data meetings with grade-level teacher teams and she maintained a set of spreadsheets on her computer to track how students were doing (School A, Document 6, 07/02/15). At one point, there were so many assessment tools in use that the principal led an effort toward what she called "data uniformity," so that, within and across grade levels, teachers were looking at similar indicators of student progress. Now, every child had a data portfolio, and, when the principal held a meeting of her teacher leaders, she said, "Bring your data along" (School A, Epstein interview, 07/02/15).

This school did not have difficulty meeting accountability expectations for student performance. The data that were collected, analyzed, and discussed tended to focus on individual students rather than subgroups defined by some shared characteristic, such as race or language status. Ms. Apple's sensemaking was likely influenced by this emphasis on the individual. Although many students in the classroom had Individualized Education Programs (IEPs), differentiation seemed to extend to all students. Differentiated reading, writing, and math assignments were given, and Ms. Donner pulled students for extra help when needed (School A, Classroom observation, 03/17/15, 04/29/15, 05/13/15, 11/06/15). The teachers created enrichment packets for the "faster" students (School A, Donner interview, 06/18/15). Ms. Apple and her co-teacher had the autonomy to teach this way, and they made sense of how their students would handle the curriculum, based on what they perceived about individual student needs.

Overall, in most instances we observed, Ms. Apple had both the opportunity and the capacity to check and refine her ongoing sensemaking about her students and to teach in ways that responded to how she saw them. She had access to enough information to guide her in moving the whole class forward in the curriculum and to respond to individual needs. She appeared confident, mostly, that, when a problem emerged, she had a pedagogical solution for it. She drew both on what was familiar in the situation, given her experience and expertise, but also on what was unfamiliar in the particularities of individual students. As one of two co-teachers with many students to teach, she bounced back and forth between what she felt she knew, what her co-teacher knew, and what they constructed together. The type, amount, and frequency of information about students produced in the classroom context seemed to suit her need for situated sensemaking.

Ms. Edwards—Vignette

Students trickled into the classroom in the morning and began tackling the daily "HOT" (Higher Order Thinking) math problem posted on the board, as they ate their school breakfasts. At 8:30 a.m., Ms. Edwards ceremoniously pulled a popsicle stick out of the "Cup of Fairness" and called the student whose name was written on it up to the board to work through the problem. As other students protested, one child called out, "It's the cup of FAIRNESS. That's the whole point! It's fair who she picked." The child at the board talked through her solution, and other students jumped in with questions and suggestions. Occasionally, Ms. Edwards prompted them to use the discussion stems posted on the walls, such as "I agree, and I would like to add—." When the student finished, Ms. Edwards asked for volunteers to explain alternative methods for solving the problem.

The students had literacy next. They were reading *Charlotte's Web*. Although Ms. Edwards worried that it was hard for her "city kids" to relate to a book that took place on a farm, it was part of the new mandated curriculum. She moved it to the second half of the year, after her students had a good chunk of second grade under their belt. Today, they were working on character maps. Ms. Edwards was circulating, but stopped at a table where students were not yet writing, to discuss what a character might be feeling when he yelled. Ms. Edwards reminded them to find evidence in the text.

Before lunch, Ms. Edwards told the students to leave their work on their desks. While they are gone, she walked around and looked at each student's work, then placed it in one of the following piles: "mostly finished," "chugging along," or "needs some help tomorrow." While she ate her own lunch, she tried to master the school's new computerized report-card system, since grades were due the next day.

Ms. Edwards had planned a writing lesson for the afternoon, but made a last-minute change. Once the children were settled on the rug, she told them sternly that she heard some things she did not like about what was happening at lunch. She expected them to always be kind and help each other, no matter where they were. She now wanted the students to write inspirational sayings that could go on the wall outside of their classroom. They discussed what the word "inspirational" meant, and students offered examples. They reviewed kind ways to critique each other's work (e.g., "Maybe you should double check how you spelled that word," or "I think you are missing the letter that makes the 'sss' sound.") and not-so-kind ways to provide critique (e.g., "I don't like this. It's boring."). While the students worked on their sayings, Ms. Edwards circulated, helping students sound out words, or urging them to "use the room" and look at the walls to find the words they were trying to spell. Those walls were covered from floor to ceiling with student work, vocabulary words, posters, and learning objectives.

Finally, Ms. Edwards sent the students off to science. She had a prep period and a stack of district-mandated performance assessments to pore over. As she read through students' responses to the writing prompt, she wondered whether her students really understood what they were asked to do.

Commentary

Ms. Edwards was a veteran teacher working in a high-accountability school that had recently placed more emphasis on analyzing and using student-performance data. She used her experience and knowledge to make sense of students' progress, even when her sensemaking seemed inconsistent with her school's new data culture. She believed in the importance of getting to know her children and helping them develop fully as kind, contributing members of the community, as the impromptu writing exercise in the vignette illustrates (School B, Classroom observation, 03/13/14, 05/05/14, 10/29/14, 05/15/15).

Since she was concerned with her students, as individuals, she looked to them as primary sources when assessing their understanding of academic work. Ms. Edwards said that she knows students are "with her" when she sees that they can both complete a task and explain how they have done it to her or to other students (School B, Edwards interview, 06/15/15).

Ms. Edwards did not ignore standardized tests and other forms of mandated performance data, but, rather, integrated them with the rest of her experience and knowledge about teaching. She interpreted the quantitative data she was asked to analyze and report on with caution, particularly when test scores were lower than she expected. She thought about the context of the assessment—were students familiar with the format? Did they know what was expected of them, or were they too confused by the directions to show what they knew about the topic? She also thought about the students themselves—was that one sick on the day they took the test? She believed that she had a bigger, broader picture of each child than was demonstrated by any one assessment score, and that she must interpret scores within the context of that larger picture (School B, Edwards interview, 06/15/15). On the other hand, Ms. Edwards allowed herself to be surprised by quantitative data that showed a student performing at a higher level than she had seen on her own, because she was always looking for the hidden talents she believed each child had (School B, Edwards memo, 07/14/17).

Her sensemaking was particularly grounded in her past teaching experience, which gave her a sense of what second-graders were supposed to know and how children of that age, in general, interacted with various curricular topics. Although her definition of the word "data" was narrow, used only in relation to standardized assessments, she actually drew upon a range of information to make instructional decisions.

> I just feel like you don't really get to know a kid looking at just data. It's so much more that you have to look at and use. If I was someone that came into my room and I looked at just the data that I have, whether it was the data in the beginning or the data toward the end of the school year, I would say—you know, I would see growth—but I would say, "What's going on with this child," or "What's going on with this one?" But, if you talked to them or if you sit with them and you see how they interact in the class, then you would see what I see. But I think the administration or just the district relies so much on data that you lose so much else about a child.
>
> *(School B, Edwards interview, 06/15/15)*

Ms. Edwards had seen many educational reforms come and go over the years. She was not necessarily opposed to any particular initiative, since they were all aimed at improving student learning. Her main complaint was that so many new initiatives were introduced so rapidly that she had difficulty keeping up with all of it. This included the new emphasis on data: "But there's a whole lot of pointless data that we have. And on a lot of the programs that came in and introduced different ways to keep track of data, it's like they came that one time and they may or may not have revisited and it was not heard of again. If we could just focus on some things as opposed to so many." (School B, Edwards interview, 06/15/15).

Making Sense of Classroom Sensemaking: A Cross-case Comparison

Ms. Apple and Ms. Edwards appeared, in many ways, to be confident, competent teachers who cared deeply about their students' academic and social well-being. Ms. Apple was able to continually interpret and recalibrate her understandings of her class, through the use of frequent, close-at-hand forms of information about her students. She had to use data for analysis in occasional data meetings with the principal, but, since the school's focus was on improving outcomes for individual students, and since she taught a grade that did not have standardized testing, her situated meaning-making took precedence in her work. In a classroom with a co-teacher and in a highly collegial grade level and school, Ms. Apple had the luxury of plenty of social interaction for sensemaking. All of this seemed to be quite productive because she also had the capacity to know how to respond to students or where to go for help when she needed it.

Ms. Edwards also engaged in ongoing sensemaking in her classroom, interpreting what she saw in her current students through the lens of her considerable store of experience and her long-held views about student development as persons and learners. This kept her grounded and protected her from being distracted by the administration's expectations for data use, which did not enhance her classroom sensemaking, except in rare instances.

The different ways these teachers approached and understood data use were affected by their own values, experiences, and school contexts. For both teachers, data use was not simply a strategy for achieving higher learning gains; it was a component of their ongoing sensemaking about their students and their own teaching. Ms. Apple seemed to embrace performance data, though not at the expense of collecting other types of data, because she was focused on academic learning and preparing her students for third-grade work. Ms. Edwards, on the other hand, approached performance data with much more caution, perhaps because she disagreed more strenuously with the accountability context of her school, and focused on different aspects of her students' development.

The teachers in our case studies learned how to integrate different types of information about students with their knowledge of pedagogy, curriculum, and themselves as teachers. This was important because most forms of data do not, on their own, suggest pedagogical strategies to use. The teachers' practice was saturated with the wisdom that enabled them to craft accounts of their contexts and work that were familiar, but they also tried to see their students from new vantage points. Many newer and less experienced teachers may not have these anchors of knowledge and experience; some older and more experienced teachers may neglect to make the familiar strange, long enough to see their students as they are. Data itself is less important than the holistic sensemaking to which it contributes.

Implications: Promising Practices for Data Use in the Classroom

Our study has implications for further developments in data use in elementary classrooms. If, as these cases demonstrate, teachers use day-to-day information about students in their ongoing classroom sensemaking, it may be prudent to help them have input into the types of information they gather, sufficient opportunities for gathering information, and more time for reflecting on it. One set of promising practices might be curriculum-embedded assessments. Whether they are single problems, performance tasks, or periodic reviews, such assessments can be helpful if teachers feel they are appropriate measures of student learning, relative to what has been or will be taught.

Instructionally embedded checks for understanding represent another promising practice. These may include student recitations of their knowledge or reasoning in small-group settings, instructional conversations with individual students, and even the Post-it note check-ins favored by Ms. Apple. Although teachers have traditionally used these forms of information gathering, they could be helped by being more deliberate about them. Planning and eliciting such assessments can seem deceptively simple; in reality, teachers who frequently use informal assessments could easily overlook some students, fail to gather crucial information about student learning, or misread evidence that contradicts their prior assessments of their students. Tools that help teachers be more systematic about gathering and interpreting data could help. At least one educational-technology start-up has recognized the value of classroom-based information and is developing technology tools to help teachers document their observational data about students (Wan, 2017).

Social supports, like co-teaching, grade-level teaming, or other collaborative or consultative opportunities, may help teachers be more thorough and reflective as they gather and consider such information. School and district administrators who support assessment and information gathering in the classroom can be most helpful when they acknowledge that information collected in the moment, including information about student social-emotional states, as well as academic performance, has value and requires time, expertise, and attention to process. This is the information teachers persist in using.

But, as our cases illustrate, information generated within the classroom does not automatically point to appropriate or necessary instructional adjustments. Teachers make sense of how to respond to data about students in light of their own experience, expertise, and access to repertoires of curriculum and pedagogy. Professional development often focuses on the collection of student data, but the ways that such information can be used to improve instruction remain implicit. Therefore, a related set of promising practices might include efforts to help teachers learn new instructional strategies for responding to student needs. Teachers constantly build their instructional repertoires, beginning in preservice programs and continuing through in-service professional development. These learning opportunities could have a greater impact if they modeled and emphasized how data-informed sensemaking about students can be coupled with the search for effective ways to teach.

Teachers' use of data for situated sensemaking in their classrooms is essential and has integrity. No use of data by educators is a panacea or magic bullet. Using aggregated data for analysis can accomplish some things, and using data for teacher learning can accomplish others. Nonetheless, being able to use information about students for classroom sensemaking is intrinsic to the professional work of teaching, and teachers should have opportunities to learn to value it and do it well.

Note

1 This work was funded with a generous grant from the Spencer Foundation, as part of their Evidence for the Classroom initiative. We are grateful for that support, and for the cooperation of the teachers, principals, and others in the four schools participating in the study.

References

Bertrand, M., & Marsh, J. A. (2015). Teachers' sensemaking of data and implications for equity. *American Educational Research Journal, 52*(5), 861–893.

Blythe, T., Allen, D., & Powell, B. S. (2015). *Looking together at student work* (3rd ed.). New York, NY: Teachers College Press.

Breiter, A., & Light, D. (2006). Data for school improvement: Factors for designing effective information systems to support decision-making in schools. *Educational Technology & Society, 9*(3), 206–217.

Bryk, A. S., Gomez, L. M., Grunow, A., & LeMahieu, P. G. (2015). *Learning to improve: How America's schools can get better at getting better.* Cambridge, MA: Harvard Education Press.

Coburn, C. E. (2006). Framing the problem of reading instruction: Using frame analysis to uncover the microprocesses of policy implementation. *American Educational Research Journal, 43*(3), 343–349.

Dudley-Marling, C., & Gurn, A. (2010). Troubling the foundations of special education: Examining the myth of the normal curve. In C. Dudley-Marling & A. Gurn (Eds.), *The myth of the normal curve* (pp. 9–24). New York, NY: Peter Lang.

Ferri, B. A., & Connor, D. J. (2006). *Reading resistance: Discourses of exclusion in desegregation and inclusion debates.* New York, NY: Peter Lang.

Flaherty, W. H. (2004). Data warehouse helps Hanover County Public Schools raise student achievement. *T.H.E. Journal, 31*(12), 38–39.

Hand, V. M. (2010). The co-construction of opposition in a low-track mathematics classroom. *American Educational Research Journal, 47*(1), 97–132.

Harry, B., & Klinger, J. K. (2005). *Why are so many minority students in special education?* New York, NY: Teachers College Press.

Huffman, D., & Kalnin, J. (2003). Collaborative inquiry to make data-based decisions in schools. *Teaching and Teacher Education, 19*(6), 569–580.

Kozleski, E. B. (2016). Reifying categories: Measurement in search of understanding. In D. Connor, B. Ferri, & S. Annamma (Eds.), *DisCrit: Critical conversations across race, class & dis/ability* (pp. 101–116). New York, NY: Teachers College Press.

Kruse, S., Louis, Seashore, K., & Bryk, A. (1994). *Building professional community in schools.* Issues in Restructuring Schools, Issue Report No. 6, pp. 3–6. Madison, WI: University of Wisconsin, Center on Organization and Restructuring of Schools.

Little, Judith Warren. (1982). Norms of collegiality and experimentation: Workplace conditions of school success. *American Educational Research Journal, 19*(3), 325–340.

Maitlis, S. (2005). The social processes of organizational sensemaking. *Academy of Management Journal, 48*(1), 21–49.

Maitlis, S., & Christianson, M. (2014). Sensemaking in organizations: Taking stock and moving forward. *The Academy of Management Annals, 8*(1), 57–125.

McDonald, J. P., Mohr, N., Dichter, A., & McDonald, E. C. (2003). *The power of protocols: An educator's guide to better practice.* New York, NY: Teachers College Press.

Olson, L. (2002). Schools discovering riches in data. *Education Week, 21*(40), 1, 16–17.

Park, V., Daly, A. J., & Guerra, A. W. (2013). Strategic framing: How leaders craft the meaning of data use for equity and learning. *Educational Policy, 27*(4), 645–675.

Protheroe, N. (2001). Improving teaching and learning with data-based decisions: Asking the right questions and acting on the answers. *ERS Spectrum, 19*(3), 4–9.

Sleeter, C. E. (1986). Learning disabilities: The social construction of a special education category. *Exceptional Children, 53*(1), 46–54.

Spillane, J. P., Reiser, B. J., & Reimer, T. (2002). Policy implementation and cognition: Reframing and refocusing implementation research. *Review of Educational Research, 72*(3), 387–431.

Talbert, J. E. (2011). Collaborative inquiry to expand student success in New York City schools. In J. A. O'Day, C. S. Bitter, & L. M. Gomez (Eds.), *Education reform in New York City: Ambitious change in the nation's most complex school system* (pp. 131–155). Cambridge, MA: Harvard Education Press.

Tyack, D., & Tobin, W. (1994). The "grammar" of schooling: Why has it been so hard to change? *American Educational Research Journal, 31*(3), 453–479.

Wan, T. (2017, June 6). *BookNook raises $1.2M seed round to facilitate small group literacy instruction.* Retrieved from www.edsurge.com/news/2017-06-06-booknook-raises-1-2m-seed-round-to-facilitate-small-group-literacy-instruction?utm_content=buffer9a6cf&utm_medium=social&utm_source=twitter.com&utm_campaign=buffer

Weick, K. E. (1969). *The social psychology of organizing.* Reading, MA: Addison-Wesley.

Weick, K. E. (1995). *Sensemaking in organizations.* Thousand Oaks, CA: Sage.

Weinstock, J. (2009). Data-driven decision-making: Mission accomplished. *T.H.E. Journal, 36*(2), 28–32.

4

USING A LEARNING TRAJECTORY TO MAKE SENSE OF STUDENT WORK FOR INSTRUCTION

Caroline B. Ebby[1]

Recent research on mathematics teaching promotes a view of ambitious instruction that is based more directly on research about student learning, and calls for teachers to make sense of student thinking as a regular part of their instruction (e.g., Franke, Kazemi, & Battey, 2007). Effective formative assessment, one of the most promising educational interventions (Black & Wiliam, 1998), involves continually collecting and interpreting evidence of student thinking, to inform an instructional response. Despite the importance of understanding student thinking for both current theories of mathematics instruction and formative assessment, helping teachers understand student thinking has not been a major focus of data use initiatives, policies, or practices (Coburn & Turner, 2012).

In this chapter, I focus on teacher sensemaking of student-learning data, or the process by which teachers give meaning to written artifacts of students' mathematical thinking. Through a case study of one fourth-grade teacher, I explore the impact of an intervention that introduced teachers of third to fifth grades to a new conceptual framework for interpreting student work, one that is based on research about the developmental progression of student learning of mathematics, on both analysis and instructional decision-making. Through participation in a series of facilitated grade-level professional learning community (PLC) meetings, teachers learned to use a learning trajectory for multiplicative thinking to interpret their own students' work.

Learning Trajectories in Mathematics Education

A wealth of research has been conducted on children's mathematical understanding, which, in recent years, has been organized into a set of developmental pathways, or learning trajectories, for various domains (Daro, Mosher, & Corcoran,

2011). In conceptualizing an integration of research on learning with research on teaching, Sztajn, Confrey, Wilson, & Edgington (2012) proposed "learning-trajectory-based instruction," teaching that draws on these progressions as the basis for instructional decisions. There is mounting evidence that knowledge and use of learning trajectories positively impacts instructional decision-making, task selection, and student achievement in mathematics (e.g., Clements, Sarama, Spitler, Lange, & Wolfe, 2011). Learning trajectories can enhance the formative assessment process by providing teachers with a clear articulation of learning goals, a framework for how student thinking develops, and activities that are likely to move students along the path toward achieving those goals (Heritage, 2008).

For this study, a learning trajectory for multiplicative reasoning from the Ongoing Assessment Project (Petit, Laird, & Hulbert, 2017) was adapted as a tool to help teachers make sense of student strategies for multiplication and division (see Figure 4.1). The trajectory illustrates the progression of student strategies, moving down the vertical dimension: from counting by ones, to adding, to skip counting, to use of visual models, and, finally, to more abstract and efficient strategies and algorithms. The trajectory also illustrates the applicability of strategies to problems with factors of different magnitudes, along the horizontal dimension. For example, although students might count to solve problems involving single-digit factors (e.g., 3 × 6), they could not reasonably count to solve multi-digit problems, such as 36 × 45. This reinforces the need to move students toward more sophisticated strategies, as expectations and rigor increase.

Central to the trajectory is the presence of visual models—specifically, the array and area model—in the transitional level. These models provide the bridge between additive and multiplicative strategies, and suggest a pathway for instruction. The trajectory also represents a progression in visual models, from an array of discrete objects organized in equal groups, to an area model with rows and columns, to an open-area model where only the dimensions and areas are represented.

Conceptual Framework

This study draws upon sociological theories of sensemaking (Dervin, 1998; Weick, 1995) to understand how teachers examined and developed understanding of evidence in student work. Central to sensemaking theory is the idea that individuals actively construct interpretations by extracting cues and making meaning of information in the environment (Weick, 1995). People also draw on their own conceptual frameworks, using previous knowledge and understanding to organize and categorize new information (Klein, Moon, & Hoffman, 2006). Conceptual frames and extracted cues are intrinsically linked, as frames filter, amplify, or dampen what cues a person attends to in a given context, and also shape actions and decisions.

The study explored the initial conceptual frameworks teachers were using to interpret and respond to student work, as well as how teachers' sensemaking

Multiplicative Reasoning Learning Trajectory

	STRATEGY			
ONES	Counting or Sharing by Ones	$3 \times 4 = 12$ ••• ••• ••• ••• 1, 2, 3, 4, 5, … 12		
ADDITIVE	Repeated Addition/ Subtraction	$3 + 3 + 3 + 3 = 12$	$12 \times 15 = 180$ $15+15+15+15+15+15+15+15+15+15+15+15$ $15+15 \; 15+15 \; \ldots \; 15+15 \; 15+15$ $30 + 30 \; \ldots \; 30 + 30$ $60 + 60 + 60$	
	Building Up	$3 + 3 + 3 + 3$ $6 + 6$ 12	$60 + 60 + 60$ 180	
TRANSITIONAL	Skip Counting	3, 6, 9, 12 or 4, 8, 12	15, 30, 45, 60, 90, 120, 150, 180	
	Array	(arrays of dots) 4 3	15 12 (grid)	
	Open Area	4 3 [12]	10 5 10 [100 50] 2 [20 10]	200 20 8 40 [8000 800 320] 8 [1600 160 64] $228 \times 48 = 10944$
MULTIPLICATIVE	Properties	$3 \times 3 = 9, \; 9 + 3 = 12$	$15 \times 10 = 150, \; 15 \times 2 = 30, \; 150 + 30$ $15 \times 2 = 30 = 90 \times 2 = 180$	$(200 \times 40) + (200 \times 8) + (20 \times 40) +$ $(20 \times 8) + (8 \times 40) + (8 \times 8) = 10994$
			Algorithms $\quad 15 \quad\quad\quad 15$ $\underline{\times 12} \quad\quad 12 \overline{)180}$ $\quad 30 \quad\quad\quad \underline{120} \;\; \times 10$ $\underline{150} \quad\quad\quad 60$ $\quad 180 \quad\quad\; \underline{48} \;\; \times 4$ $\quad\quad\quad\quad\;\; 12 \;\; \times 1$ $\quad\quad\quad\quad\;\;\; 0$	$\quad\;\; 228$ $48 \overline{)10944}$ $\quad \underline{\;9600\;} \; 200$ $\quad 1344$ $\quad \underline{\;\;960\;} \;\; 20$ $\quad\;\; 384 \;\; 5$ $\quad\;\; \underline{240}$ $\quad\;\; 144 \;\; 2$ $\quad\;\;\; \underline{96}$ $\quad\;\;\; 48 \;\; 1$ $\quad\;\;\; \underline{48}$ $\quad\quad\; 0$ $\quad 228$ $\underline{\times 48}$ 1824 $\underline{9120}$ 10944 *Menu* $48 \times 10 = 480$ $48 \times 20 = 960$ $48 \times 2 = 96$ $48 \times 100 = 4800$ $48 \times 200 = 9600$ $48 \times 5 = 240$
	Fluency	Fact Recall ($3 \times 4 = 12$) ° ° °		

FIGURE 4.1   A Learning Trajectory for Multiplicative Reasoning[2]

processes changed over time through the introduction and use of the learning-trajectory framework. As a promising data use practice, the utilization of a learning trajectory supports teachers in extracting and interpreting cues in relation to student strategies (how they are solving the problem), underlying conceptual understanding, and sophistication of reasoning. In this chapter, I focus on a case of one teacher who showed continuous and significant change in the way she analyzed her own student work, highlighting both sensemaking opportunities during the PLC meetings and changes in the sensemaking of her own students' work over time.

Methods

Research-Data Sources

The research data for this case study were collected as part of a larger study about the professional learning of 18 grade three, four, and five teachers in two elementary schools. The intervention involved initial professional development and a series of facilitated grade-level PLC meetings, where teachers collaboratively looked at student work with the learning trajectory at three times during the school year. The PLC meetings were videotaped and transcribed. A series of four semi-structured cognitive interviews were used to understand how teachers were interpreting their own student-learning data and drawing on evidence to formulate instructional responses over time. Teachers were asked to bring a class set of student work on a multiplication or division problem to the interview. First, they were asked to sort the work in a way that made the most sense them, while talking aloud about their process. Second, they were asked to highlight at least one example from each category and talk about the work in terms of strengths and weaknesses. Last, teachers were asked to explain instructional responses for the examples discussed and for the whole class. The interviews were audio recorded and transcribed, and student work samples were collected.

Through purposeful sampling, one case was selected as an information-rich example (Patton, 1990) that tracks change in a teacher's analysis of student work over time. Although not necessarily a typical case, it illuminates some of the conditions that support connections between the learning-trajectory framework and a teacher's analysis of student-learning data.

Research-Data Analysis

Analysis of the interview data was conducted in two stages. First, an analytical memo was produced for each teacher (Strauss & Corbin, 1990) to track how the teacher categorized and made sense of student work for instruction. Next, the memos were used to generate inductive codes, in relation to: 1) sorting schema,

2) analysis of student work, and 3) instructional response. Categories for sorting schema included *correctness* (whether the answer was correct and the presence of errors), *proficiency* (judgement of performance, often using labels such as advanced, proficient, etc.), and *strategies* (how the student solved the problem). As shown in Table 4.1, teachers' interpretations of student work ranged along a continuum of depth, from a focus on surface characteristics (answer or neatness), to a descriptive focus (how the student solved the problem), to a conceptual focus (what the student understood). A final, but less frequently encountered level of interpretation, was characterized by drawing together descriptive, conceptual, and developmental aspects of student work. Similarly, a set of codes was developed for planned instructional responses, ranging from general (reteaching content, grouping students), to procedural (focus on procedural mastery, fluency, or efficiency), to conceptual (deepening understanding or connecting procedural and conceptual understanding), to developmental (building on student understanding to move toward more sophisticated strategies and understanding). Once the codes were established, all of the interviews were double coded. The research team met to discuss any discrepancies that emerged and agreed on a final code. These codes were then translated into rubric scores for each sample of student work discussed, and those scores were averaged to construct a profile for each teacher over time. The fourth-grade teacher reported on in this chapter was selected as a case study based on her steady increase in mean rubric scores, for both analysis and instructional response, over the year of the intervention.

The PLC videos were transcribed and analyzed using open coding (Charmaz, 2006) to characterize the focus of discussion, activities, and facilitator press. The case-study teacher's involvement was also coded, in relation to sharing student work, raising questions, responding, initiating new topics, or changing the direction of the discussion.

TABLE 4.1 Levels of Teachers' Analysis of Student Work and Planned Instructional Response

Level	Focus of Analysis of Student Work	Focus of Planned Instructional Response
General	Surface aspects (correct answer, format) or overall judgment	Not specific to mathematical content or understanding
Procedural	How students solved the problem	Teaching a specific procedure or skill
Conceptual	Conceptual understanding connected to use of strategy	Developing conceptual understanding
Developmental	Situating strategy and understanding within a developmental progression	Moving students from current understanding to more sophisticated strategies and/or understanding

Learning to See and Build on Student Learning: The Case of Ivy Monroe

Ivy Monroe[3] was one of four fourth-grade teachers at an urban K–8 charter school with a diverse student population. She was in her fourth year of teaching and her third year of teaching fourth grade at that school. Before the intervention, Ivy gave formative assessments regularly, but analyzed her students' work from a correctness and procedural frame. Over the intervention year, she began to focus more on student strategies and conceptual understanding, and eventually integrated conceptual and procedural understanding to recognize sophistication of strategy as a developmental process. This shift did not happen immediately after the introduction of the learning trajectory, rather it occurred incrementally throughout the year, as the learning trajectory was clarified and reinforced through the three facilitated PLC meetings. Her development, beginning with baseline data collected in the spring of the year prior to the intervention, and then through three rounds of PLC meetings and interviews (fall, winter, and spring), is traced to illuminate some important themes and contributing factors.

Before the Intervention: Looking for Correct Answers and Procedural Errors

For the baseline interview, Ivy analyzed work on a problem from an exit slip, where students had to solve a decontextualized two-digit multiplication problem (49 × 63) using the open-area model. She had made corrections on the student work and sorted it based on whether the answer was correct and, if not, what kind of errors were made. She noted that only 10 students ("less than half the class") had the correct response. The remaining piles she made included "simple mistakes," "students who aren't multiplying the correct numbers in the correct places," and "errors in multiplying multiples of 10." The student work in these last two categories showed evidence of using the open-area model procedurally, and either multiplying the wrong combinations of numbers, adding factors, or making place-value errors. Ivy seemed to recognize that these errors were showing a lack of conceptual understanding, but her ideas about what to do about this were limited. She focused on the need for additional practice and review, but did not provide any specific ways to address misunderstandings.

In the example shown in Figure 4.2, she noted that the student correctly broke up the factors into tens and ones (49 = 40 + 9 and 63 = 60 + 3) and correctly calculated the product of 60 × 40 as the first partial area, but then seemed to have multiplied random combinations for the other three areas.

> This is right, this is written correctly, but they don't seem to understand how to use, kind of like, the columns and the rows in order to figure out which factors to multiply in which part. And then, here she seems to have

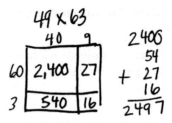

FIGURE 4.2 Incorrect Student Solution for 49 × 63 Using the Open-Area Model

> gotten totally lost. Like she knows she has to multiply different numbers at the ones and the tens from the two different numbers, but she seems to not understand where each part goes.
>
> *(Interview, 05/23/14)*

Note that her analysis of the student work remained at the procedural level—"which factors to multiply" and "where each part goes"—rather than focusing on the conceptual underpinnings of the visual model or properties of multiplication. She concluded: "This is a student I'd definitely pull out for re-teaching with my assistant or with me," but did not give any details about the focus of this remediation.

After looking at her student's work, Ivy was surprised by the results of this formative assessment:

> I guess because [of] the classwork that they had been doing that day and the day before, it had seemed that they were getting it correct, and I thought that they were doing better than they were. And then, when I gave them this, it was not what I was expecting. I was expecting more of them to get the right answer.
>
> *(Interview, 05/23/14)*

Throughout the interview, she recognized that many of her students were not demonstrating understanding of the open-area strategy that she was having them use, but, without a conceptual frame from which to make sense of their understanding or how it develops, she focused on general recommendations.

In sum, at the beginning of the study, Ivy was sorting student work based on correctness, and focusing her analysis primarily on what students did and what errors they made, rather than on what their strategies suggested about their underlying understanding or how to build on that understanding. Her instructional recommendations remained at a general or procedural level, focusing on remediation, grouping students for instruction, or reinforcing a specific strategy or method.

At the beginning of the following school year, the intervention began with a half-day professional-development session focused on multiplicative reasoning and the learning trajectory at Ivy's school. The content included the development of student understanding and strategies, important underlying ideas and concepts, grade-level expectations, multiplicative problem structures, formative assessment, and instructional strategies for moving students along the trajectory. Teachers also worked in groups to sort a sample set of student work using the trajectory, with the following questions guiding their analysis:

- What different strategies are students using to solve the multiplicative problem?
- Where are those strategies on the learning trajectory?
- What do those strategies suggest about students' understanding of multiplication?
- What needs are evident in the student work?

This routine for sorting student work was designed to intentionally focus on extracting cues related to student strategies and understanding, rather than only correctness and errors. The trajectory and routine were designed to work together to structure teachers' sorting, analysis, and instructional response, in relation to data on student learning, to focus more on student thinking than on correctness or overall performance. At the end of the session, teachers were asked to administer a formative-assessment item to their class during the beginning weeks of school and to bring the student work to the first PLC meeting to sort and analyze with this same routine.

Fall: Learning to See Different Strategies in Student Work

For the first PLC meeting in early October, the fourth-grade teachers brought student work on two related multiplication word problems of different magnitude ("How many wheels are there on 6 cars?" "How many wheels are there on 18 cars?"). The facilitator asked them to share different strategies they were seeing in their students' work. They took turns projecting examples and engaged in discussion to make sense of both students' strategies and underlying thinking. The facilitator named and recorded strategies on chart paper as they emerged to reflect the order of the learning trajectory (see Figure 4.3). The facilitator also modeled and clarified the learning-trajectory language and pressed teachers to talk about the underlying understanding, also listing those on the left side of the chart (e.g., equal grouping, place value, and properties of multiplication).

The last half of the meeting focused on instruction: how to move students along the trajectory, the importance of visual models, and how to continue to deepen the understanding of students who were already using multiplicative strategies.

Shortly after this PLC, Ivy participated in an interview where she brought student work on an exit ticket, consisting of a multistep single-digit multiplication problem and a related division problem. In a manner similar to which she had sorted in the baseline interview, she made four piles based on correctness and errors: those that had correct answers to both problems, those that had only the

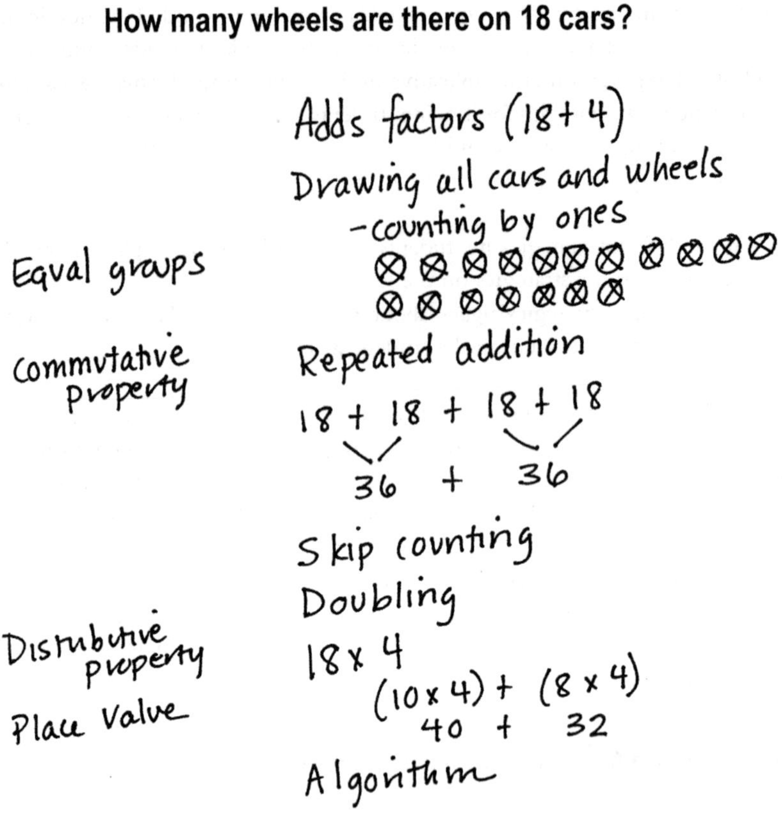

52 Ebby

How many wheels are there on 18 cars?

Equal groups

Commutative property

Distributive property

Place Value

Adds factors (18 + 4)
Drawing all cars and wheels
— counting by ones
⊗ ⊗ ⊗ ⊗ ⊗ ⊗ ⊗ ⊗ ⊗ ⊗
⊗ ⊗ ⊗ ⊗ ⊗ ⊗ ⊗

Repeated addition
18 + 18 + 18 + 18
  ∨   ∨
  36   + 36

Skip counting
Doubling
18 × 4
 (10 × 4) + (8 × 4)
   40   +   32
Algorithm

FIGURE 4.3 Facilitator's Recording of Strategies and Concepts as That Emerged in the PLC Discussion

multiplication problem correct, students that added rather than multiplied the factors, and students who multiplied, but used the wrong factors. As she talked through examples from each pile, however, she drew on the learning trajectory to identify more specific strategies.

For example, in analyzing work where a student had multiplied the wrong factors, she focused on what the work suggested about the student's understanding of multiplication:

> I mean, she was definitely able to create an array, six times six, and she got the answer correct. So, she kind of knows how to model a multiplication situation and, on the side, you can see she was like, skip counting by sixes, and then figured out, okay, I have four sixes and I need to do two more, twelve, plus six more.... So, she started to figure out, like, how to skip count and how to use factors.
>
> *(Interview, 11/07/14)*

In addition to recognizing the student's use of the array and repeated addition, she recognized that an appropriate next step would involve moving from repeated addition to a more efficient strategy, like skip counting.

Looking more closely at the work in the pile of correct solutions, Ivy created an additional category for a student who had used skip counting. She acknowledged some strengths in his work: "He understands how to add groups. He's not, like, drawing each individual dot he's circling. He's figuring out that he can add four at a time." She then explained that she would have him work on using related problems, such as 4 × 5, to figure out 4 × 6, working toward fact fluency, automaticity, and efficiency. Although Ivy had initially sorted this example into the correct pile, further analysis of the strategy allowed her to see where there was room for improvement.

When asked about using the trajectory, Ivy described how she learned to "see different strategies and how they work differently for different kids," and the importance of encouraging efficiency:

> Which one will be faster if we count by sixes, if we count by threes. If I count every three, is that going to be faster, or if I count every six? . . . What if I just figure out how many are in half and I double it—how can I use that?
>
> *(Interview, 11/07/14)*

At this point in time, the trajectory seemed to be helping her identify and distinguish differences in the ways that students made sense of and approached multiplicative problems, and also gave her an awareness of the importance of efficiency. Although her sorting showed that her use of the trajectory was not yet automatic, participating in the interviews seemed to prompt her to draw on it for analysis.

Winter: Making Conceptual Connections

The second PLC meeting took place in January, and teachers were asked to give students a division problem where the remainder had to be interpreted ("How many 9-inch bows can be made from 105 inches of ribbon?"). The discussion began by talking about the nature of the problem and the significance of having students work with a continuous, rather than discrete, quantity. The facilitator had them anticipate some of the strategies students might use. They then moved into sharing and making sense of different strategies—e.g., multiplication, skip counting by nines, building up—while the facilitator named and recorded them. Ivy noted that although many of her students could carry out the steps of division, they were often confused about what the quantities meant in the problem context. For example, a student might perform all the steps, end up with a remainder of six, and think that six was the answer to the question.

Later, when the facilitator modeled an open array to represent a student's doubling strategy, Ivy remarked, "My kids get so confused by that, and I draw it all the time, but it doesn't help them" (PLC, 01/14/15). The facilitator pointed out how understanding of arrays and open-area models develops over time, as reflected on the trajectory, and highlighted the importance of underlying concepts. Another teacher described ways to help students understand the open-area model.

At the end of the session, the facilitator introduced the partial-quotients method in response to teachers' concerns that students did not understand the traditional long-division algorithm. After talking about the first step ("How many groups of nine are in 105?"), Ivy made an important conceptual connection between the factors (9 and 11) and the dividend (105), exclaiming, "It's like an array!" (PLC, 01/14/15; see Figure 4.4).

$$9\overline{)105}^{\,11} \qquad\qquad \begin{array}{c}?\\ 9\,\boxed{105}\end{array}$$

FIGURE 4.4 Connections between division and the area model

Note that she was making sense of exactly what she stated her students were struggling with—the quantities and the meaning of the model. This PLC represented an important opportunity for Ivy to solidify her understanding of different strategies on the trajectory in relation to division, but also to make some conceptual connections between the open-area model, procedures, and the quantities in a division problem.

In the interview that followed this PLC, Ivy brought student work on a two-digit by one-digit multiplication problem ("19 students each brought in 6 cans"). This time, she sorted the work by strategy, embedding both correct and incorrect solutions within the piles she made, and her students' work showed much more variety in strategy use than in previous interviews. In her analysis of examples in each pile, she paid attention to the strategy and also made some assertions about underlying conceptual understanding. Throughout the interview, she mentioned open area as a visual model to help develop conceptual understanding.

In discussing the following example in Figure 4.5, Ivy stated that the student broke apart the factors of 19 by place value to multiply 6 × 10 and 6 × 9, but then went on to double the answer. She explained that she was happy that the student chose "easy numbers to work with," knew her facts, and "knows she's supposed

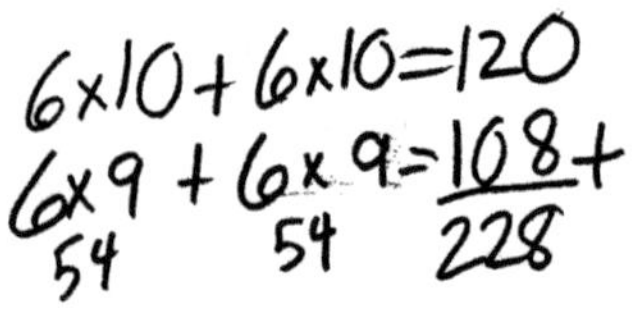

$$6\times10 + 6\times10 = 120$$
$$6\times9 + 6\times9 = 108 +$$
$$5454228$$

FIGURE 4.5 Incorrect Student Solution to 19 × 6

to break it apart and then add the products and the partial products together" (Interview, 01/22/15).

At the same time, she acknowledged that doubling the resulting expression showed some misunderstanding. When asked what she would do next with this student, she focused on the use of the visual model to help build conceptual understanding for the procedure:

> Maybe referring it, like creating an array to visually model it, too, so she understands where this breaking apart is coming from, so she understands she doesn't have to double it, necessarily, or shouldn't double it.
>
> *(Interview, 01/22/15)*

At the end of the interview, Ivy reflected on how the learning trajectory was guiding her choice of strategies to share, discussion of efficiency, and use of visual models:

> Especially during warm-ups, when we're doing a multiplication question, I see kids solving it different ways. I like to call on different kids to show us how they solved it, to show a variety of ways to break it up, and have them—Like, if they're breaking up an array, show that, oh, she multiplied, she did this one, he did this, she did this. Which one do you think is the fastest way to solve it? Who got there faster? Or what's easier, 10 × 6 or 12 × 6? That kind of stuff. We've done a lot of that. We've also started moving away from closed arrays to open arrays, to kind of show, well, we know this is this, we don't need to draw every single line. Although I think, for some of them, it would be beneficial to still have the closed arrays, to keep working with those.
>
> *(Interview, 01/22/15)*

In addition, Ivy drew on the trajectory to note some growth she had been able to see in her class: "There's fewer students doing repeated addition now than did it two months ago, which is encouraging" (Interview, 01/22/15).

Spring: Connecting Conceptual and Procedural Understanding

For the third PLC meeting, which took place in April, teachers were asked to give a problem that focused more specifically on students' conceptual understanding: a partially completed open-area model was given, and students had to think about the relationship between multiplication and division to identify the missing partial products and factors. For various reasons, only one teacher brought student work to this PLC meeting, but she found the results very illuminating: none of her students answered the problem correctly, and most of them demonstrated a complete lack of understanding of the relationship between the model and the operations of multiplication and division. The facilitator decided to have teachers explore what it is that students should understand around the open-area model, and how the model relates to multiplication algorithms, place value, and magnitude, and algebra. All four teachers seemed eager to deepen their own understanding of multiplication and the area model.

For the following interview, Ivy gave her students a decontextualized two-digit multiplication problem ("34 × 68"), like the one she had given the previous spring for the baseline interview. She noted that she had been focusing on the open-area model in her instruction, but, rather than require that students all use that model, she had left it open for them to use any strategy. She went on to sort the student work by strategy (open area, traditional algorithm, use of distributive property, using a related problem).

In her analysis of these different strategies, Ivy made sense of the procedures students were using, but also recognized the sophistication of student thinking in relation to the trajectory and connected their strategy use to their understanding of the operation. For example, she noted that one student correctly broke up 34 × 68 into 34 × 60 and 34 × 8, but then had to repeatedly add 34 to do these calculations:

> He was thinking about it in kind of a sophisticated way, but he's using repeated addition to calculate the actual products . . . and he got the right answer, so he shows a lot of credibility to break apart the tens and ones, to break apart your numbers, but his fact fluency just isn't very high.
>
> *(Interview, 06/05/15)*

She went on to explain that this student needed to work on multiplication of multi-digit numbers and that working with the open-array model to further break up 34 × 60 would be helpful for him, to move away from repeated addition.

Although most of her students were using the open-area model successfully (in contrast to the baseline interview, where more than half solved it incorrectly), Ivy also recognized two students who were showing misconceptions. Her analysis of the misuse of procedures showed how far she had come in terms of making sense of student thinking over the year. As shown in Figure 4.6, the student had drawn the open-area model correctly, but then added the factors of 30 and 60, instead of multiplying them.

Ivy noted that the student showed some level of understanding: "He understands sort of what's happening in each box." She also noted, however, "He's doing things like multiplying 30 times 60, [and] getting 90, because he's just adding them together. I don't think he's completely understanding, again, the multiples of 10" (Interview, 06/05/15). As she continued to analyze the work, she noticed that he was using repeated addition to calculate some of the products and that might explain why he had added 30 and 60.

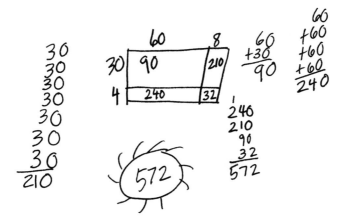

FIGURE 4.6 Incorrect Student Solution to 68 × 34

She recognized, however, that this was more than just a procedural issue, or one of not knowing the correct steps to follow:

> The 60 plus 30 worries me . . . just because I think, in this point in the year, I think repeated addition is one thing. But to just add two numbers they're supposed to be multiplying seems to be a pretty big oversight and misunderstanding of the problem.
>
> *(Interview 06/05/15)*

In addition to recognizing the severity of the error, Ivy was able to articulate specific recommendations for building his conceptual understanding of the model. (Recall that, at the end of the previous year, her instructional response was simply to pull a student out for reteaching.)

> He also needs to work on just, maybe, modeling the example of what's going on, so I might also go back to a closed array with him. And thinking about, like, well, what is 30 groups of 60? What does that mean? We're not just adding 30 plus 60 because that would only give us a very small portion of what's here. We have to multiply them to calculate how many tiles are on the floor. We have to calculate how many squares are actually in that box. I think he knows what the measurements are of the individual boxes, so that's good. I think, just maybe, working on visualizing what's inside of those boxes, what it actually means.
>
> *(Interview, 06/05/15)*

By the end of the year, Ivy was drawing on the learning trajectory both to identify strategies and to think about the potential next instructional steps. Prior to the intervention, Ivy understood the open-area model as another method or procedure for multiplication, and interpreted errors as a matter of not following the correct steps. Over the year, she learned to see it as a visual model that could help students develop deeper understanding of multiplication. During the last interview, it was apparent that she recognized different strategies, looked for conceptual understanding, and also integrated conceptual understanding with efficiency of strategy.

Reflecting Back on the Year

Ivy's reflections on her experiences over the year illuminate some important aspects of using a learning trajectory that contribute to its promise as a practice for teachers' data use. First, she explained how the learning trajectory had shifted the way teachers were looking at student work, from focusing on correctness to focusing on specific needs:

> I think it's been really useful because, oftentimes as a teacher, you know you should look at the work and group it like this, and think about what each kid is really showing you. But, so frequently in teaching, it's just, you have so many other things happening that it just becomes, is it right or wrong? And who got it wrong? Okay, and those kids, work with those kids as a group. When, really, we should look at it like, the kids who are getting it wrong are doing a lot of different things, and [they are] not necessarily compatible, to put in the same small group.
>
> *(Interview, 06/05/15)*

As Ivy noted, sorting student work by strategy allowed teachers to move beyond identifying students for small-group remediation, to get a more refined understanding of what errors and misconceptions were evident in the student work, and, in turn, this led to ideas for differentiated support. In contrast, when student work is sorted only by correct answers, teachers learn who needs extra help, but not what kind of specific help they need.

She also explained that, by focusing on strategies, this routine illuminated common strengths and needs that otherwise might not be visible:

> I think you can see trends, and you can kind of see trends even across the different piles. You saw trends that kids had in common, needs they had in common—even though some of them are going to get it right, some are going to get it wrong, some are using starter problems, some are using arrays—that you might not see otherwise.
>
> *(Interview, 06/05/15)*

Ivy reflected on how the learning trajectory helped her understand the overall development of multiplicative thinking. She recognized that, in the past, she had focused on getting students to a level of mastery that was not necessarily appropriate, given their current understanding:

> I would have kids, especially in the beginning of the year, who were still counting individual groups. And my answer would always be, like, well, we have to get them to at least memorize their facts. But then, by doing that, you're, kind of, skipping a whole couple of steps, in terms of skip counting and thinking about grouping, versus counting individual circles, or what have you. And helping, kind of, like, move them along, versus just trying to make them skip three steps, which is just going to make them more confused and have not very good number sense at all.
>
> *(Interview, 06/05/15)*

She also remarked that the use of the learning trajectory had changed how she talked to her students, and helped her understand how to support struggling students: "How to help them figure out why it's wrong or why they might have made that mistake. Help them getting clearer on their thinking." At the same time, she acknowledged that it helped her understand "how to help advanced students not be bored in math without giving them a totally separate lesson" (Interview, 06/05/15).

Learning Trajectories as a Promising Practice for Teachers' Data Use

Table 4.2 illustrates changes in Ivy's sorting schema, analysis of student work and instructional response, along with the focus of the PLCs over the yearlong intervention. As a conceptual framework, the learning trajectory supported a change in the way she interpreted her students' work and broadened the nature of the cues that she extracted, from surface features to evidence of strategies and understanding. The learning trajectory also supported her sensemaking and led to growth in her ability to make specific instructional recommendations to help improve both conceptual and procedural understanding around multiplication and division. Table 4.2 also shows how making sense of different aspects of the trajectory in the PLC meetings (strategies, underlying concepts, visual models) was evidenced in Ivy's analysis of her own students' work.

As Ivy reflected, when teachers analyze student-learning data through a correctness lens, sensemaking focuses on identifying those students who have not yet met the performance standard, but there is little information gleaned about how to help them reach that standard. The learning trajectory gives teachers a conceptual framework from which to pay attention to and make sense of student strategies and conceptual understanding, and this helps them generate more specific and refined instructional responses to move students along a continuum toward the goal of multiplicative reasoning. Moreover, unlike more traditional approaches

TABLE 4.2 Changes in Sorting, Analysis, and Instructional Response Over Time

Time	PLC Focus	Sorting Scheme	Analysis	Instructional Response
Baseline		Correctness	Identifying errors; recognition of lack of conceptual understanding	Additional practice and review
Fall	Clarifying trajectory and underlying concepts	Correctness	Using learning trajectory to identify strategies within piles	Encouraging efficiency of strategy
Winter	Division—conceptual connections	Strategy	Making connections between visual model and strategy	Using the open array to develop conceptual understanding
Spring	Making sense of open-area model	Strategy	Considering both conceptual understanding and efficiency of strategy	Developing understanding of open-area model and encouraging efficiency

to using student-learning data, the discussion of instructional responses is not limited to students who do not show mastery of a given standard.

The themes in Table 4.2 also highlight some important milestones in the trajectory for the teacher's use of student-learning data. At first, the learning trajectory acted as a conceptual tool to help shift her sorting frame and the extraction of cues, allowing Ivy to recognize multiple strategies in her students' work. As she began to allow for and encourage multiple strategies in her instruction, her students' work also reflected more variety in relation to strategy. A second important shift occurred when Ivy began to understand the learning trajectory in terms of the development of conceptual understanding; this shift allowed her to draw on the framework for both analysis and instructional response. By the end of the year, she was demonstrating an emerging ability to integrate strategy, efficiency, and conceptual understanding in her thinking about student learning and instruction.

Implications

Developing procedural fluency with understanding is an important goal of current reforms in mathematics education. Learning trajectories can enhance the interpretive process central to effective formative assessment and instructional improvement, shifting the focus from students who "get it or don't get it" to addressing specific student needs and moving all students along a continuum toward the learning goal. As promising practice for the use of student-learning data, using learning trajectories to make sense of student work has the potential for a deeper impact on classroom instruction and student learning.

This practice requires shifting our current notions of data use, however, broadening the scope of the data to provide evidence of student thinking rather than just performance (e.g., looking at student work, rather than percent correct). It also introduces an interpretive framework that interrupts normative practices based on frames of achievement, correctness, and mastery. For example, student work is sorted, rather than graded or scored. These shifts require a substantial investment in teacher learning and capacity building. The intervention described in this case study provided opportunities for teacher learning through traditional professional development, but also through guided practice and interpreting data on student learning in a collaborative setting over time. The presence of a facilitator with expertise in the learning trajectory was also critical. Ivy herself reflected on the importance of having an outside expert "to hold us accountable" and focus the discussion (Interview, 06/05/15).

It is also important to acknowledge that these shifts will not occur simply by giving teachers a new routine or framework to use. The case study illustrates the importance of working with the learning trajectory over time, with different goals, content, and problem types, in a context that can support continuous teacher learning. The teacher's understanding of the learning trajectory deepened over time and through repeated use in practice, and not all teachers showed the same kind of continuous growth that Ivy demonstrated. One of Ivy's grade partners took up the learning trajectory right away, while another was just beginning to move away from a deeply embedded mastery learning perspective by the end of the year. It is important to recognize how teacher learning, like student learning, is on a progression; professional-learning opportunities need to respect both where teachers are in the journey and what the next appropriate step might be in a process of continuous learning. Further research can help illuminate more of these kinds of patterns and milestones in teacher learning, as well as explore the impact of using learning trajectories to interpret data on student learning, classroom instruction, and student performance.

Notes

1 The author would like to thank the Spencer Foundation for their support of this research and acknowledge the contributions of Rowan Machalow and Cecile Sam to the data collection, coding, and analysis.
2 This framework was adapted from the *OGAP Multiplicative Progression* (Petit et al., 2017).
3 All names of people and places are pseudonyms

References

Black, P. B., & Wiliam, D. (1998). Assessment and classroom learning. *Assessment in Education, 5*(1), 7–74.

Charmaz, K. (2006). *Constructing grounded theory: A practical guide through qualitative research.* London: Sage.

Clements, D. H., Sarama, J., Spitler, M. E., Lange, A. A., & Wolfe, C. B. (2011). Mathematics learned by young children in an intervention based on learning trajectories: A large-scale cluster randomized trial. *Journal for Research in Mathematics Education, 42,* 127–166.

Coburn, C., & Turner, E. (2012). The practice of data use: An introduction. *American Journal of Education, 118*(2), 99–111.

Daro, P., Mosher, F. A., & Corcoran, T. B. (2011). *Learning trajectories in mathematics: A foundation for standards, curriculum, assessment, and instruction.* Philadelphia: Consortium for Policy Research in Education.

Dervin, B. (1998). Sense-making theory and practice: An overview of user interests in knowledge seeking and use. *Journal of Knowledge Management, 2*(2), 36–46.

Franke, M. L., Kazemi, E., & Battey, D. (2007). Mathematics teaching and classroom practice. In F. K. Lester Jr. (Ed.), *Second handbook of research on mathematics teaching and learning* (pp. 225–256). Charlotte, NC: Information Age Publishing.

Heritage, M. (2008). *Learning progressions: Supporting instruction and formative assessment.* Los Angeles, CA: National Center for Research on Evaluation, Standards, and Student Testing, University of California, Los Angeles.

Klein, G., Moon, B. M., & Hoffman, R. R. (2006). Making sense of sensemaking 1: Alternative perspectives. *IEEE Intelligent Systems, 21*(4), 70–73.

Patton, M. Q. (1990). *How to use qualitative methods in evaluation.* Newbury Park, CA: Sage.

Petit, M., Laird, R., & Hulbert, E. (2017). *Multiplicative reasoning framework.* Retrieved from https://ogapmathllc.com/resources-and-related-publications/

Strauss, A., & Corbin, J. M. (1990). *Basics of qualitative research: Grounded theory procedures and techniques.* Thousand Oaks, CA: Sage.

Sztajn, P., Confrey, J., Wilson, P. H., & Edgington, C. (2012). Learning trajectory based instruction: Towards a theory of teaching. *Educational Researcher, 41*(5), 147–156.

Weick, K. (1995). *Sensemaking in organizations.* Thousand Oaks, CA: Sage.

5

FROM FOCUSING ON GRADES TO EXPLORING STUDENT THINKING

A Case Study of Change in Assessment Practice

Stephanie Rafanelli, Hilda Borko, Matthew Kloser, and Matthew Wilsey

The Next Generation Science Standards (NGSS) have established an inflection point not only for science teaching but also assessment and accountability. Changes recommended by NGSS raise questions about the types of student data that teachers are now collecting and how they are using these data to inform their instruction. Moreover, given the NGSS focus on scientific practices and the creation of multiple ways—models, explanations, and arguments—for students to show evidence of their thinking, how can professional-development programs support teachers as they tackle the complex task of adapting instruction appropriately, based on student data? Data from science classrooms, when used formatively, can significantly improve teaching practice and lead to increased student learning (Black & Wiliam, 1998; Furtak, 2009). However, some scholars argue that an emphasis on high-stakes standardized testing has negatively impacted effective implementation of formative assessment (Stiggins, 2005; Wiliam, Lee, Harrison, & Black, 2004). Despite an urgent need to better understand classroom assessment, practitioners and researchers lack a strong evidentiary base for identifying which teachers use student data, what data they use, when they use it, and how they make sense of student performance to impact their instructional choices (Coburn & Turner, 2011). As Yin and colleagues (Yin et al., 2008) point out, few studies provide comprehensive descriptions of how multiple assessment components are used across extended curricular units in actual teaching contexts. Furthermore, we have yet to explore ways in which professional-development (PD) experiences focused on effective data use can shape these practices.

This chapter explores one science teacher's assessment and data use practices before, during, and after participation in a yearlong professional-development experience focused on these practices. Case studies, such as the one described in the quote that follows, are particularly useful when examining phenomena in a real-world context (Flyvbjerg, 2006; Houghton, Casey, Shaw, & Murphy, 2013; Yin, 2013). They afford the researcher a powerful and intricate glimpse into a complex system (Eisenhardt, 1989, Merriam, 1998). Shulman (1983), Siggelkow (2007), and others have argued convincingly for the value of case studies as existence proofs, providing images of what can be accomplished, rather than documenting what is typically the case. Specifically:

> One major virtue of a case study is its ability to evoke images of the possible.... It is often the goal of policy to pursue the possible, not only to support the probable or frequent. The well-crafted case instantiates the possible, not only documenting that it can be done, but also laying out at least one detailed example of how it was organized, developed, and pursued.
> *(Shulman, 1983, p. 495)*

We offer an example of the possible as we explore changes in one middle-school science teacher's assessment practices.

Theoretical Framework

The multidimensional nature of this project draws on and connects three conceptual frameworks: 1) dimensions of effective science-assessment practice (Furtak, 2009; Martínez, Borko, Stecher, Luskin, & Kloser, 2012; National Research Council, 2001); 2) a theory of teacher data use (Boudett, City, & Murnane, 2013); and 3) a framework for effective professional development (Desimone, 2009).

Effective science-assessment practices form the foundation of teachers' understanding of high-quality student-performance data. Based on the literature and the Framework for K–12 Science Education (2012), we developed nine "Dimensions" of effective science-assessment practice, which could be organized by the three questions articulated in the National Research Council's (2001) work on science assessment: 1) Where are you going? 2) Where are you now? and 3) How can you get there? The Dimensions include: 1) set clear learning goals; 2) align assessments to learning goals; 3) assess frequently; 4) vary assessment; 5) measure with appropriate cognitive complexity; 6) reflect scientific practices and core ideas; 7) involve students in their own assessment; 8) provide specific feedback to students; and 9) use data for instructional decision-making (see Table 5.1). For each Dimension, we created a rubric that outlines the continuum of assessment practice.

Our framework for teachers' use of student data derives from Boudett et al. (2013). This framework recognizes that data use is an active, iterative process in which student data, which is affected by the quality of assessments, must be transformed into information that can be used to improve instruction. Effective teachers do not merely gather data, report results, and then continue to move through

TABLE 5.1 Central Questions and Nine Dimensions of Effective Science Assessment

Central Questions	Dimensions of Effective Science Assessment
Where are you going?	1. Set Clear Learning Goals
	2. Align Assessments to Learning Goals
Where are you now?	3. Assess Frequently
	4. Vary Assessment
	5. Measure with Appropriate Cognitive Complexity
	6. Reflect Scientific Practices and Core Ideas
	7. Involve Students in Their Own Assessment
How can you get there?	8. Provide Specific Feedback to Students
	9. Use Data for Instructional Decision-Making

their curriculum. They consider the information derived from the data in light of instructional options that are most likely to help students close the gap between their current understanding and the learning goal. The process, as envisioned by Boudett et al. (2013), involves a spiraling sequence of actions, including digging into student data, examining instruction, developing an action plan, planning and implementing assessment, and beginning the process anew. Once teachers have represented the data in helpful ways, they can prioritize needs and adjust future instruction. This process is unnatural for many teachers and requires support at the classroom, department, or school level.

To shape the PD experience focused on assessment and data use, we incorporated five consensus features of effective professional development (Desimone, 2009): 1) the PD focused on the content—the assessment was based on science core concepts; 2) the PD helped teachers use students' ideas to inform their instructional decisions and actions; 3) participating teachers were engaged actively and collaboratively in a professional learning community; 4) the PD was situated in the teachers' practice through the use of a portfolio tool, called the Quality Assessment in Science (QAS) Notebook; and 5) the intensive summer PD and monthly school-year PD allowed teachers to reflect extensively on new ideas around science assessment and data use, and on what occurred in their classrooms throughout the school year. Informed by these three frameworks, our project explored the changing assessment practices of middle-school science teachers.

Methods

Project Description and Participants

Twelve middle-school science teachers from four schools in two different states participated in the Quality Assessment in Science Professional Development (QAS PD) project. In spring 2015, teachers provided baseline information through interviews about their assessment practice, their feedback practices, and how they used assessment data for instructional decision-making. Each teacher then collected a baseline 10-day QAS Notebook. The Notebooks included artifacts from each class period—assignments, tests, quizzes, teacher feedback—as well as artifact annotations and reflections on the teacher's practice.

All the teachers participated in a three-day summer professional-development institute conducted by the project team, followed by a half-day workshop during the first week of the school year. During the summer PD, participants were introduced to the nine Dimensions of assessment practice and the *Data Wise* (Boudett et al., 2013) framework for using assessment results. They used the Dimensions as a framework for analyzing their baseline Notebooks and identifying goals for improving their assessment practices during the upcoming school year.

The teachers collected two five-day Notebooks during the 2015–2016 academic year—one in each semester. They attended monthly professional learning community (PLC) meetings facilitated at their schools by the project team. During these meetings, they used artifacts from the five-day Notebooks to explore their assessment practices, guided by prompts provided by the research team. In late spring 2016, participants collected a final 10-day Notebook on the same topic as the baseline Notebook, which was used to compare their assessment practices before and after the professional-development experience. Teachers also participated in a concluding interview about their assessment practice, providing their perceptions of effective science assessment and identifying perceived changes in their practice over the year. Using their final Notebook as evidence, teachers were specifically asked to discuss Dimensions in which they saw growth and Dimensions in which they hoped to grow more in the future.

Abby[1], the teacher selected for the current case study, is a veteran middle-school science teacher who has been at her current school for more than a decade. Though interested in the project from the beginning, Abby asked many questions about the nature of the research over two introductory meetings before agreeing to join a colleague in forming a team. Abby's assessment practice was initially dominated by restricted-response quizzes and tests. During the research project, she willingly opened her practice to reflection and critique, wanting to grow in efficacy. Because of her engagement with the project and clear evidence of growth over time, we chose Abby as a focal case, an intriguing "vision of the possible."

Data Sources

The QAS PD project included four main types of data: 1) the teachers' two 10-day QAS Notebooks; 2) pre- and post-project interviews; 3) audio recordings of PD and PLC sessions; and 4) conceptual models of assessment practice. This chapter draws on the first three data types, which are discussed in more depth in the sections that follow.

QAS Notebooks

The QAS PD project used a structured portfolio collection of teachers' assessment artifacts as the central tool in a yearlong professional-development experience. The portfolio, the QAS Notebook, was designed to collect evidence of science-classroom activities and materials that can be used to describe and measure assessment practices. For each Notebook, the teachers collected assessment artifacts from 10 consecutive days of instruction, including samples of student work. Accompanying each artifact and set of student-work samples, they provided structured annotations about the purpose of the artifact and how it was used, if at all, to inform instruction. Annotated artifacts for each day were placed in a daily folder. The Notebook also contained an initial folder in which teachers placed unit and lesson plans, and a concluding folder for more extensive reflections on assessment practice (for a more complete description of the QAS Notebook, see Martínez et al., 2012).

Interviews

Prior to the collection of the baseline Notebooks, participants were interviewed about their science-assessment practices. The interview used a semi-structured format that investigated each main assessment type—summative, formative, and benchmark—by iteratively asking a series of probes about each assessment example that the participant named. Probes targeted the participant's understanding of what each assessment afforded, and whether and how each assessment informed future instruction. Participants also answered questions about the types of feedback used in class. Finally, participants were asked to identify perceived strengths and weaknesses in their own assessment practice.

Summer Institute and PLC Sessions

All teachers participated in an intensive (~25 hours) three-day summer professional-development institute conducted by the project team, focused on developing assessment and data use literacy. During the summer PD, participants were introduced to the nine Dimensions of assessment practice and the *Data Wise* framework (Boudett et al., 2013) for using assessment results, and were engaged in activities to apply these new frameworks to practice. The teachers used the Dimensions to analyze their own baseline Notebooks, reflect on their current practice, and identify goals for improving their assessment practices during the upcoming school year. The PD continued once a month, between September and April, with PLC meetings facilitated by the project team at participants' schools. Each session addressed one or more Dimensions of assessment practice. PLC sessions were activity based and involved participants working with classroom artifacts collected for the two five-day Notebooks. For example, one session began with participants rating their own Notebook along several Dimensions, followed by a discussion of strengths, challenges, and new ideas. Subsequently, participants reflected on one challenging area of assessment, and committed to trying one or more of the ideas by writing their plan on an exit card. Another session focused on classroom-assessment data. Participants used their own class data and were guided through an activity to analyze the scores using a pre-designed spreadsheet with a variety of possibilities for data representation.

Analysis

Notebooks, interviews, and PLC transcripts were analyzed by the first two authors using an analytic coding scheme we developed, based on the nine Dimensions of effective assessment practice. Working independently, we examined each artifact in the two Notebooks and used a spreadsheet to record evidence that reflected or contradicted each Dimension. We also coded the interviews and PLC transcripts along the Dimensions and added notes summarizing the coded data onto the spreadsheet. The researchers then compared and reconciled evidence in the spreadsheets and identified emergent themes that appeared across the data sources. This chapter presents our analysis of changes in one teacher's assessment practices.

A Veteran Teacher's Changing Assessment Practice

> I plan on having the students take a summative assessment at the end of the unit in the form of a paper-and-pencil test. The questions on the test are from a test bank that is based on the California Standards. As we progress through the unit, I will employ formative assessment in the form of reviewing their work during guided practice, spot checking homework assignments, and using class discussions to gauge their understanding.
>
> (Initial Reflection, Notebook 1)

Abby was one of eight science teachers at a middle school with just over 1,000 students on the West Coast. Her four classes had an average of 30 students per class; they met three times a week, once for 45 minutes, followed by two block sections of 90 minutes each. The school culture appeared to be genial and supportive. Abby noted a lack of school-wide or team-level discussions of assessment practices and use of student data. "As far as school wide, we've talked about homework policies and we've talked about dress codes, we've talked about scheduling assessments, so the kids don't have too many tests the same day, but we've not really had discussions about the type of assessments" (Concluding interview, 05/19/16). Abby noted that she occasionally shared ideas or puzzled over student challenges with a team member, but did not remember ever talking "about the summative assessments." The school was working to adopt the NGSS, and although Abby did not explicitly identify disciplinary core ideas or scientific practices, she did mention lab work, computation, data collection, and using equipment, in her initial interview.

Over more than a decade teaching middle-school science, Abby developed a clear and efficient assessment practice. She described making daily observations of students as they worked in class, collecting homework occasionally to assess for completion, and capping each unit with a multiple-choice test that used items drawn from a test bank. When asked whether and how she would use student data in the initial reflection questions of the baseline Notebook, Abby wrote, "I'd like to use the data from the assessments to make changes to improve the instruction, but I don't have a plan."

Over the course of a year, Abby showed different degrees of change across the Dimensions, perhaps reflecting the complexity of assessment practice. The most extensive growth was evident along the following three Dimensions: 3) assess frequently, 4) vary assessment, and 9) use data for instructional decision-making. Smaller signs of change were present for two Dimensions: 5) measure with appropriate cognitive complexity, and 6) reflect scientific practices and core ideas. In what follows, we discuss evidence of both larger and smaller changes in Abby's assessment practice, as well as Dimensions for which no change was evident.

Substantial Change

Dimension 3: Assess Frequently

Abby's initial interview revealed a pattern of assessment that she explained as being, "probably less than once a week" (Initial interview, 04/08/2015). As discussed previously, Abby typically assessed student work for completion and rarely collected daily work. Her responses on the initial interview and artifacts in the baseline Notebook underscored Abby's focus on daily informal class observation and weekly individual conversations with students as primary formative-assessment techniques. The difference between Abby's baseline and final Notebooks showed strong evidence of an increase in the frequency of assessment. Within the same 10-day period, she included 10 formative assessments in her final Notebook, compared with five in the prior year. In the final Notebook, structured formative assessments were conducted each day. New assessments, including brief exit tickets and longer homework tasks, allowed students multiple opportunities to calculate, describe, and explain motion. During PLC meeting #2, Abby noted the shift she had made in frequency of assessment, explaining, "I'm including more of what I would call 'snapshots' to check on student learning, like exit tickets . . . previously when I've taught this unit, I've just done the instruction, but I haven't really tried to see how it's landing" (PLC meeting 2, 11/19/2015). Moreover, when asked in the final interview to identify the Dimension in which she grew the most, she responded, "Well, I would say frequency of assessment would be my first area. I've definitely increased the frequency of my assessments. I'm doing it more often" (Concluding interview, 05/19/2016).

Dimension 4: Vary Assessment

Data from the initial interview and baseline Notebook revealed little variety in the type of assessment Abby conducted prior to participation in the study. She identified science notebooks, quizzes, and tests as assessment tools, and noted that tests were entirely multiple choice. Artifacts in the baseline Notebook confirmed an emphasis on verbal exercises designed to reinforce reading comprehension and note-taking skills. In the final Notebook and PLC work, artifacts and reflections revealed strong evidence for increased attention to variety in the forms of assessment. One assessment, a Newton's Second Law exit ticket, provided students with a variety of opportunities to show what they knew. For example, students could: write three things they learned about Newton's Second Law, illustrate their understanding of Newton's Second Law with a diagram, or create a poem including important facts about Newton's Second Law. Abby discussed new elements of variety in her assessments during several of our PLC meetings. For instance, during PLC meeting #4, she shared an example of a new exit ticket that asked students to diagram a physical model and to analyze the strengths of a different diagram. In the past, she explained, she asked students to verbally explain the model discussed in the reading. During PLC meeting #5, Abby described changing her cell-model assessment to allow students choice between creating a physical model, writing and performing a song or skit, drawing a comic, or designing and presenting a digital piece. In her final interview, she explained why she believed that variety in forms of assessment was important: "I think life has different challenges. Sometimes you have to write things and sometimes you have to calculate things and sometimes you have to read a map or make some visual interpretation" (Concluding interview, 05/19/2016). Evidence from the Notebooks indicated that Abby's practice of varying assessment developed significantly over the course of the project.

Dimension 9: Use Data for Instructional Decision-Making

When asked during the initial interview whether assessments informed her curricular choices, Abby responded, "Not as much as I would like it to . . . I wish I could say that it really did shape my curriculum" (Initial interview, 04/08/2015). She also emphasized her focus on summative assessments and infrequent use of formative assessments, accompanied by little feedback. Reflections included in the baseline Notebook underscored the lack of connection between assessments and adaptation of instruction. Annotations on two of the five assessments indicated that no changes to instruction were planned. Although annotations on three assessments did indicate an instructional change, the changes were minor, low-level shifts, such as, "Have students look at figures 3 & 4 and re-read," and "Change wording in instructions."

Data from the PLC meetings revealed a clear change in Abby's use of assessment for instructional change. During PLC meetings #2 and #3, Abby discussed how exit tickets and classroom discussions revealed gaps in student understanding and led her to add new visual aids and different activities to help students master the concepts at hand. Furthermore, in PLC meeting #4, Abby described how she used an online simulation to clarify misunderstandings revealed on student review sheets. She explained, "Instead of looking at pictures, a model that was moving seemed to be a lot more understandable for them . . . I saw an improvement in the answers when I collected them again" (PLC meeting 4, 01/07/2016). Abby adapted her instruction in response to student review work, and found final review sheets and test answers to be better, as a result. During our final PLC meeting, Abby noted the importance of formative assessment as a tool for informing her teaching. She described her new approach to formative assessment as creating a "student feedback loop, so that you're getting some information and you're communicating to the students and then you're coming back and seeing if they're getting it and, hopefully, maybe checking again, before you finally get to feeling like you're ready to get to the summative assessment" (PLC Meeting 6, 03/31/2016).

The final Notebook included evidence of Abby's increased use of formative assessments as a source of information for adapting instruction. In addition to doubling the number of formative assessments, Abby noted changes to future practice and curriculum based on seven of the ten assessments. For example, in her notes regarding an assessment of projectile motion and gravity, Abby indicated she would "more deliberately connect demonstrations, PowerPoint, video. Some students can't connect without more support." On another assessment, Abby identified an immediate change in her instruction, declaring she would "check in with students who are omitting units and have them correct their work." Annotations noted multiple instances of checking in more systematically and frequently with students as they worked, and allowing students to revise some assignments after receiving feedback. Identifying what she finds most helpful in making instructional decisions, Abby stated, "I think the formative assessment is what I'm really keeping an eye on" (Concluding interview, 05/19/2016).

Small Change

Dimension 5: Measure with Appropriate Cognitive Complexity

Abby's initial interview suggested a focus on recall, summary, and application, with little mention of assessments that included more complex levels of Bloom's Taxonomy (Krathwohl, 2002). She explained that her multiple-choice tests were designed to see if students "were able to answer a question based on a particular

72   Rafanelli et al.

standard" (Initial interview, 04/08/2015). She discussed making sure students had mastered terms, were able to use units correctly, and could do basic calculations. Abby demonstrated an awareness of more complex tasks when she noted that she substituted an argument paper for one multiple-choice assessment, and explained that it gave her a better view of her students' ability to analyze evidence. Similarly, assessments in Abby's baseline Notebook showed a focus on recall and summary of information from readings. A typical example from that Notebook, shown in the figure that follows, asked students to read a passage and answer several questions (see Figure 5.1). The prompts directly echoed explanations in the text without asking students to apply or synthesize any material.

The student sample, marked as "high achievement" work, involved only the least complex level of Bloom's Taxonomy: recognizing and remembering relevant knowledge. Initially, Abby's artifacts consistently prompted students to remember facts and activities, summarize text, or answer closed-ended lab questions.

Abby's final Notebook, in contrast, included two new artifacts with higher levels of cognitive complexity. The Newton's Second Law exit ticket, discussed previously as an example of Dimension 4 (see Figure 5.1), allowed students to choose their assessment. Although the first two choices were lower-level tasks, the remaining tasks met Bloom's criteria for higher levels of complexity by requiring application, evaluation, and/or creation. A second assessment, which replaced a task of labeling and interpreting diagrams that was used the previous year, asked students to create a cartoon that illustrated Newton's Third Law and apply it to a novel situation (see Figure 5.2).

In the annotation accompanying the task in her final Notebook, Abby wrote, "I found that looking at their cartoons was some of the most useful performance data because it was the most open-ended assessment and revealed their thinking." In her final interview, Abby expanded on this note, saying, "I added what I thought would be open-ended things so that it'll be a little more of a stretch for them." The two instances described here suggest that Abby recognized the need

Orbiting and Gravity

Read textbook pages 381 – 382 and then answer the questions.

1. What helps keep the planets orbiting the sun?
   gravity applies centripetal force on the planets which keeps them orbiting the sun.

2. Explain why an object in orbit needs centripetal force acting on it. In what direction does a centripetal force act?
   The centripetal force pulls everything twards the center, so in orbit, the centripetal force pulls it twards the center.

FIGURE 5.1   High-Achievement Student Gravity Assessment, Initial Notebook

Newton's Third Law Cartoon

Purpose: To construct a comic strip that illustrates Newton's Third Law of Motion and applies it to a situation.

Requirements:

- Must be neatly drawn.
- Must be colorful (include at least two colors in each pane).
- The comic must be logical and display your knowledge and understanding of Newton's Third Law.
- Be creative! The situation must tell a story, writing definitions is not appropriate.
- Include the following keywords in your comic strip
    1. Newton's Third Law
    2. Action
    3. Reaction

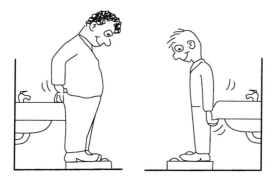

FIGURE 5.2 Newton's-Third-Law Cartoon, Final Notebook

to challenge students, but that her practice was only moderately affected. That is, Abby appeared to make incremental changes that allowed students to "stretch" to higher levels of cognitive complexity on assessments.

Dimension 6: Reflect Scientific Practices and Core Ideas

Although Abby rarely noted scientific practices explicitly, there was some evidence of change over the course of the project, in relation to this Dimension. Abby mentioned some scientific practices in her initial interview, without identifying them as being part of NGSS. For example, she described working with a literacy coach to develop an argument paper as an assessment. NGSS includes arguing from evidence as a critical scientific practice, however, Abby did not identify it as an important science skill. When asked what information she gained from the argument assessment, she contended, "It gave me an idea of where they were, as far as writing arguments and their writing ability, which, as a science teacher, was not particularly helpful" (Initial interview, 04/08/2015).

The baseline and the final Notebooks showed little explicit mention of the NGSS scientific practices, however, Abby's participation in the PLC meetings revealed small but definite growth in this Dimension. For example, in PLC meeting #2, Abby shared a new exit ticket designed to assess students' understanding of the development of the atomic model. Rather than giving her past homework assignment that asked students to summarize the reading, Abby gave students an exit ticket, asking questions about different atomic models and how each new historical development revealed flaws in a prior model. When articulating why she liked this new assignment, in which the evaluation of models was explicitly addressed, Abby explained that students seemed to be "understanding the significance of the experiment and why it [suggested that] Thomson's model didn't work anymore, that the plum-pudding model couldn't work and wouldn't explain what they were seeing" (PLC meeting 2, 11/19/2015). Although Abby did not mention the task's direct connection with the NGSS practice of developing and using models, she clearly valued the task.

When asked in the concluding interview how the science standards influenced her planning, Abby responded, "Students should have a richer science experience than just being able to do well on this multiple-choice test" (Concluding interview, 05/19/2016). Although she did not explicitly mention specific NGSS scientific practices in the interview, Abby showed awareness of and enthusiasm for tying future assessments that were more closely aligned to the Standards.

No Change

There was no clear change in four Dimensions: 1) set clear learning goals, 2) align assessments to learning goals, 7) involve students in their own assessment, and 8) provide specific feedback to students. However, the data offer evidence that Abby was thinking deeply about the first three of these Dimensions, suggesting the possibility of future growth in each domain. The first two Dimensions—setting clear goals and aligning assessments to those goals—were present in both Notebooks, yet showed no explicit change. Abby included a daily sheet noting Learning Objectives and California State or NGSS standards, with class activities or documents connected to each objective. Her baseline and final Notebooks had identical daily-goal sheets. In the initial interview, Abby explained her hope that "tests would give me an idea if they were mastering these standards" (Initial interview, 04/08/2015). However, at the conclusion of the project Abby expressed uncertainty about the clarity of her course's goals and standards. Abby's uncertainty and her articulation of future challenges as she addresses NGSS goals may lead to future growth in her practice of setting and aligning goals.

In contrast to Dimensions 1 and 2, no evidence of Dimension 7 was present in either the baseline or final Notebook. However, Abby did mention an interest in student self-reflection through the use of rubrics, at the end of PLC meeting #3. Moreover, when asked in the concluding interview to select one Dimension in which she hoped to improve next year, Abby responded, "I think it would be getting students to use the assessment data, thinking more about what they're learning and what they're getting out of it, just empowering them" (Concluding interview, 05/19/2016). Although no evidence of involving students in their own assessment was present in the Notebooks, Abby's continued interest in promoting student involvement suggests the possibility of future change.

The final Dimension in which the data showed no noticeable growth was feedback to students. In the initial interview, when asked what kind of feedback she gave students, Abby acknowledged, "You know, they don't get very much" (Initial interview, 04/08/2015). Her baseline and final Notebooks corroborated her interview, with only two brief examples of feedback evident from 10 days of student artifacts in the former, and one example in the latter. There was no evidence of change on providing feedback throughout the project.

Discussion

Although a single case, Abby's changes in practice offer an optimistic example of how professional-growth opportunities can impact what occurs in the classroom. The dramatic change in practice seen across three Dimensions and more modest, yet noticeable, change evident across two other Dimensions supports the contention that the type of professional-development program our research team designed—informed by the theoretical and empirical literatures on assessment, data use, and effective PD—may be a powerful structure with which to support science teachers as they develop new assessment practices. Given the challenges posed by the adoption of the NGSS, it is imperative that researchers explore new ways of helping teachers understand how to effectively collect, analyze, and act upon student data. The NGSS identify core ideas, crosscutting concepts, and scientific practices that students should master during their K–12 education, but offer little guidance to educators as to how students can or should be assessed on each performance expectation (Harris, Krajcik, Pellegrino, & McElhaney, 2016). This research project provides new ideas for aiding teachers in assessing and supporting students in the development of scientific practices and deep scientific understanding.

We separated the Dimensions for the purpose of analysis, however, it is important to note that the themes were often intertwined. For example, Abby's exit ticket shown in Figure 5.1 demonstrated change in variety of assessment, attention to cognitive complexity, and the use of formative assessment as a tool for adapting instruction. Further, in her final interview, Abby connected cognitive complexity, scientific practices, and variety, when explaining how she hoped to get a better picture of what her students understood: "Multiple-choice tests I did just don't reveal very much about their thinking, and I think having things where they're writing, or maybe drawing, or making a model or a diagram, gave me a lot more information" (Concluding interview, 05/19/2016). Through connecting the scientific practice of supporting ideas with evidence to more cognitively complex opportunities afforded through a variety of assessment forms, Abby articulated a more interconnected vision of assessment at the conclusion of the project than was evident in her initial interview. Thus, providing teachers with opportunities to develop even a small number of new assessments can be a promising practice for addressing multiple dimensions of effective assessment.

Understanding classroom assessment practices and use of student data are critically important for teachers in an increasingly data-driven educational environment. Marsh, Pane, and Hamilton (2006) identify "focused training on analyzing data and identifying and enacting solutions" (p. 10) as a key recommendation for schools and policymakers. We saw clear changes in the way Abby understood and implemented formative assessment. Through the process of examining student data, in an effort to reflect on instruction and create an action plan, supported by PD drawing from Boudett et al.'s (2013) framework for working with student data, Abby increased her data literacy and made adjustments to her teaching practice. Moreover, the project afforded Abby the time and focused content recommended by scholars of effective PD, and her work was grounded in her own classroom practice and supported by both summer work and consistent, school-year meetings (Desimone, 2009).

The scope of the current project was designed to be effective, yet manageable, in light of teachers' heavy schedules. As Guskey (2002) and other scholars have noted, teacher change is gradual and difficult. Cognitive-load theory posits that individuals, when faced with complex attentional demands, such as those in a classroom, must focus attention on and practice a limited set of actions until expertise is developed (Van Gog, Ericsson, Rikers, & Paas, 2005). Through practice, teachers acquire facets of expertise and can perform those tasks automatically, freeing attention for the development of expertise in new areas. It is reasonable to expect that teachers need support and time to develop a limited number of new assessment skills and may develop more as time goes on. As Feldon (2007) explains, educators who "participate in programs that do offer extended and well scaffolded practice opportunities tend to be more consistent and more effective in their teaching" (p. 130).

It is likely that Abby experienced a full cognitive load while working to change practice along some Dimensions, while also navigating the existing complexities of her classroom practice and life beyond school. As she develops expertise in those Dimensions of change, her attention will be freed to focus on change along different Dimensions. However, it may also be that the particular Dimensions along which Abby changed involved practices that were easier to shift. Perhaps the four Dimensions along which no change was visible are more challenging, and require different levels of support to induce growth. Future research might explore teacher change in assessment in a multiyear professional -development program, to identify whether patterns of growth are related to particular teachers' practice or are connected with specific Dimensions of assessment.

Although the administrations at each school supported the project work and allowed teachers and facilitators to meet on the school site once a month for an hour, teachers were not excused from normal teaching, meeting, conferencing, and planning activities. The project showed indicators of teacher change at both urban and suburban schools, however, and proved feasible with a three-day summer institute, a half-day workshop, and eight one-hour PLC meetings spread over the school year. Evidence from the current case supports our proposal that the work discussed here offers a set of promising PD practices, which may be a means of supporting teachers' targeted use of assessments and student data across a variety of school settings. By setting structured and facilitated reflection of teachers' classroom artifacts—the daily, micro acts of assessment—within a framework of science-assessment practice and theory of teacher data use—broader, macro educational frameworks—the project supported positive growth in assessment practice and use of student data for instructional decision-making.

At the same time, it is important to acknowledge that the process of change must continue to be well scaffolded to be effective (Feldon, 2007). The structured reflections and team participation during PLC meetings served as both support for engagement in new assessment practices and accountability. When asked if she thought she would continue collecting a Notebook once the project ended, Abby responded, "I won't be as diligent, I'm pretty sure, but I think I will—it's something I've learned there is some value in, collecting some of these artifacts." Despite Abby's enthusiasm for the project, her comments suggest that reflecting on assessment with the Notebook will diminish without support from the structured PLC.

The field of science education lacks a strong body of theoretically informed scholarship connecting PD practices with assessment research. This case offers evidence for the potential of one summer PD, supported by a year of monthly meetings, in promoting initial changes in attitudes toward and practices of assessment. Although the findings are not necessarily generalizable, they afford a view of a PD process that ties artifact collection, reflection, and an established conceptual framework to changes in science assessment and teaching practice.

Acknowledgements

This work is supported by a grant from the Spencer Foundation. Any opinions, findings, and conclusions or recommendations expressed in this material are those of the author(s) and do not necessarily reflect the views of the Spencer Foundation. We thank all of the teachers who participated in this project and shared their teaching with their colleagues and our project staff.

Note

1 All names of people and places are pseudonyms.

References

Black, P., & Wiliam, D. (1998). Assessment and classroom learning. *Assessment in Education: Principles, Policy, and Practice, 5*, 7–73.

Boudett, K. P., City, E. A., & Murnane, R. J. (2013). *Data wise: A step by step guide to using assessment results to improve teaching and learning.* Cambridge, MA: Harvard University Press.

Coburn, C. E., & Turner, E. O. (2011). Research on data use: A framework and analysis. *Measurement: Interdisciplinary Research & Perspective, 9*, 173–206.

Desimone, L. M. (2009). Improving impact studies of teachers' professional development: Toward better conceptualizations and measures. *Educational Researcher, 38*, 181–199.

Eisenhardt, K. M. (1989). Building theories from case study research. *Academy of Management Review, 14*, 532–550.

Feldon, D. F. (2007). Cognitive load and classroom teaching: The double-edged sword of automaticity. *Educational Psychologist, 42*, 123–137.

Flyvbjerg, B. (2006). Five misunderstandings about case-study research. *Qualitative Inquiry, 12*, 219–245.

Furtak, E. M. (Ed.) (2009). *Formative assessment for secondary science teachers.* Thousand Oaks, CA: Corwin Press.

Guskey, T. R. (2002). Professional development and teacher change. *Teachers and Teaching, 8*, 381–391.

Harris, C. J., Krajcik, J. S., Pellegrino, J. W., & McElhaney, K. W. (2016). *Constructing assessment tasks that blend disciplinary core ideas, crosscutting concepts, and science practices for classroom formative applications.* Menlo Park, CA: SRI International.

Houghton, C., Casey, D., Shaw, D., & Murphy, K. (2013). Rigour in qualitative case-study research. *Nurse Researcher, 20*, 12.

Krathwohl, D. R. (2002). A revision of Bloom's taxonomy: An overview. *Theory into Practice, 41*, 212–218.

Marsh, J. A., Pane, J. F., & Hamilton, L. S. (2006). *Making sense of data-driven decision making in education: Evidence from recent RAND research.* Santa Monica, CA: RAND Corporation.

Martínez, J. F., Borko, H., Stecher, B., Luskin, R., & Kloser, M. (2012). Measuring classroom assessment practice using instructional artifacts: A validation study of the QAS notebook. *Educational Assessment, 17*, 107–131.

Merriam, S. B. (1998). *Qualitative research and case study applications in education: Revised and expanded from "case study research in education.* San Francisco, CA: Jossey-Bass Publishers.

National Research Council. (2001). *Classroom assessment and the national science education standards.* Washington, DC: National Academies Press.

Shulman, L. S. (1983). Autonomy and obligation: The remote control of teaching. In L. S. Shulman & G. Sykes (Eds.), *Handbook of teaching and policy* (pp. 484–504). New York, NY: Longman.

Siggelkow, N. (2007). Persuasion with case studies. *Academy of Management Journal, 50*, 20.

Stiggins, R. (2005). From formative assessment to assessment for learning: A path to success in standards-based schools. *The Phi Delta Kappan, 87*, 324–328.

Van Gog, T., Ericsson, K. A., Rikers, R. M., & Paas, F. (2005). Instructional design for advanced learners: Establishing connections between the theoretical frameworks of cognitive load and deliberate practice. *Educational Technology Research and Development, 53*, 73–81.

Wiliam, D., Lee, C., Harrison, C., & Black, P. (2004). Teachers developing assessment for learning: Impact on student achievement. *Assessment in Education: Principles, Policy & Practice, 11*, 49–65.

Yin, R. K. (2013). *Case study research: Design and methods.* Thousand Oaks, CA: Sage.

Yin, Y., Shavelson, R. J., Ayala, C. C., Ruiz-Primo, M. A., Brandon, P. R., Furtak, E. M., . . . Young, D. B. (2008). On the Impact of Formative Assessment on Student Motivation, Achievement, and Conceptual Change. *Applied Measurement in Education, 21*, 335–359.

6

USING DATA MEANINGFULLY TO TEACH FOR UNDERSTANDING IN MIDDLE-SCHOOL SCIENCE

Melissa Braaten, Chris Bradford, Sadie Fox Barocas, and Kathryn L. Kirchgasler

Data-driven improvement initiatives feature prominently in schools. Some initiatives target mathematics and literacy achievements (e.g. Datnow, Park, & Kennedy-Lewis, 2012; Horn, Kane, & Wilson, 2015) others target attendance, grade-level advancement, and behavior referrals (e.g, Mandinach, 2012). Data-centric initiatives do not always include meaningful data use valuable for instructional adaptations from teachers' points of view, however. Teachers in areas outside of mathematics and literacy find themselves in a complicated position—they feel responsible for supporting accountability goals, but unsure about other educational priorities beyond the scope of data-driven initiatives.

Our study of science teachers' data use raises two questions explored in this chapter:

1) How does a team of teachers reconfigure data use into a more meaningful activity, by focusing on different forms of data and different ways of using data than what is typical in school-wide data use initiatives?
2) How does a team of teachers reclaim learning goals in science and focus on teaching for understanding, even though that is not a school-wide priority?

This case study tells the story of a middle-school teaching team that used promising practices for meaningful data use when teaching science for understanding. By *teaching for understanding*, we mean that science teachers focused on deepening understanding through an iterative process of building and refining students' explanatory models, rather than emphasizing rote factual recall or demonstrations of academic skills. Even though this team's case was unusual, examining how they worked together to use data meaningfully and reclaim science learning goals might offer a possible pathway for meaningful data use and science teaching.

Multiple Meanings of "Data" and "Data Use"

Before moving forward, we want to be clear about how these teachers defined "data" and "data use" in their practice. This clarification is important because these concepts came to have at least two levels of meaning. One level of meaning was shared within teacher teams and contrasted significantly from another level of meaning, held as part of school- and district-wide data-driven reforms.

Within teacher teams, "data" about students' learning meant any information offered by students, providing insight into *what* students understood and *how/why* students understood things in a certain way. For example, a student telling a story about how car batteries become "drained" and wondering if all batteries can "drain" was viewed as data by teachers who saw not only a student's working hypothesis but also clues about sensemaking in the connection from one system to another.

Such information was not considered "data" by the school- and district-wide data-driven initiatives, where "data" was defined more narrowly, including only those pieces of information that could be quantified, usually through externally developed interim assessments (e.g., NWEA, 2016). Importantly, these officially sanctioned forms of "data" focused on knowledge and skills targeted by data-driven initiatives, which prioritized a limited set of outcomes: mathematics and literacy performance, improved attendance, and reduced behavior-referral rates for certain racial subgroups of students (Braaten, Bradford, Kirchgasler, & Barocas, 2017).

Just as "data" carried multiple levels of meaning for teams, "data use" also carried multiple levels of meaning. The most common use of data in official data-driven initiatives involved moving students into and out of various academic interventions designed to remediate deficits, and moving groups of students over the bubble of a particular academic benchmark (e.g., Booher-Jennings, 2005). Data use in official data-driven initiatives did not include ideas about flexibly adapting future instructional designs to be responsive to students' unfolding ideas, nor did the official image of data use include ideas about how teachers might capitalize on students' strengths. This team of teachers, then, offers a compelling case study because their definition of "data use" was centrally focused on adaptive and responsive science teaching, where students' contributions—struggles and strengths—were used as key pieces of information for recrafting instruction to move science learning forward.

Theoretical Perspective

Data Use as Contested Sensemaking

We use a sensemaking perspective to understand the complicated work of teacher teams grappling with multiple accountability and improvement initiatives and a jumble of pedagogical frameworks (e.g. Coburn, 2001; Maitlis & Christianson, 2014). By *sensemaking*, we mean the ongoing processes by which groups of people interpret information, including data, goals, and expectations, in order to negotiate meaning and actions together (Weick, 1995). By taking this theoretical perspective, we look at how educators make and remake activities, tools, routines, discourses, and expectations as part of their daily practice, in order to coordinate complex work.

Sensemaking is always contested terrain. Because activities, tools, routines, discourse, and expectations do not fit neatly together, people have to negotiate meaning in shifting situations (Feldman & Pentland, 2003; Maitlis & Christianson, 2014). Instead of viewing data use as a rational and technical activity—with clear definitions, decision rules, and problem-solving pathways—a sensemaking perspective presumes that activities like data use will be messy and full of contradictions, disagreements, and uncertainty. This means that multiple levels of meaning can evolve within and across an organization (Coburn, 2001).

Teaching Science for Understanding

Teaching science to deepen students' understanding of science through a continuous process of sensemaking—also known as "ambitious science teaching"—is quite different from teaching science aimed at knowledge recall or rote performance of skills (Ambitious Science Teaching Development Group, n.d.; Carlone, Haun-Frank, & Webb, 2011; Windschitl & Calabrese Barton, 2016). Teaching science for understanding rests on continual use of overlapping forms of formative assessment, supported by scaffolding and highly interactive and responsive learning experiences for students (Kang, Thompson, & Windschitl, 2014; Kang, Windschitl, Stroupe, & Thompson, 2016). In this case study, we are focused on how a teacher team employed an ambitious-science-teaching framework to guide their use of student data when adapting instruction to support students' growing understanding.

Ambitious science teaching requires seeing students as sensemakers, capable of the complex intellectual work of revising ideas over time through disciplinary practices of science and engineering (e.g., NGSS Lead States, 2013; NRC, 2011; Schwarz, Passmore, & Reiser, 2016). This perspective, common in science-education research and reform efforts, remains uncommon in typical school practice, which continues to frame learning in terms of right versus wrong answers to knowledge-recall questions or in terms of correct versus incorrect demonstrations of discrete science, math, or literacy skills (e.g., Banilower, Smith, Weiss, & Pasley, 2006; Trygstad, 2013). In this case study, we are focusing primarily on how teachers used promising practices to make sense of students' learning and to make principled adaptations to instruction, even when other goals were emphasized in the school and district.

How We Studied Data Use in Glacier City School District

This case study is part of a larger ethnographic study of science teachers' day-to-day practice during the first two years of a district-wide push to make data-driven changes in schools. Our research team worked as embedded observers, following 36 science teachers and nine school-level leaders through daily routines at two middle schools and one high school in Glacier City School District[1] (GCSD). We used detailed field notes to capture descriptions of science-teaching practices, including how teachers planned, adjusted, assessed, and reflected. We attended meetings, professional development, and informal collaborations alongside science teachers, using field notes to record and describe the substance of those meetings.

We conducted follow-up interviews with teachers after classroom observations, and formal, extended interviews with all participants annually. Finally, we collected artifacts, including teacher- and student-created materials, templates and tools distributed during meetings, photos of whiteboards and data walls, and digital copies of leaders' slideshows, school and district newsletters, local news stories, and GCSD documents communicating data-driven initiatives.[2] This case study focuses on one eighth-grade teaching team from Hickory Middle School (HMS), selected because they were unique in using data to make nuanced instructional adjustments that were responsive to students' contributions during science classes (Stake, 1995).

Understanding the Contexts of GCSD and HMS

Glacier City School District is located in a midsized Midwestern U.S. city. At the time of this study, GCSD served 27,000+ students, half of whom were from low-income families. Over 100 languages were spoken and about 30% of students were English-Language Learners. Just over 50% of students in GCSD identified as people of color. Glacier City was newsworthy for having among the worst disparities between students of color and Caucasian students in nearly every possible indicator of academic performance, social and economic well-being, and health care. To address the academic component of these disparities, GCSD implemented initiatives, including intensive efforts to "move the needle" on high-priority data for local and statewide accountability, such as achievement in mathematics and literacy.

When data for this study were collected, Hickory Middle School served approximately 650 students in grades 6–8; 75% of students lived in low-income households. About one-third of HMS students were learning English as an additional language. About 75% of HMS students identified as people of color. During the time period of the study, HMS was considered to be barely "meeting expectations" for literacy and mathematics achievement, and was considered to be "at risk." As with most schools in GCSD, HMS had significant disparities in academic performance between students of color and their Caucasian peers, and between English learners and their English-only peers.

Meet the Z-Team

The Z-Team consisted of four teachers working with approximately 60 eighth-grade students (one-third of the eighth-grade students at HMS). The Z-Team included three veteran teachers who had taught at HMS for 5–15 years. All academic subjects were taught by the team, with team members determining who would take the lead in planning, teaching, and assessing each subject area. Mrs. Paszekski tended to take the lead during social-studies teaching, and worked collaboratively to support literacy, social/emotional learning, and community-building activities. Mr. Donovan took the lead during mathematics and science teaching, and worked collaboratively throughout the rest of the day supporting language learners. Mr. Vasquez took the lead during literacy teaching, and worked collaboratively to support social/emotional learning and community building. Mr. Vasquez also circulated all day to support students with special-education needs, as the Z-Team's expert in special education.

During the time of the study, the Z-Team also included a student teacher, Mr. Brant, who took the lead teaching science, and collaborated closely with Mr. Donovan. Mr. Brant was a student in a local teacher-preparation program, and the first author was his university instructor. The Z-Team welcomed Mr. Brant and happily allowed him to take the lead in science teaching because of his expertise in physics, particularly in the area of circuits and electricity, which all of the team members felt was outside of their own content knowledge.

A Promising Case of Using Data Meaningfully

This promising case study focuses on an extended nine-week science unit addressing energy transformations in circuits and electrical systems. Mr. Brant redesigned kit-based instructional materials to create modeling-based inquiry units, engaging students in proposing, testing, refining, and justifying explanatory models for different electrical systems (e.g., flashlights, solar panels supplying a home with energy, cell phones, etc.). Mr. Brant used ambitious science-teaching practices grounded in a set of planning tools, classroom-discourse routines, and formative-assessment heuristics that he brought into HMS from his teacher-preparation program (Ambitious Science Teaching Development Group, n.d.; Windschitl, Thompson, Braaten, & Stroupe, 2012). We organized this case study as a series of windows into classroom-science interactions and Z-Team planning and debriefing interactions.

Day 1: Introducing the Coin Battery

Mr. Brant began the unit with a Z-Team routine of "warm-up writing" about a focus question: "What is a battery? Please explain as if you were trying to tell a younger brother or sister." This question was projected in front of the classroom, along with a Learning Target: "Begin to explore how a battery works." This Learning Target differed from those typical of HMS because it pointed to an ongoing, exploratory image of learning science in school. Typical Learning Targets emphasized acquisition of a single piece of factual knowledge (e.g., "Define 'electrical current.'") or performance of a single skill (e.g., "Write a summary paragraph."). As students took seats in rows of desks, they began writing responses. Mr. Brant circulated, asking, "Do you know how to get started? Ok, great, get to it!" He then moved to the front of the classroom and asked to hear from students about their ideas.

STUDENT 1: I have an answer!
MR. BRANT: Great! And you sound proud of it. Can you tell us your idea?
STUDENT 1: A battery is an item that is used to power something, such as cell phones, iPods, [long list of items powered by batteries].
MR. BRANT: Can anyone add on?
STUDENT 2: A battery is something we use to make things work or turn on. They can be square or round. Big or small. Small like AAA or big like a car battery.
STUDENT 3: Car batteries aren't big!
MR. BRANT: How big are car batteries?
[Students used their hands to gesture the size of car batteries, while looking around at other students' gestures.]
STUDENT 4: Batteries have two terminals and they have an electrical charge, positive/negative, red/black.

Mr. Brant showed photos of batteries students suggested in response to the warm-up question, anticipating examples of batteries from devices students used daily in school. Mr. Brant included phone and music technologies, as well as computer and handheld video games in his examples, because Mr. Brant shared these interests with his students. After spending time talking about familiar batteries, Mr. Brant showed an unusual type of battery, using an image from a YouTube video that showed a battery made from a stack of coins, wires, and wet cardboard. In the image, the coin battery was powering an LED light.

MR. BRANT: When you watch this YouTube, see if there's something in here that surprised you. This surprised me, for sure; I didn't know how to make a battery out of random stuff.

Mr. Brant silenced the voice-over audio, so that he, rather than the engineer in the video, could generate conversation with students. Mr. Brant explained later that this decision was strategic. The engineer used dense, technical language to constantly explain how coin batteries and LEDs work, preempting opportunities for students to build curiosity, pose their own questions, or propose tentative ideas.

MR. BRANT: Ok, so he's picking out pennies based on the year and then he's sanding off one side of the penny.

STUDENT 5: Why is the inside [of the penny] silver?
MR. BRANT: Now, he's stacking them with cardboard soaked in vinegar . . . and, then, check it out, he's lighting it up! Can you write down what happened and what you saw that you didn't expect?
STUDENT 6: Are we gonna try it?
STUDENT 7: Are you gonna explain it?
MR. BRANT: YOU'RE gonna explain it.
STUDENT 3: It's ghetto—who would do that?
STUDENT 1: You could use it when you're babysitting. Like, you could use it to make something for lighting up a Polly Pocket.

Students began writing, but continued talking about the video, expressing that this kind of homemade battery was "ghetto," or less desirable, less legitimate than high-tech batteries in phones and video games. Other students made remarks like Student 1, suggesting ways that a make-your-own battery might be interesting to explore. Ultimately, optimistic students swayed the class; students wanted to watch the video again, and wanted to make their own coin batteries. Mr. Brant agreed to put the video on "repeat," so that it played multiple times. He invited students to come up to the screen and play the role of narrator while everyone else finished writing.

Mr. Brant arranged students into groups of four, turning desks to face each other. Mr. Brant drew an example diagram of the coin battery and directed students to start drawing a diagram on their posters, too. Meanwhile, Mr. Donovan and Mr. Brant began circulating, to help student groups get started.

Mr. Brant told the class, "Here's four things to put on your poster: 1) observation, 2) expectations, 3) questions, 4) drawings. Put your guesses, not just things that you know as facts."

Mr. Brant visited each group, interacting with students about their ideas and making notes about ideas on his seating-chart template. To conclude the class period, Mr. Brant asked students to rearrange the desks into rows and revisit their warm-up, adding any new ideas that they now had about batteries.

Mr. Brant gathered each group's coin-battery diagrams and students' individual responses to the warm-up question. He placed these papers in a clipboard, along with his seating-chart notes about the group's discussions.

Between Days 1 and 2: Analyzing Students' Contributions to Inform Instruction

Between days one and two, Mr. Brant and Mr. Donovan met during the Z-Team's daily planning time, to talk through student work from day one. Mr. Brant had taken the student work home after day one to review students' contributions. Mr. Brant began the meeting by sharing what he noticed from this initial look at students' work.

MR. BRANT: Ok, so, if there's a "check plus" (✓+), that didn't mean something like getting the "right" or "wrong" answers. It means that their thinking was really visible. I wanna communicate to them that THAT is what I wanna see in their work—is their thinking visible?

MR. DONOVAN: Looks like half got "check pluses."

MR. BRANT: This student brought up electrons, but most said basically the same stuff.

MR. DONOVAN: Yeah, as I was looking over shoulders, I saw that they were saying [that] the setup conducts electricity, but no one really had ideas about where the electricity is coming from.

MR. BRANT: I saw the word "conducts" or "conductor" a lot. I wanna give these back and have them add more ideas and draw more.

MR. DONOVAN: So, are you gonna show the video again?

MR. BRANT: I think I wanna show the still image of the stack [of pennies that make up the coin battery], and maybe ask first, "Where do you think the electricity is coming from?" Then, the goal will be to come up with some ways to change the stack and test to see what happens. Also, to learn to use the voltmeter—at first, it won't really matter, but, down the road, when we're doing subsequent activities, they'll really need the numbers on the voltmeter. First, I want them to do just one change, like just change the vinegar, or just change the number of pennies.

MR. DONOVAN: Let's come up with some guiding questions about whether or not to change more than one thing at a time. And whether or not it's valuable to the claims—you know, like, will we know what caused the change?

MR. BRANT: [Flipping through the samples of student work with Mr. Donovan.] Look at this—José had this idea about the guy on the video "charging it up" and, in fact, that's what the sandpaper does!

MR. DONOVAN: Almost like static electricity or something?

MR. BRANT: Yeah! And José was noticing that!

MR. DONOVAN: Wow! That's a big deal—a really good observation. Ok, so, we'll do what you said for a warm-up, and then the Learning Target will be the things about variables and experiment designs. Do you have other questions that you want them to talk about in their groups? We've been talking about trying to get them working more together, especially kids who aren't usually [active, vocal] participants.

MR. BRANT: Yeah, like, what do you think I should try?

MR. DONOVAN: So, like, when they are doing "Think-Pair-Share," I listen in and strategically choose some kids, to have them share later—kids who often don't speak up. Or I guess you could call on them with sticks.

Mr. Brant and Mr. Donovan brainstormed potential strategies for generating more student-to-student interactions, including creating some talking "jobs" for each student in a group (e.g., paraphrasing group ideas, asking clarifying questions, noting connections and contrasts in group-members' ideas). They also planned ahead for an upcoming lesson, where they would regroup students to read informational texts about electricity, metals, and circuits. Mr. Brant and Mr. Donovan decided to be strategic about building groups that would "manufacture expertise," by positioning students as experts within groups. Mr. Brant noted that José was a good example of this kind of expertise and suggested that José could be a good leader for a group focused on electrical charge. We will follow up on this part of Mr. Brant and Mr. Donovan's planning later in this case study. But, first, we will follow Mr. Brant into day two, to see how the class unfolded.

Day 2: "Where Does Electricity Come From in the Coin Battery?"

On the second day of investigating electricity in coin batteries, Mr. Brant strategically adjusted the warm-up question and discourse routines used when working with students, to extend their initial models and learn more about how students were thinking about electricity. Notice how Mr. Brant and Mr. Donovan put their plans into action, drawing upon details discussed while examining students' work together. Mr. Brant launched day two by using the warm-up question that he and Mr. Donovan generated from their meeting: "Where do you think the electricity comes from?" In groups of four, students reanalyzed a photo of the coin battery, focusing their attention on the origin of the electricity in this system. This was a missing component of students' initial models. Instead of treating it as an error or deficit in students' initial ideas, Mr. Brant and Mr. Donovan treated this missing component as the next idea to work on with their students.

MR. BRANT: [Speaking to one group of four students.] Where do you think the electricity comes from?
STUDENT 1: Maybe it's like static electricity, like when you touch a doorknob and it sparks, and whatnot.
STUDENT 2: Maybe it's like *in* the vinegar?
STUDENT 3: Or *in* the pennies?
STUDENT 4: [Speaking on behalf of her whole group.] We think electricity comes from the vinegar and pennies, or it has something to do with the pennies being shaved off.
MR. DONOVAN: [Speaking to another group of four students.] Did you all think about the question up there? Where does the electricity come from?
STUDENT 5: Positive and negative ends.
MR. DONOVAN: Ok, but where does it start from?
STUDENT 6: Maybe from the cardboard—it's carbon, right? Hmm, where *does* the energy come from?
STUDENT 7: Like a chemical reaction of the vinegar and copper and carbon. The outside of the penny is copper, but the inside looked like something else,

something kind of silver. Lemme go ask Mr. Vasquez. [Student 7 runs over to Mr. Vasquez, who is working on his computer at the back of the classroom.] What kind of metal is inside of pennies? [Mr. Vasquez helps Student 7 look up this information using the computer. Student 7 then runs back to his group.] Zinc! It's zinc! The other metal inside of pennies is zinc.

MR. VASQUEZ: Yep, that's what it says. In newer pennies, it's zinc. I didn't know that.

STUDENT 7: [To the other members of the group.] I found it out. The chemical reaction might be because of zinc.

After the student groups generated ideas about where electricity could come from in coin batteries, Mr. Brant drew another coin-battery diagram on the whiteboard, much like diagrams created the previous day. He then gathered all of the ideas generated by the student groups and added them to the diagram. Mr. Brant also created a list on the side of the whiteboard of "things we need to know," which included questions posed by students. For example, students wanted to know what vinegar was made of and if it could be a part of a chemical reaction with the metals in the coins or with the cardboard. Students also wanted to know where the electricity in static electricity comes from, citing numerous experiences with static electricity as they put on their clothes, especially in the winter, as they touched metal door knobs, and as they jumped on trampolines.

At the end of the class session, Mr. Brant snapped photos of whiteboards and jotted notes onto his seating chart, capturing observations about areas of student "expertise" and anticipating regrouping students into reading groups. Student 7, for example, showed keen interest in learning more about properties of metals involved in this chemical reaction. Mr. Brant commented to Mr. Donovan that it might be smart to create a reading group focused on metals and chemical reactions.

Between Days 6 and 7: Analyzing Students' Explanatory Models After Reading Informational Texts

About a week into the electricity unit, Mr. Brant and Mr. Donovan reorganized small groups of students with *manufactured expertise*, allowing each group to focus on reading informational text, in order to serve as experts about chemical reactions, electrical charge, properties of metals, and LEDs. Mr. Brant and Mr. Donovan again met during Z-Team planning time to review student work, focusing specifically on the updated explanatory models, reflecting students' ideas from firsthand experiments, and their reading groups. Meanwhile, Mr. Vasquez and Mrs. Paszekski worked at their computers at the back of the room. Initially, they were facing their computers and working on their own, but, as the conversation between Mr. Brant and Mr. Donovan proceeded, Mr. Vasquez and Mrs. Paszekski turned their chairs toward the conversation and began participating from the back of the room.

MR. BRANT: Well, ok, so, in these models, now . . . there's a lot of good stuff. Like, you can see how they're adding stuff from their experiments and stuff from their reading groups. But, I guess, ok, look, so, see how this group has these particles drawn here and here, and there's particles making up the penny, the cardboard, the vinegar, the wires, and then these plus and minus signs? So, this is the only group really showing particles and electrical charge in their models. Everyone else has words like "electrons" or "positive charge" or "negative charge," but I'm still just not sure if these other groups are connecting those words to the actual particles, like, the actual chemistry of the materials.

MR. DONOVAN: Huh. Yeah, I see it now. I wouldn't have noticed that.

MRS. PASZEKSKI: Me neither. I don't know anything about electricity. Thank God you're doing this!

MR. VASQUEZ: Right?! I'd have no clue.

MR. BRANT: So, I'm thinking of doing this card-sorting activity for the warm-up, to start getting them thinking about sizes of things. And then, like, how could I get them to, like, catch on to the particles ideas that these guys have?

MR. DONOVAN: What did that group read? Is that where they got the idea?

MR. VASQUEZ: That's what I was wondering, too.

MR. BRANT: Yeah, probably. It was in a diagram in their text.

MR. VASQUEZ: Could you regroup them again? Have that group split up and teach the other groups?

MR. BRANT: Like, the rest of a "jigsaw" group? Yeah, that might help. Kind of, like, "Hey, you're the experts, now. Go and spread the word to everyone else." Yeah, I like that.

MR. VASQUEZ: Man, it is awesome to see [Student] and [Student] getting to be experts. Just awesome.

MR. DONOVAN: Yeah, and did you hear [Student] speaking up yesterday? More words than I've ever heard her say about anything academic. Amazing.

Meaningful Data and Meaningful Use of Data

What made the Z-Team's use of student data more meaningful than the uses that were more common in their school and district? We think that the answer to this question has at least three dimensions: 1) the data themselves were more meaningful to the teachers, 2) the Z-Team had constructed meaningful routines—promising professional practices—for using data to make inferences about student learning and conjectures about instructional adaptations, and 3) the use of student data was integrated into a larger framework for science teaching—promising pedagogical practices—oriented toward deepening students' understanding of science.

Importance of Meaningful Data

Mr. Brant and the Z-Team specifically focused on types of data that were meaningful as sources of information necessary for science teaching. Recall that Mr. Brant gathered multiple pieces of qualitative data, including student work (e.g., students' drawings of tentative explanatory models, students' responses to warm-up questions) and seating-chart notes capturing students' daily science-classroom discourse. These sources of data were meaningful for the Z-Team because they were closely connected to curricular goals and useful within a short time cycle. Importantly, the data required analysis and interpretation in order to offer some clues about students' science ideas, language, and experiences. Mr. Brant acknowledged this explicitly when he explained that his system of writing check plus on student work was not focused on straightforward evaluation of right versus wrong answers, but was, instead, focused on highlighting aspects of drawing and writing, where students made thinking visible for analysis and interpretation.

Importance of Routines for Meaningful Use of Data

One of the most promising professional practices for meaningful data use was visible when Mr. Brant and Mr. Donovan used shared planning time to analyze and interpret data gathered during the previous science class. Mr. Brant prepared in advance by looking through students' work, making note of salient contributions from individual students, as well as identifying patterns or trends in contributions across the entire class. As a result, Mr. Brant arrived at Z-Team meetings with some inferences about students' ideas and some conjectures about how these ideas could be further expanded in upcoming lessons. This gave the Z-Team's planning routine an inquiry-oriented character, motivating Mr. Vasquez and Mrs. Paszekski to join in from the sidelines, to help interpret students' work and add ideas about adaptations to upcoming science lessons.

Sitting in on these daily conversations was exciting because the teachers approached their analysis of students' work from an inquiry stance. This inquiry stance was composed of a number of promising professional practices: 1) the Z-Team used conversations about student data as a chance to pursue questions about how students develop and refine explanatory models, 2) Z-Team teachers used data-centered conversations to continually revisit commitments to creating participatory and equitable learning experiences, and 3) Z-Team teachers used a wide variety of student data as an opportunity to gather evidence about students' sensemaking, language use, and connections that were useful for further science learning. Such asset-based interpretations of student data were rare for teachers at HMS, where the norm was to look for gaps, weaknesses, or performance below a benchmark during other data-centric meetings. The Z-Team's inquiry stance and asset-based interpretations of student work were just one part of a larger framework for science teaching that set this team's use of data apart from the data use practice seen more commonly at their school. We turn, next, to these promising pedagogical practices at the heart of the Z-Team's work with students.

Importance of a Larger Pedagogical Framework

The Z-Team's meaningful data use was embedded within a larger pedagogical framework—the ambitious-science-teaching framework—that aims at deepening students' understanding of core science ideas through the construction, testing, revision, and justification of evidence-based explanatory models. Mr. Brant brought this pedagogical framework to the Z-Team from his teacher-preparation coursework. Mr. Donovan, Mr. Vasquez, and Mrs. Paszekski welcomed the highly interactive, modeling-based-inquiry approach to science teaching as a useful way to organize science units.

Promising pedagogical practices were visible in Mr. Brant's science teaching. As Mr. Brant reorganized science units, he foregrounded close attention to students' unfolding ideas, use of language, and connections to other experiences as central ingredients for building and refining explanatory models together as a class. By drawing upon a set of coherent classroom-discourse routines, formative-assessment practices, and scaffolding tools, Mr. Brant made adaptations to upcoming lessons, in response to what he was hearing and seeing from students. Mr. Donovan quickly picked up on Mr. Brant's routines, and also began using discourse routines and formative-assessment practices to help students steadily revise their explanatory models and justify claims with evidence.

This was quite different from the instructional responses typically put forward, in the context of data use efforts, elsewhere in HMS, where data use did not aim at teaching for understanding, but, instead, aimed at recall of factual information or performance of discrete literacy and mathematics skills. Pedagogical responses at HMS consisted of reteaching to directly transmit information, repeated practice of isolated skills, or separating students from the classroom community for more extended remediation in literacy or mathematics.

Implications for Teacher Teams and Leaders Seeking Meaningful Data Use

Schools working to improve the quality of teaching and narrow disparities in students' educational experiences and outcomes often employ data-centric initiatives as a central component of a theory of change. As the Z-Team case study illustrates, meaningful data use by a team of teachers can anchor thoughtful science teaching that is attentive and responsive to students' unfolding science ideas. We must emphasize, however, that out of 36 teachers and three schools studied during this time period, only Mr. Brant and his Z-Team used these forms of student data to propel science teaching aimed at developing students' understanding.

This promising case has implications for teacher teams and leaders seeking more meaningful data and data use in their educational practice.

Teacher teams and school leaders could benefit from examining three dimensions of meaningful data use important for the Z-Team's practice. Posing the following questions as a way of reframing data use within teacher teams and school-wide data teams could help educators make data use more meaningful:

- What makes the data that you currently use meaningful for daily adjustments to plans for instruction, discourse routines, and responsiveness to students' sensemaking resources? If some data are not meaningful for these purposes, how could other data be gathered and used, instead?
- What promising professional practices are already part of your repertoire? For instance, what routines do you currently use to analyze and interpret the information you gather about students' sensemaking? If analysis and interpretation currently consist only of seeing scores as below, at, or above a benchmark, how could your data-analysis routines be altered to become inquiry-oriented conversations used to puzzle through questions about teaching and learning?
- What promising pedagogical practices are already part of your repertoire? For instance, what curricular and instructional adaptations do you currently make in response to student data? What larger pedagogical frameworks or local theories of instruction underpin those adaptations? If your current responses are dominated by reteaching or remediation to address deficits, how could you build a new repertoire of instructional responses that leverage students' sensemaking resources to benefit the entire learning community?

Acknowledgements

We would like to thank the Spencer Foundation for their support of this work and for making space for thoughtful and careful discussion between all of the scholars involved in the Evidence for the Classroom initiative. In addition, we are deeply grateful to the teachers and school leaders who opened their classrooms and schools each day for two years allowing us to learn how teachers experience increased emphasis on data use, accountability, and high-stakes evaluation. This work required extensive access to both the public features of work in schools and the backstage, private features of work in schools. Thank you to all of the educators involved for trusting us with your candor about your deeply emotional, complex, and stressful work.

Notes

1 All names of people and places are pseudonyms.
2 For more detailed descriptions of the larger study design and research methodology, please see Braaten et al. (2017).

References

Ambitious Science Teaching Development Group. (n.d.). *Tools for ambitious science teaching*, viewed 2 December 2016. Retrieved from http://ambitiousscienceteaching.org/

Banilower, E. R., Smith, P. S., Weiss, I. R., & Pasley, J. D. (2006). The status of K-12 science teaching in the United States. *The Impact of State and National Standards on K-12 Science Teaching*, 83–122.

Booher-Jennings, J. (2005). Below the bubble: "educational triage" and the Texas accountability system. *American Educational Research Journal, 42*(2), 231–268.

Braaten, M., Bradford, C., Kirchgasler, K., & Barocas, S. (2017). How data use for accountability undermines equitable science education. *Journal of Educational Administration, 55*(4), 427–446.

Carlone, H. B., Haun-Frank, J., & Webb, A. (2011), Assessing equity beyond knowledge- and skills-based outcomes: A comparative ethnography of two fourth-grade reform-based science classrooms. *Journal of Research in Science Teaching, 48*(5), 459–485.

Coburn, C. E. (2001). Collective sensemaking about reading: How teachers mediate reading policy in their professional communities. *Educational Evaluation and Policy Analysis, 23*(2), 145–170.

Datnow, A., Park, V., & Kennedy-Lewis, B. (2012). High school teachers' use of data to inform instruction. *Journal of Education for Students Placed at Risk (JESPAR), 17*(4), 247–265.

Feldman, M. S., & Pentland, B. T. (2003). Reconceptualizing organizational routines as a source of flexibility and change. *Administrative Science Quarterly, 48*(1), 94–118.

Horn, I. S., Kane, B. D., & Wilson, J. (2015). Making sense of student performance data: Data use logics and mathematics teachers' learning opportunities. *American Educational Research Journal, 52*(2), 208–242.

Kang, H., Thompson, J., & Windschitl, M. (2014). Creating opportunities for students to show what they know: The role of scaffolding in assessment tasks. *Science Education, 98*(4), 674–704.

Kang, H., Windschitl, M., Stroupe, D., & Thompson, J. (2016). Designing, launching, and implementing high quality learning opportunities for students that advance scientific thinking. *Journal of Research in Science Teaching, 53*(9), 1316–1340.

Maitlis, S., & Christianson, M. (2014). Sensemaking in organizations: Taking stock and moving forward. *The Academy of Management Annals, 8*(1), 57–125.

Mandinach, E. B. (2012). A perfect time for data use: Using data-driven decision making to inform practice. *Educational Psychologist, 47*(2), 71–85.

National Research Council (NRC). (2011). *A framework for K-12 science education: Practices, crosscutting concepts, and core ideas*. Washington, DC: National Academies Press.

NGSS Lead States. (2013). *Next generation science standards: For states, by states*. Washington, DC: National Academies Press.

Northwest Evaluation Association (NWEA). (2016). *Measure student progress with MAP, NWEA MAP*, viewed 2 December 2016. Retrieved from www.nwea.org/assessments/map/

Schwarz, C., Passmore, C., & Reiser, B. (2016). *Helping students make sense of the world using next generation science and engineering practices*. Arlington, VA: NSTA Press.

Stake, R. E. (1995). *The art of case study research*. Thousand Oaks, CA: Sage.

Trygstad, P. J. (2013). *2012 national survey of science and mathematics education: Status of elementary school science*. Chapel Hill, NC: Horizon Research.

Weick, K. E. (1995). *Sensemaking in organizations*. Thousand Oaks, CA: Sage.

Windschitl, M., & Calabrese Barton, A. (2016). Rigor and equity by design: Seeking a core of practices for the science education community. In D. H. Gitomer & C. A. Bell (Eds.), *AERA handbook of research on teaching, 5th edition*, 1099–1158). Washington, DC: American Educational Research Association.

Windschitl, M., Thompson, J., Braaten, M., & Stroupe, D. (2012). Proposing a core set of instructional practices and tools for teachers of science. *Science Education, 96*(5), 878–903.

7

USING STANDARDIZED-TEST DATA AS A STARTING POINT FOR INQUIRY

A Case of Thoughtful Compliance

Brette Garner and Ilana Horn

Under federal accountability policies, schools face increased pressure to raise test scores, as a demonstration of student learning. In this way, standardized-test scores are used to hold teachers, principals, schools, and districts accountable for ensuring that all students learn. In the wake of this policy climate, data-driven decision-making has gained popularity (Mandinach, 2012); many teachers are now required or encouraged to use data—including standardized-test data— to inform instruction. Yet, the details of this process vary across contexts (Datnow & Hubbard, 2015), as educators decide what data to use, how to analyze them, what conclusions to draw from them, and how to respond instructionally. Although educators in some schools credit data use for dramatic improvements in students test scores (Villavicencio & Grayman, 2012), there are many documented instances in which educators' data use practices were at odds with consensus views of good and equitable teaching (e.g., Booher-Jennings, 2005; Horn, 2016).

Theoretical Lens

In this chapter, we build on literature that has identified learning opportunities, resources, and professional development that supports or hinders productive data use in practice (e.g., Horn, Kane, & Wilson, 2015; Nelson, Slavit, & Deuel, 2012). We conceptualize *productive data use practices* as those that can lead to instructional improvement by supporting teachers' learning and improvement of practice (Horn et al., 2015). As teachers attend to students' mathematical understanding, they can design instruction responsive to students' learning needs. In our work, we investigate the ways in which workgroups' conversations prepare teachers to engage in such responsive, conceptually rich instruction.

We investigate *professional-learning opportunities* in teachers' conversations by identifying how activities and environments stand to support new forms of practice and understanding (Greeno & Gresalfi, 2008). To operationalize learning opportunities, we look at how conversations: 1) provide conceptual resources for understanding teaching, and 2) mobilize teachers for future work (Horn et al., 2015). Within workgroup conversations, learning opportunities are further shaped by the conceptual resources that participants bring to bear in conversation, including epistemic stances, representations of practice, activity structures, and frames.

In prior work, we found that even well-functioning teacher workgroups do not always support rich learning opportunities (Horn, Garner, Kane, & Brasel, 2017). Both research and practice would benefit from clearer accounts of what it looks like when teachers' conversations stand to support teacher learning. For this reason, we investigate the following research question: How does a middle-school-mathematics-teacher workgroup analyze assessment data in ways that support instructional improvement and student learning?

Research Design and Methods

We situate our study of teachers' collaborative learning within a larger design research project investigating instructional improvement in middle-school mathematics in urban school districts in the United States. Starting in 2007, the Middle-School Mathematics in the Institutional Setting of Teaching (MIST) project investigated large-scale efforts to support instructional improvement in middle-school mathematics. Our research team identified four urban school districts investing in viable strategies to meet these goals. We focused on instructional improvement, from the district office to schools and classrooms, collecting a variety of qualitative and quantitative data to document this work. Since we tracked the quality of instruction over time, we used and developed numerous measures of instructional expertise. In 2011, we narrowed our focus from four to two school districts, partnering with Districts B and D because of their investments in high-quality mathematics curriculum and intensive teacher professional development. As part of their professional-development efforts, both districts required that teachers meet regularly in collaborative workgroups. Workgroups were typically organized around content area and grade level (e.g., seventh-grade mathematics teachers) and met three or four times per month.

Following the best-case logic of the larger study, we purposively sampled teacher workgroups from participating schools in each of our districts. We used an internal sampling technique, asking key district informants to recommend groups that collaborated well (Bogdan & Biklen, 1992). We interviewed participants to further refine our selection, since local ideas of strong workgroups did not always align with our own. For example, teacher workgroups might be viewed as "strong" at the local level because colleagues provided each other emotional support, but may not have worked in ways that would likely improve instruction. To identify potentially strong collaborations, we sought out workgroups with unusual resources, like facilitators with pedagogical expertise or promising meeting protocols. We theorized these resources as "catalysts" for teacher learning. In the end, we identified 6–8 teacher workgroups per year. Because of high rates of teacher turnover, we engaged in this selection process each year. Over the course of the study, we observed 24 workgroups in a theoretically purposive sample (Yin, 2013).

Our primary data came from our corpus of video recordings of teacher workgroups from the 2011–2015 school years. We recorded between four and six meetings from each group each year, for a total of 111 meetings. Elsewhere (Horn et al., 2017), we categorized our corpus of meetings based on the learning opportunities available. Approximately 30 meetings involved data use, though most of these were distinct from the work of instructional planning. We considered this a finding, in that the most common data use activities were distinct from lesson planning, and, instead, focused on remediation and designing intervention activities. We supplemented the video data with semi-structured interviews of most participants, in which we asked about typical activities during collaborative time, the helpfulness of the activities, as well as their descriptions of the group's organization, to understand the broader scope of their collective activity and their subjective experiences of participation.

In this chapter, we present a case study of the Magnolia Middle School[1] sixth-grade-math-teacher workgroup as they analyzed data under the guidance of instructionally expert facilitators (Yin, 2013). Lindsay Millard, an instructional coach provided by the state Department of Education, and Gerard Donovan, an assistant principal and former math coach, led the Magnolia workgroup. Other group members included two sixth-grade mathematics teachers (Shonda and Deanna) and a special-education teacher, Tasha. Another school-based instructional coach, Tabitha, occasionally attended meetings.

Magnolia Middle School was located in a large urban district in the southern United States. Most of the approximately 800 students at Magnolia were students of color (including about 40% black and 25% Latinx) taught by primarily Caucasian teachers; approximately 20% of students were emergent bilinguals. Nearly 90% of students received Free and Reduced-Price Lunch, indicating that their families were in lower income brackets. Like many urban schools, Magnolia faced great pressure under the No Child Left Behind (NCLB) Act. Magnolia failed to meet achievement goals in mathematics each year of NCLB. At the time of our data collection, Magnolia had already undergone multiple years of state-mandated restructuring, which, in part, resulted in Coach Lindsay's involvement at the school. Other studies have found that schools in similar situations—with high proportions of students from historically marginalized communities and facing great pressure under test-based accountability policy—often engage in distortive data use practices (Booher-Jennings, 2005; Diamond & Cooper, 2007; Horn,

2016). The Magnolia sixth-grade workgroup stood out as exceptional, however, in spite of these accountability pressures.

The Magnolia workgroup was atypical in that they had an unusually high concentration of mathematics instructional expertise. In interviews, Mr. Donovan and Coach Lindsay described sophisticated visions of high-quality math instruction (VHQMI; Munter, 2014), meaning that their ideas about good teaching aligned with the consensus represented in such documents as *Principles to Actions* (National Council of Teachers of Mathematics, 2014) or *Adding It Up* (National Research Council, 2001). In addition, they expressed productive visions of students' mathematical capabilities (VSMC; Jackson & Gibbons, 2014), reflecting an asset-based orientation toward students and their students' potential as learners. Furthermore, the teachers were using a rigorous mathematics curriculum and received high scores on the Instructional Quality Assessment (IQA; Boston & Wolf, 2005).

In addition to the facilitators' expertise, the Magnolia workgroup's ways of using student-assessment data stood out for its design to support teachers' learning. Like many schools facing sanctions due to standardized-test scores, district and school leaders asked Magnolia teachers to use these data to inform their teaching. Unlike many workgroups facing such mandates, the Magnolia group integrated their data use into instructional planning. During weekly 40-minute meetings, Magnolia's workgroup developed common assessments, analyzed students' responses, and discussed instructional strategies in three-week cycles. Teachers analyzed data (including multiple-choice data and student work) from both district benchmark assessments and workgroup-designed common assessments. They intentionally used assessment data to inform future instruction. We came to refer to them as a *thoughtfully compliant* workgroup. That is, they followed the mandate to use data to inform instruction, but they did so in ways that stood to improve their instruction.

These atypically optimal conditions make the Magnolia workgroup an excellent site to study the learning opportunities well-designed data use might offer. For these reasons, we conceptualize this as a best-case analysis, given the expertise and dedicated time available to the workgroup. Examining teachers' data use under such conditions allows us to not only account for organizational and structural issues that typically undermine data use but also to dig deeper into details of their practice.

The Magnolia group met for approximately 40 minutes each week; we collected video data from four of their meetings over the course of one school year. To study how the workgroup supported teachers' learning opportunities, we used discourse analysis as a tool for analyzing video data of the workgroup's interactions during their data use meetings. Within each meeting, we analyzed Episodes of Pedagogical Reasoning (EPRs; Horn, 2007) to examine the teachers' professional-learning opportunities. EPRs are topically bounded segments of interaction in which teachers discuss issues relevant to their instruction. Within

EPRs, we operationalize learning opportunities as: a) the pedagogical concepts that are developed, and b) the ways in which teachers are mobilized for future work. In other analyses (Horn et al., 2017), we identified the Magnolia meetings as ones with consistently—and unusually—rich learning opportunities, particularly as compared to other meetings in the larger corpus. Because of this, we examined the Magnolia workgroup's conversations closely in order to understand the ways in which they used assessment data to support instructional improvement and deeper student learning.

Findings: Promising Practices for Instructionally Meaningful Data Use

The Magnolia workgroup used assessment data as a starting point for deeper inquiry into student learning. To comply with the district's mandate for data-informed instruction, each teacher used data from their districts' interim assessments to identify approximately 10 students who were on the cusp of proficiency, sometimes called bubble kids (Booher-Jennings, 2005). Under the guidance of the workgroup's expert facilitators, Coach Lindsay and Mr. Donovan, the teachers developed their own open-ended assessments and closely analyzed the work from this subset of students, in order to examine their conceptual understanding. They reasoned that, if they could uncover the thinking of students on the cusp of understanding, they would likely uncover misconceptions that were pervasive throughout the rest of the classroom. The facilitators then pressed teachers to connect their analyses to instructional strategies that could be used in future lessons to respond to students' thinking. By integrating their data use with their instructional planning, the Magnolia teachers were positioned to improve their instruction and support student learning.

As we described in our case selection previously, although many workgroups used assessment data to inform instruction, the Magnolia group's approach was highly atypical. Many workgroups used data to identify content to reteach or students who needed interventions, without going into greater detail about *how* to reteach or *why* students were struggling (Horn et al., 2015; Horn, 2016). Based on our analysis of the Magnolia workgroup's data use, we present a set of promising practices for productive use of student-assessment data. To illustrate each practice, we share representative excerpts from one of the four meetings we analyzed. We selected excerpts from the same meeting, to highlight the coherence across the three promising practices.

Promising Practice 1: Quality Over Quantity

Often, teachers have a large quantity of data to analyze. Assessments can include dozens of questions with responses from over 100 students. Workgroups are typically limited in the amount of time they have to meet; the Magnolia teachers met for about 40 minutes each week, which was fairly typical in our sample. With a great deal of data and limited time, there is a natural tension between looking at all of the data (quantity) and thinking deeply about any of it (quality).

The Magnolia workgroup addressed this tension by purposively selecting a subset of students whose data they could analyze more deeply. They used district interim assessments, administered every six weeks, to have teachers each identify 10 bubble kids who were just on the cusp of mastery. They reasoned that these students' understandings were likely prevalent in their classrooms. Mr. Donovan described their approach in the following way:

> We have our bubble kids, and we're looking at the student work from them, and then we're gonna see whether or not they mastered [the standard] or not. And the important part with this is our bubble kids are kids closest to proficiency. . . . If we're looking at their misconceptions, there's a good chance that those misconceptions permeate throughout the room. . . . Because these are the kids who're the closest kids for getting it naturally. . . . So, it's not that we're forgetting about the other kids, it's just, if you don't have high numbers of kids mastering the standards, with these kids, then, more than likely, your whole room's suffering, and we need to reteach and do some interventions.
>
> *(Meeting transcript from 02/19/13)*

Mr. Donovan's description closely matched the group's approach during their weekly meetings. Although the specific students identified as bubble kids shifted over time, the teachers brought in work from 10 bubble kids every three weeks. They selected students that (based on common assessments) were close to mastering the material at hand, and analyzed their work in order to determine student thinking around that material. Rather than cursorily summarize the responses of hundreds of students, the teachers used their limited time to closely analyze a purposive sample of data, as illustrated through the other promising practices.

We note that the Magnolia group's use of the term *bubble kids* differed greatly from other uses that were documented in the literature. Some educators have used bubble kids to engage in educational triage (Booher-Jennings, 2005). In these settings, students who were close to passing state end-of-year tests were given additional support (e.g., after-school tutorials or targeted in-class interventions), but: 1) no help was offered to those who were deemed unlikely to pass at the end of the year, and 2) regular instruction was left unchallenged and unchanged. The Magnolia group's approach was dramatically different: they used bubble kids as the canaries in their classroom coal mines. Working under the assumption that these students would exhibit misconceptions that "permeated throughout the room," the Magnolia teachers analyzed the bubble kids' work to address their understandings through instruction, thus increasing learning opportunities for all of their students.

Promising Practice 2: Look Beyond Aggregated Data to Consider Student Thinking

When teacher workgroups try to analyze large amounts of data, they typically focus on quantitative data. They look at aggregated results from multiple-choice items (e.g., "32% of students answered #14 correctly.") and make inferences about what students know (e.g., "Most students haven't mastered the standard for #14.") without considering students' underlying thinking (Horn et al., 2015). Although this is an efficient process for looking across many students' responses and identifying potential problem areas, quantitative data lacks sufficient detail for it to allow teachers to discern *why* specific content and assessment items are difficult for students.

After using quantitative data to identify a small number of focal students, Coach Lindsay and Mr. Donovan asked teachers to bring in the selected students' work from open-ended assessment items. This qualitative data provided rich representations of student thinking, thereby supplementing the quantitative data from the multiple-choice assessments. With a relatively small set of focal data, the Magnolia workgroup was able to collectively investigate students' ideas.

In a meeting on February 19, 2013, the Magnolia workgroup analyzed a task requiring students to solve problems involving unit rate. In the task, a fictitious student, named Joe, babysat at a rate of five dollars per hour. Figure 7.1 illustrates part A of the task, which asked students to fill in missing values in a table. Students were also asked to graph the data on a coordinate plane and determine how much money Joe would earn after seven hours of babysitting. In the first part of the meeting, Deanna and Shonda sorted their bubble kids' work into piles of students who mastered the standard and those who did not. Mr. Donovan recorded a "yes" or "no" for each bubble kid.

Mr. Donovan noted that seven of Deanna's 10 bubble kids demonstrated mastery of the standard; he asked her about the three who had not done as well, Jaime,

---

Joe is babysitting to earn money, so he can attend a summer camp. The following table shows how much money he earned each day for one week.

Joe's Babysitting Service					
Day of the Week	Monday	Tuesday	Friday	Saturday	Sunday
Money Earned (dollars)	10	20		30	25
Time (hours)	2		3	6	

A. Joe charges the same amount of money per hour of babysitting. Complete the remaining values in the table above.

FIGURE 7.1 Part of a Task Assessing Students' Ability to Use Unit Rate to Solve a Problem

Derek, and Tommy. Deanna turned to Jaime's work. She described that he had correctly found the unit rate (five dollars per hour) and used it to find out how much money Joe would earn after babysitting for seven hours. Jaime did not correctly find the missing value in the table, however. Another student, Derek, made a similar mistake. Mr. Donovan asked Deanna what Jaime and Derek struggled with on the task. See Table 7.1 for their discussion and Figure 7.2 for references to Jaime's work.

Deanna and Coach Lindsay noted that Jaime had filled in 2.5 and 6.5 hours in the bottom row of the table (Figure 7.2). At first, Deanna thought that "he's just guessing" (Table 7.1, turn 6), but then Coach Lindsay noted that he might have used an additive relationship (turn 7). Coach Lindsay interpreted Jaime's work

TABLE 7.1 The Workgroup Analyzed Jaime's Work

Turn	Participant	Talk
1	Mr. Donovan:	So, is it extending the pattern? Is the struggle with repeated addition or multiplication? Or is it just, like, are you seeing numbers that make no sense or—
2	Deanna:	His [Jaime's] doesn't make—I mean, he has 2.5, 6.5. At least, that's not—
3	Coach Lindsay:	Could I see it?
4	Deanna:	He got the first. It doesn't even look like he finished.
5	Coach Lindsay:	Two, 2.5, three. Okay, but 2.5 is halfway between—
6	Deanna:	Right. So, he's just guessing.
7	Coach Lindsay:	And then, six. So, but this is additive. He's not seeing the relationship between 10 and two.
8	Deanna:	Right. He's looking.
9	Coach Lindsay:	He's seeing, I've got a pattern along the bottom and I need to add—
10	Deanna:	Right.
11	Coach Lindsay:	—I need to add, I need to add an equal interval every time.
12	Deanna:	Mmm hmm.
13	Coach Lindsay:	So, in a sense, they have the concept, or they have the procedure for finding unit rate, like, what, like, I can divide—maybe what would be helpful is to make the connection between, how do you find unit rate, what is the one thing that holds true with all of those relationships on the table? Because it's not about the numbers—
14	Deanna:	Right.
15	Coach Lindsay:	—counting up, you know—
16	Deanna:	Right.
17	Coach Lindsay:	—multiples, but, along the top and the bottom, there's the relationship between the two, and that has been two, that coordinating of the two units instead of just thinking about time.

104 Garner and Horn

Joe is babysitting to earn money so he can attend a summer camp. The following table shows how much money he earned each day for one week.

Joe's Babysitting Service					
Day of the Week	Monday	Tuesday	Friday	Saturday	Sunday
Money Earned (dollars)	10	20	**25**	30	**25**
Time (hours)	2	**2.5**	3	6	**6.5**

A. Joe charges the same amount of money per hour of babysitting. Complete the remaining values in the table above.

FIGURE 7.2 Jaime's Responses (in Boldface) to Part A of the Task

to mean that he saw a blank space between two and three in the table, and filled in the value that is halfway between (2.5). Figuring that the variable for time increased by 0.5 (albeit with a few columns missing between three and six), Jaime filled in 6.5 as the number to come after six. Coach Lindsay took this as evidence of an additive relationship, since it was based on adding "an equal interval every time" (turn 11). As she elaborated on her interpretation, Coach Lindsay emphasized the importance of students understanding the relationship between money and time, rather than focusing on one variable (turns 13–17).

As the rest of the conversation unfolded, Mr. Donovan, Deanna, and Shonda built on Coach Lindsay's analysis that Jaime saw an additive, rather than multiplicative, relationship. Mr. Donovan noted that the table in Figure 7.1 was atypical, since it showed data for different days of the week, rather than displaying the amount of money earned after babysitting for one hour, two hours, three hours, etc. Deanna and Shonda agreed with this distinction; Shonda also noted that some of her students made similar mistakes.

In this exchange, the workgroup determined that Jaime (and other bubble kids) demonstrated procedural understanding—that is, they were able to use the unit rate to determine the amount of money earned after a certain amount of time. They did not demonstrate sufficient conceptual understanding, however, since they relied on an additive relationship to complete the table. Rather than taking students' answers on the interim assessment as straightforward evidence of whether they had mastered unit rate, the Magnolia workgroup seriously considered *what* students understood (and did not understand) about the mathematical content. Specifically, though Deanna ultimately determined that Jaime did not fully understand unit rate, she identified a specific point of confusion around additive and multiplicative relationships. She identified what Jaime did understand—namely, the procedure for finding a unit rate. The workgroup's interpretation of the bubble kids' work allowed them a more nuanced understanding of students' mathematical development than if they had looked at answers alone.

Promising Practice 3: Linking Interpretations to Instructional Practice

When teachers do not (or cannot, based on available data) consider student thinking around mathematical content, they typically design interventions that involve reteaching specific content to groups of students. Often, such groups identify content to review and plan to reteach the content: 1) in ways similar to the original lesson, or 2) geared toward a specific item on the assessment. Occasionally, teachers might modify their original method by sharing instructional tips and tricks, but these strategies often fail to engage the details of student thinking. Without determining why content was difficult for students and what strengths students can build on, teachers are unlikely to make changes in their instruction that support student learning (Horn et al., 2015).

At Magnolia, however, a deep consideration of students' understandings of particular content allowed the facilitators to press for instructional responses that linked to the group's interpretations. In the same February meeting introduced previously, Coach Lindsay broached this topic first (see Table 7.2).

After Coach Lindsay asked how to get students "back on track" (Table 7.2, turn 49), Shonda described a strategy that worked for some of her students (turns 50–54). She encouraged students to make their own table, one that showed hours increasing by one and dollars earned increasing by five. That, she said, helped them recognize incorrect answers that were "out of order" (turn 52) and correct their graphs (turn 54). Coach Lindsay noted that Shonda's strategy supported students' understanding of additive relationships (e.g., that each one-hour increase in time was associated with a five-dollar increase in earnings), but that it was unlikely to address the group's concerns about multiplicative relationships (e.g., that there is a constant ratio of time to money).

Mr. Donovan then brought up the notion of problem solving—a recurrent theme for each of Magnolia's math-teacher workgroups. He hypothesized that some students may have approached the task in discrete parts, without reading the entire task first and making connections among the different sections. Students who approached the task in such a way were not using the problem-solving principles that the Magnolia teachers had been working on in recent weeks. After a brief discussion around the importance of problem solving, Coach Lindsay again turned the conversation to instructional responses (see Table 7.3).

Coach Lindsay emphasized that students "need to do something with" unit rate in order to "make meaning" of the strategy and "make that connection" between a procedure and the underlying mathematical concept (Table 7.3, turns 91, 94). In these turns, she pressed teachers to make instructional choices that support students' mathematical thinking and reinforce problem-solving approaches (including "attacking" a problem, which was a local term for a specific strategy). In response, Shonda suggested giving students a similar task later in the week:

TABLE 7.2 The Workgroup Discussed Ways to Support Students' Understanding of Unit Rate

Turn	Participant	Talk
49	Coach Lindsay:	Okay. So, what, then—the question is, what're we gonna ask them to get them back on track?
50	Shonda:	I had— So, when we went over it, I said, "What you should've done was made your own table. When you showed your work, you should've made your own table and did your 'one, two, three, four, five, six, seven.'" And then, once they did that, when we went over this, they understood that, "Okay, it's going up by," I forget however many it was. Was it 10 or five?
51	Deanna:	They're multiplying, yeah.
52	Shonda:	And their— Their interpretation: "Well, it went up by however so many. And the three was out of order."
53	Coach Lindsay:	Right.
54	Shonda:	So then, once they saw that they make their own table, then they were able to correct the graph.
55	Coach Lindsay:	And I— I think that that's a nice strategy for them to see the additive relationship, but I don't know if that really helps them interpret the context. Because I think that— I think that what that still— I think that what that's still focusing on is that you have to have the numbers in order to figure out what's happening, and, really, what we want them to focus on [is] the unit, the unit rate, and the relationship between 10 and two.
56	Deanna:	Right.
57	Coach Lindsay:	So, I think the next step would be to draw their attention to, "What is the relationship between money and time? And if I know money, but I don't know time, then how can I use that relationship to figure out one or the other?" Because in real life, you're not gonna have an ordinal table.
58	Shonda:	Uh huh.
59	Coach Lindsay:	In real life, you're gonna have these situations where, I don't even know what the context is, but, in real life, you're gonna have the situation where they're babysitting on Tuesday, and you babysit for a lot longer than you did on Wednesday. So, I think that it's good for them to see the connection between the order, to, to make sense of it. But I don't, I don't— I caution in staying with that, and leaving it there, because what that perpetuates is the additive relationship that we're trying to get away from.

In response to Shonda's suggestion of providing an additional unit-rate task, Coach Lindsay pressed for greater specificity in their plan. She suggested that additional problems would be helpful, but that students would need "guidance without [the teacher] showing them what to do" (Table 7.4, turn 98). Since

TABLE 7.3 Coach Lindsay Pressed Teachers to Support Students' Mathematical Thinking

Turn	Participant	Talk
91	Coach Lindsay:	So, I'm wondering what can we do at this point, and what sort of— Because we've been— It's easy to go over it and do all the talking, but they [the students] need to do something with this.
92	Deanna:	Right.
93	Shonda:	Mmm hmm.
94	Coach Lindsay:	They need to make meaning out of it. So, what can we do, what sort of experiences can we give them, so that they can make meaning of using the strategy using, "Are you attacking?" And then, also make that connection between, what is unit rate, and how can unit rate help me complete a table when it's not in order?

TABLE 7.4 The Workgroup Discussed Potential Instructional Responses

Turn	Participant	Talk
95	Shonda:	I'm going to give them a similar question on Friday.
96	Coach Lindsay:	Mmm hmm.
97	Shonda:	We went over this on, I guess, Friday last week. And we went through, just exactly as you said, we found the ones where we had the two numbers to find our unit rate, and we took it as a whole question. So, giving them another problem, I mean, is that what you're thinking to do, or something?
98	Coach Lindsay:	Yeah, I mean, giving them another problem, but I'm wondering what role you want to play in the whole thing. It sounds like you've already gone over it. So, what can— Like I said, they need some sort of— They can redo a problem, but they need to have some guidance without you showing them what to do. You know what I mean? Like maybe— Have they already gotten their papers back, or did you collect [them] again?
99	Deanna:	I haven't given them back.
100	Coach Lindsay:	Oh, okay, this is good. So, maybe what we could do is give—write comments on their papers—give them feedback on their papers, and then give them another problem that looks very similar, a similar context. And maybe they could then apply— Because you've gone over it with them, and then they would have their feedback on their paper, to use to solve the new problem. And maybe they could do it as a warm-up, or something.

Deanna and Shonda had not yet returned the students' papers, Coach Lindsay suggested giving students feedback as a way to provide support, without giving students a procedure to follow. Deanna then described what she planned to do in her classroom (see Table 7.5).

Deanna built on Coach Lindsay's suggestion, as she planned to have students analyze an exemplar response ("the level four") and compare their work to it (Table 7.5, turns 101, 105). Mr. Donovan suggested using a different context, to further support student thinking around the use of unit rate (turns 106, 108). As the meeting wrapped up, Deanna and Shonda agreed to use a different context for the new unit-rate problems they would give to students. The group also briefly discussed some other specific strategies that Deanna and Shonda might find helpful, like having students explain their thought processes to each other.

By linking the group's interpretations of student thinking to their plans for future instruction, the Magnolia workgroup supported its teachers in designing instruction responsive to students' learning needs. They went beyond planning to merely reteach content, to planning to address specific points of misunderstanding. This positioned Deanna and Shonda to support students' thinking and deeper

TABLE 7.5 The Workgroup Continued Discussing Potential Instructional Responses

Turn	Participant	Talk
101	Deanna:	I was going— They haven't gotten this back yet, but we did the problem and they did it in their notebooks. So, I was going to give them back their paper and they were going to compare what they did on their test, compared to the problem that we did in class, and they were going to look and see where—
102	Coach Lindsay:	Right, that's right.
103	Deanna:	Like, where they went wrong and—
104	Coach Lindsay:	Yeah. I think that's great.
105	Deanna:	They haven't gotten anything— That's why I haven't written anything, because I wanted them to see what the level four *[the highest level on the task rubric]* looked like, and then what they did, and their—
106	Mr. Donovan:	And I think, when we do it, we have to put it in a different context. Like, don't make it a babysitting problem, because what happens is, then, they—
107	Deanna:	Right. Well, yeah, right.
108	Mr. Donovan:	You know, make it, like, mowing lawns, or any other context, so they're just seeing—
109	Coach Lindsay:	Right. So, maybe what they could do is do what you're saying, where they compare and they identify what they did wrong on their own paper. So, it's almost like they're scoring their own paper, but, then, give them a new situation that's similar.

conceptual understanding, and also positioned Deanna and Shonda to improve their own instruction.

Discussion

Across our large corpus of teacher-workgroup meetings, Magnolia was the only group to approach data analysis in a manner that deliberately supported rethinking instruction in ways that responded to students' understandings of key ideas. To achieve this, they augmented quantitative large-scale assessment data with rich qualitative data, in the form of student work. The quantitative data helped them target which students' thinking to investigate, and the qualitative data supported that investigation. All too often, when teachers and instructional leaders talk about being data driven, they use a very narrow definition of data as quantitative information from multiple-choice questions, with the notion that all the data needs to get equal attention. By starting with multiple-choice-assessment data and supplementing them with student work, the Magnolia workgroup invested their time strategically to inform their instruction. This allowed for a more detailed and nuanced analysis than if they had used quantitative data alone.

We also note the unusual instructional support and expertise available to the Magnolia teachers. Mr. Donovan and Coach Lindsay were instructional leaders with many years of experience in both mathematics teaching and instructional coaching. In interviews, they demonstrated impressive expertise, describing ambitious visions of high-quality mathematics instruction, confidence in students' mathematical capabilities, and thoughtful ways to support teachers' development. This expertise translated to their interactions with the workgroup. In meetings, they pressed teachers to reflect on their instruction and supported them in designing instructional responses that addressed students' learning needs. Undoubtedly, Mr. Donovan's and Coach Lindsay's expertise and experience made these rich learning opportunities possible. It is our hope that this analysis of how they brought these opportunities about can inform other educators seeking to support meaningful data use.

Implications

This case of thoughtful compliance is instructive in many ways to both practitioners and policy makers. In particular, the uniqueness of Magnolia's approach to data use in our sample suggests that U.S. accountability-policies' levers are not pressing teachers toward instructional improvement. To work in that vein, Magnolia's team developed practices that emphasized quality over quantity, looked beyond aggregated data to consider student thinking, and, crucially, linked these interpretations to instructional practice. Nothing in accountability policies, as currently devised, supports these promising data use practices. The implications for educators are clear: to work toward instructional improvement, they will have to go beyond commonplace data use practices and mobilize instructional expertise to carefully interpret various data, attend to student thinking, and, then, link that thinking to subsequent instruction. If policy makers want accountability structures to truly serve the goals of instructional improvement, newer instantiations of these initiatives should consider their current shortcomings, providing the time and personnel resources required to make meaningful use of student data.

Acknowledgements

We thank those who have helped make this work possible, including Lindsay, Gerard, and the other Magnolia teachers for welcoming us into their school. Britnie Kane, Jason Brasel, Jonee Wilson, and Mollie Appelgate provided valuable feedback and research assistance. This work was also supported by funding from the Spencer Foundation and the National Science Foundation.

Note

1 All proper names are pseudonyms.

References

Bogdan, R. C., & Biklen, S. K. (1992). *Qualitative research: An introduction to theory and methods (2nd ed.)*. Needham Heights: Allyn & Bacon.

Booher-Jennings, J. (2005). Below the bubble: "Educational triage" and the Texas accountability system. *American Educational Research Journal, 42*(2), 231–268.

Boston, M., & Wolf, M. K. (2005). *Assessing academic rigor in mathematics instruction*. Center for the Study of Evaluation, National Center for Research on Evaluation, Standards, and Student Testing.

Datnow, A., & Hubbard, L. (2015). Teachers' use of assessment data to inform instruction: Lessons from the past and prospects for the future. *Teachers College Record, 117*(4).

Diamond, J. B., & Cooper, K. (2007). The uses of testing data in urban elementary schools: Some lessons from Chicago. *Yearbook of the National Society for the Study of Education, 106*(1), 241–263.

Greeno, J. G., & Gresalfi, M. S. (2008). Opportunities to learn in practice and identity. In D. C. Pullin, J. P. Gee, E. H. Haertel, & L. J. Young (Eds.), *Assessment, equity, and opportunity to learn* (pp. 170–199). Cambridge: Cambridge University Press.

Horn, I. S. (2007). Fast kids, slow kids, lazy kids: Framing the mismatch problem in math teachers' conversations. *Journal of the Learning Sciences, 16*(1), 37–79.

Horn, I. S. (2016). Accountability as a design for teacher learning sensemaking about mathematics and equity in the NCLB era. *Urban Education*. doi:10.1177/0042085916646625

Horn, I. S., Garner, B., Kane, B. D., & Brasel, J. (2017). A Taxonomy of Instructional Learning Opportunities in Teachers' Workgroup Conversations. *Journal of Teacher Education, 68*(1), 41–54.

Horn, I. S., Kane, B. D., & Wilson, J. (2015). Making sense of student performance data: Data use logics and mathematics teachers' learning opportunities. *American Educational Research Journal, 52*(2), 208–242.

Jackson, K., & Gibbons, L. (2014, April). *Accounting for how practitioners frame a common problem of practice—students' struggle in mathematics.* Paper presented at the annual meeting of the National Council of Teachers of Mathematics, New Orleans, LA.

Mandinach, E. B. (2012). A perfect time for data use: Using data-driven decision making to inform practice. *Educational Psychologist, 47*(2), 71–85.

Munter, C. (2014). Developing visions of high-quality mathematics instruction. *Journal for Research in Mathematics Education, 45*(5), 584–635.

Nelson, T. H., Slavit, D., & Deuel, A. (2012). Two dimensions of an inquiry stance toward student-learning data. *Teachers College Record, 114*(8).

Villavicencio, A., & Grayman, J. K. (2012). *Learning from "turnaround" middle schools: Strategies for success.* New York, NY: Research Alliance for New York City Schools.

Yin, R. K. (2013). *Case study research: Design and methods.* Thousand Oaks, CA: Sage.

8

BEYOND MATCHMAKING

Considering Aims for Teacher Data Use

Margaret Evans, Priya LaLonde, Nora Gannon-Slater, Hope Crenshaw, Rebecca Teasdale, Jennifer Green, and Thomas Schwandt

In an address to the American Psychological Association, Mandinach (2012) shared a narrative about a group of educators who wished to enhance the academic outcomes of a group of low-performing students. After analyzing a slew of student data on the students' health, behavior, and attendance, administrators and teachers were still stumped on identifying any meaningful ways to better support the students. Eventually, they examined transportation data and noticed the lowest-performing students were also the students who traveled the farthest by bus. Noticing this correlation, administrators reworked the bus routes to shorten students' commutes and increase their time at school.

This narrative captures a theme in the literature on data-driven decision-making (DDDM): with the right student data, educators can identify and eliminate barriers to student learning. By using student data, teachers-turned-detectives can examine evidence until they find the culprit for low student performance. Indeed, multiple scholars have documented teachers practicing DDDM in this way, where educators examined diverse sources of data, investigated root causes of low student performance, and, eventually, identified and removed barriers to students' academic success (Dillon, 2010; Lachat & Smith, 2005; Park, Daly, & Guerra, 2013).

Yet, other accounts of teachers' DDDM portray a less intriguing practice. For example, Moody and Dede (2008) observed educators who engaged in DDDM, with the target of complying with district accountability policies. In these schools, educators focused on the standardized student data prioritized by the district. This narrow conceptualization of what counted as student data led to rather superficial decisions, such as "teaching to the test" and focusing on "bubble kids" (i.e., those students who were close to meeting performance goals set by external stakeholders), in order to meet district accountability requirements (Moody & Dede, 2008, p. 237).

As illustrated in the examples from Mandinach (2012) and Moody and Dede (2008), educators practiced DDDM in diverse ways. Teachers' purposes for engaging in DDDM influenced the type of student data they analyzed and the decisions made from that data. In other words, teachers' aims for DDDM promoted particular inquiries and decisions while stifling other possibilities.

This idea that teachers' data use aims promote certain types of inquiries while stifling others is the theme of this chapter. In this chapter, we present a case study of DDDM and how this practice operated at Greenbrook Elementary [pseudonym]. Specifically, we report on two distinct data use aims employed by teachers at Greenbrook Elementary. We then analyze these data use aims and consider the potential for each aim to support a promising practice for DDDM.

Picking the Right Bullseye

Research on data use suggests school leaders and teachers need an *explicit* shared aim or target for data use (Hargreaves & Braun, 2013; Simmons, 2012). A clearly articulated data use aim fosters a shared understanding of the desired outcomes for educator data use (Park et al., 2013) and avoids the pitfall that the aim is to merely become "data driven" (Booher-Jennings, 2005, p. 240). Further, explicit aims for data use bring meaning to the practice. Without a clearly defined aim for which to target data use practices and decisions, DDDM can become an "activity trap," where educators perform a set of acts out of compliance, as opposed to acting with purpose (Timperley & Earl, 2009, p. 125). Also, with the abundance of student data available to educators, an aim for data use can bring clarity to deciding which data sources are the most informative (Timperley & Earl, 2009). Data use aims could also support the careful consideration of data use routines and frameworks employed in schools. Data use aims can guide the selection of data sources, the types of decisions made from data, and, ultimately, the extent to which DDDM will influence educational practices and students' education (Coburn & Turner, 2011; Park et al., 2013).

As aims for data use impact the process and potential outcomes of DDDM, it is important to consider the nature of these aims. Moody and Dede (2008) described three diverse data use aims observed in the Milwaukee school district: accountability, school improvement, and teacher reflection. A portion of schools in the district used data for accountability purposes. This data use aim often fostered educators' analysis of standardized data and the identification of weaknesses, and created "products" to prove their compliance to stakeholders (Moody & Dede, 2008, p. 236). When educators aimed data use at school improvement, small groups of teachers often analyzed multiple sources of student data to identify and rectify school-wide problems. Finally, when teachers aimed data use at reflecting on their practice, they identified lines of inquiry that were important to them or their students, and looked to diverse sources of data to explore their inquiries (Moody & Dede, 2008).

Other research has highlighted the aim of equitable educational opportunities and outcomes for all students in a school or district (Bernhardt, 2009; Dillon, 2010; Johnson & La Salle, 2010; Park, Daly, & Guerra, 2013). This research emphasized educators' values and school-leaders' capacity to invest all teachers in the goal of students' equitable access to learning opportunities. For example, in Park and colleagues' (2013) case study of a historically low-performing, large urban district, they found that the superintendent framed student-data use as a tool to evaluate students' opportunities to learn. Data use was one component of his reform plan that was characterized by the slogan "commitment over compliance," where commitment meant "doing the right thing for students" and compliance meant meeting federal regulations (Park et al., 2013, p. 656). Bernhardt (2009) studied a school whose teachers practiced DDDM to enhance the outcomes of students of color. These educators collected "perception data" from parents and students, to ensure that their data use aim of equity was guided by the voices of all important stakeholders (Bernhardt, 2009, p. 25). These examples highlight how particular aims bind teachers to certain kinds of data, decisions, and modes of inquiry that aligned to these aims.

Matchmaking Versus Investigating

Given the myriad of data use aims, Darling-Hammond (1994) offered a way to classify these aims into two distinct categories. First, educators aim to "*matchmake*," or use student data to sort students into preexisting educational tracks. Meaning that the educational offerings at the school remain static, and student data are used to determine which current educational offering best meets students' needs (as indicated by assessment data). For example, educators use data to select tracks for high-school students, like a remedial track versus a college-preparatory track (Barrett, 2009; Darling-Hammond, 1994; Oakes & Guiton, 1995). At the elementary level, educators may "matchmake" by using student data to select a limited number of students for an after-school tutoring program (Booher-Jennings, 2005; Earl, 2009).

Oakes and Guiton (1995) coined the term matchmaking when they observed teachers using data to match high-school students to predetermined curricula or educational tracks. For example, in Oakes and Guiton's (1995) study, high-school teachers consulted new-students' assessment data to identify which educational track—college prep, general education, or vocational education— was most appropriate for students. The underlying principle in matchmaking is that students' test scores indicate which course or educational track they need. This data use aim assumes that: a) the existing educational offerings and learning environment(s) are sufficient, and b) that test scores provide a valid indicator for matching students to a curriculum (Oakes & Guiton, 1995).

In contrast to using student data to sort students into preexisting educational offerings, educators may use student data to evaluate or investigate the quality of students' learning environment (Darling-Hammond, 1994). In this approach, which we refer to as *investigating*, teachers may use student data to reflect on their practice, identify systemic barriers to student learning, and make informed decisions about curricula, their teaching strategies, and students' learning environment. For example, Koschoreck et al. (2001) observed a team of teachers who abandoned their current reading curriculum in light of low test scores, and created a reading program tailored to their current students' strengths and needs. In another example, Park et al. (2013) observed a district where leaders recognized that high-school offerings created a scarcity of college-prep courses. Therefore, the school leaders redesigned the curriculum and "de-tracked" the school. When aiming to investigate, teachers use student data to make informed decisions about the extent to which a school's policies and academic offerings align with students' academic needs.

In this chapter, we position matchmaking and investigating as two distinct data use aims, which drove teachers toward different data-driven inquiries and decisions. Positioning these two aims as a heuristic dichotomy, we offer an analysis of how these aims fostered different data-driven inquires and decisions at a low-performing school.

Methods

Since the majority of research on DDDM has occurred outside of schools (Little, 2012), the literature contains "shockingly little research" on how educators engage with data in their workplace (Coburn & Turner, 2012, p. 99). To address this issue, researchers are studying DDDM in situ (see Kallemeyn, 2014 as an example). As a part of a larger effort[1] to understand DDDM, as it functions in educational settings, our research team conducted a case study on the phenomena of DDDM by observing two grade-level teams of teachers (six total) at Greenbrook Elementary[2]. Each grade-level team included three teachers and at least one instructional coach or administrator.

This research employed a case-study approach to "thoroughly understand" the case of DDDM (Stake, 1995, p. 9). Our unit of analysis was the phenomenon of DDDM, as opposed to the teachers who participated in DDDM. The teachers were our primary "informants through whom the case can be known" (Stake, 1994, p. 234).

We intentionally identified a low-performing school as an apt context to study DDDM. Like many schools in the U.S., Greenbrook had a history of low scores on standardized tests, specifically with long-standing achievement differences between Caucasian, more affluent students, and African American students from neighborhoods with too few resources. Since DDDM is, at times, impacted by accountability measures and policies (Hargreaves & Braun, 2013; Ingram, Louis, & Schroeder, 2004), Greenbrook offered a typical case for investigating the nature of DDDM in schools that face heightened levels of pressure to meet state and federal accountability standards. Also, we selected Greenbrook because the elementary-school context offered the advantage of teachers working closely with students. The homeroom teachers instructed the same group of students all day and, thus, they had knowledge of students' strengths, personalities, cultures, and more.

The primary method used in this case study was observations of two grade-level teams of teachers as they made sense of and decisions from student-performance data. Per district policy, elementary teachers met biweekly in grade-level teams to collaborate on DDDM. We observed these grade-level meetings for the duration of one academic year, for a total of 23 meetings, with each meeting lasting approximately 30 minutes. For each grade-level meeting, one researcher audio recorded the meeting and created detailed field notes. In the field notes, we documented the type of student data educators examined, summaries of the grade-level-team conversations with important dialogues transcribed, the ways in which student characteristics came to bear in these conversations, and any instructional decisions made by teachers during the meetings. Each of the 23 field notes averaged four single-spaced pages in length. These field notes constitute our primary research data.

To supplement our understanding of observations of teachers' DDDM in grade-level meetings, we also interviewed teachers individually and in their teacher teams. Each teacher (six total) agreed to an individual interview, where researchers asked clarifying questions related to the grade-level team meetings, such as:

- What supports has this teacher received for making sense of student-performance data?
- In what ways do data contribute to teaching effectiveness for this teacher?
- In what ways do student characteristics influence or contribute to teacher data use?

In addition to individual interviews, researchers facilitated an end-of-study group interview with each grade-level team. These semi-structured group interviews lasted approximately 60 minutes and offered teacher participants a voice in the analysis of researcher data. Specifically, we presented the teachers with preliminary findings and asked them to challenge, question, or confirm our initial analysis of researcher data. Teachers' responses in the end-of-study group interview were transcribed and became a part of the body of researcher data analyzed for this study.

To analyze researcher data, we drew from Darling-Hammond (1994), who distinguished between using student data to match students to preexisting educational tracks and using student data to reflect upon and investigate teaching and learning. Using these two data use aims as a heuristic dichotomy, we categorized the researcher data collected from Greenbrook into instances when teachers aimed to "matchmake" and instances when teachers aimed to investigate teaching and learning. The following offers an account of this analysis.

Findings

Matchmaking at Greenbrook

In grade-level meetings at Greenbrook, both teacher teams followed a predictable set of steps when making decisions from student-performance data. These steps were not discussed at the meeting, as the team was familiar with this process.

Step 1: The principal or instructional coach provided teachers with student-performance data from a reading-fluency test (see Table 8.1). Each row of student data was highlighted in the colors green, yellow, or red, depending on how students scored. Students whose test scores were highlighted with the color red were the lowest performing students, and they were classified as "well below average." By contrast, students whose data were highlighted "green" were classified as "average."

Step 2: The team looked at student data and identified students who were classified as English-Language Learner (ELL), students in special education (SPED), and/or students in the gifted program (GT).

Step 3: The team sorted students who were low performing, but not classified as ELL or SPED, into predetermined instructional groups (see Figure 8.1).

Step 4: Teachers identified a small group of high-performing students for enrichment.

Step 5: The principal/instructional coach moved onto other issues that may or may not include data.

The time spent on steps 1–4 in these meetings decreased over the course of the school year. For example, in September, one grade-level team spent 44 minutes on this process and, by April, they went through all four steps in 12 minutes.

Essentially, the aim of data use in grade-level meetings was to match students to a preexisting curriculum or educational environment, or matchmaking, as described by Oakes and Guiton (1995). The grade-level meetings consisted of educators using color-coded data to sort students into corresponding preexisting educational offerings (see Figure 8.1). Similarly to diagnosing patients in the medical profession, students were tested, diagnosed, and then placed into treatment,

TABLE 8.1 Example of Student-Performance Data with Fictitious Student Data

Student Name	Corrects	Errors	Accuracy	Performance Summary	Potential Instructional Action
Student A	125	10	92%	Average	Continue Program
Student B	100	5	95%	Below Average	Further Assess & Consider Intervention
Student C	35	12	66%	Well Below Average	Begin Problem Solving

118 Evans et al.

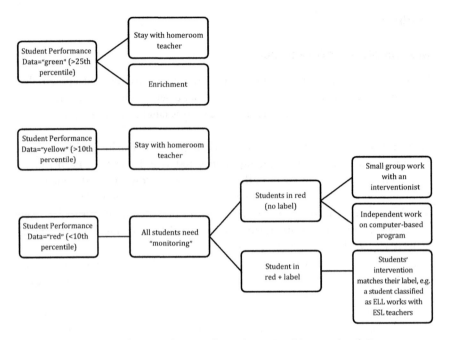

FIGURE 8.1 Matchmaking Students with Predetermined Instructional Groups

or an educational program or curriculum that matched their diagnosis. Fluency-assessment data resulted in a diagnosis of red, yellow, or green, and students of a particular "color" or test score were matched to a corresponding curriculum (see Figure 8.1).

Considering Matchmaking as a Data Use Aim

On the one hand, this aim of matchmaking students of the same test score with the same educational treatment has some support in research. Multiple evaluations of educational programs have documented that students of similar abilities can benefit from receiving the same empirically based instruction, or "standard treatments" (Fuchs & Fuchs, 2006; Fuchs, Mock, Morgan, & Young, 2003, p. 95; Marchand-Martella, Ruby, & Martella, 2007; What Works, 2013). Fuchs and Fuchs (2006) asserted that matching students of similar ability to standardized, empirically validated programs can benefit students because: a) teachers have a clear understanding of how to address students' needs, because it is spelled out by a protocol or educational program, and b) "the fidelity of implementation is easier to assess and ensure" than a non-standardized program (p. 96). Marchand-Martella et al. (2007) observed that a school's adoption of standardized educational programs enabled teachers to learn and implement the same types of teaching skills and instructional strategies. They argued that teachers were then able to offer a high-quality education to all students, as all teachers taught in a manner that was empirically based (Marchand-Martella et al., 2007).

The research on standard treatments offers some support of this aim of matchmaking exhibited in Greenbrook's grade-level meetings (Fuchs & Fuchs, 2006; Fuchs et al., 2003; Marchand-Martella et al., 2007; What Works, 2013). For example, the lowest performing students were often matched to Lexia, a software program that has research to support its effectiveness in raising students' reading test scores (McMurray, 2013). In this way, the lowest-performing readers were offered a research-based intervention that was supposed to enhance their reading scores.

Although matchmaking has some empirical support to suggest it is a promising practice, the case of Greenbrook offers insights into why the matchmaking data use aim is limited and potentially problematic. The case of Greenbrook suggests that the data use aim of matchmaking stifled valuable conversations around teachers' instruction, trends in students' data, and potential barriers to student learning.

For example, in grade-level meetings, students were matched to educational treatments, but the instructional strategies and learning environments of these treatments were rarely, if ever, discussed, in our observations. Regardless of whether students' performance improved, remained the same, or dropped, teachers did not discuss instructional strategies or the learning environment, in grade-level meetings. In interviews, the majority of teachers expressed dissatisfaction with this aspect of their data use conversations, such as in the following transcript from the fourth-grade-teacher team end-of-study interview:

TEACHER 1: What is frustrating is that, when we go to collaboration, we are not talking about the data, really, besides when we are dividing the kids up.
TEACHER 2: We are not planning.

Perhaps not surprisingly, the lack of conversation around instruction in DDDM meetings corresponded with teachers stating that data use meetings did not impact their instruction. In both end-of-study group interviews, the majority of teachers indicated that data use meetings and students' data did not impact their instruction. For example, a fourth-grade teacher stated, "I don't change my instruction much. Everything I do instruction-wise is the same for everyone." Another fourth-grade teacher stated, "I teach the same way all year." Overall, in individual and group interviews, five out of six teachers in this sample stated that the student-performance data examined in grade-level meetings did not impact their instruction; student data only drove the ways in which they grouped students.

The data use aim of matchmaking may have also stifled inquiry into blatant trends in students' data. Even when trends were obvious in student-performance data, the team did not discuss possible interpretations of or resolutions to troubling trends, such as indicators of an achievement gap. The following excerpt from a data use meeting with fourth-grade teachers, a school administrator, and an instructional coach is representative of how trends like the achievement gap fell outside of the matchmaking data use aim:

SCHOOL ADMINISTRATOR: As part of my evaluation, I had to write goals, and most of my goals are focused on my reading and math assessment. They are only attending to my African American and SPED students. So, for fourth grade, currently one out of seven students [with special needs] made our target for [the fluency standardized assessment] and only three out of our 25 African American students hit the goal, so my goal is to increase that by at least 10% by the winter. In math, only two of our seven SPED students made our goal, and only two of our 25 African American students [made it].

FOURTH-GRADE TEACHER: [Whispers] That's scary!

SCHOOL ADMINISTRATOR: So, then, on top of that, I picked out some SPED students and African American students to keep an eye on. My SPED students, who are also African American—student one, student two, and student three. And my African American students are student four, student five, and student six. So, I may be coming in and checking in on those students periodically, following their fluency test or progress monitoring.

Almost the exact same conversation took place in the third-grade team meeting, where the school administrator also identified a large proportion of African American students and students with special needs who were below grade level.

In alignment with the matchmaking data use aim, the focus of both of these grade-level data use conversations was individual students, and the most appropriate educational treatments for each individual student. After presenting glaring evidence of an achievement gap, the conversation never turned to discussing this trend.

In both grade-level meetings, what was not discussed was the most revealing. The team did not question why students with special needs and African American students were much more likely to score below grade level than their Caucasian, unlabeled counterparts at this school. Also, the teams did not discuss how teachers, the school administrator, and the instructional coach could address these students' academic needs. No changes were proposed to the instruction students received and/or school policy.

Throughout an entire school year of observations, the grade-level teams never discussed the glaring achievement gap, in data use meetings. The data use aim of focusing on individual students' scores and placements dominated data use, to the extent that teams excluded flagrant patterns in achievement from the conversation.

Although teachers did not discuss the root causes of the achievement gap at Greenbrook in data use meetings, they candidly discussed this issue in other settings. In interviews, teachers pointed out particular school-wide policies and norms that potentially created undue hardships for groups of students. For example, four out of six teachers discussed in individual interviews the discrepancy between educational opportunities for the majority of Caucasian students in the gifted program and the majority of African American students in the general-education classrooms. Further, in observations of grade-level teams, teachers did not discuss the data of low-performing students who were classified as special-education students. Students in special education were identified at the beginning of data use meetings as SPED, and then literally never discussed again. In alignment with the matchmaking data use aim, the team did not need to discuss students with special needs, as these students had a diagnosis and a corresponding treatment. In the end-of-study interview, the fourth-grade teachers explained the rationale for not discussing students with special needs in DDDM conversations.

TEACHER 1: They are already getting SPED services and working with SPED teachers, so it is already decided on what they do. We don't necessarily have to do anything more with them.

TEACHER 2: Someone is going to give them services.

TEACHER 1: They already have those in their IEPs, what they are doing. Again [said with a sarcastic laugh], you get that feeling, well, they are ESL, they are not my problem. SPED, they are already being take care of. I am just being honest, you get that way. And then, when you get those tests back and they [students] don't do very well, well, they are SPED. And it is looked at that way here [referring to a school norm].

TEACHER 1: Uh huh. [In agreement with Teacher 2.]

TEACHER 2: It gets those kids down. Those SPED kids and those ESL kids are not held [responsible] the same as the general-ed kids [referring to a norm at this school]. Because it is easy to say, well, they didn't do well because they are SPED.

Teachers' Alternatives to Matchmaking

In interviews, most teachers were critical of the matchmaking aim employed at grade-level meetings. Privately, teachers expressed interest in a fundamentally different aim for data use. Four out of six teachers described ideal data use as identifying trends in student data and then responding to those trends by changing instruction or the learning environment. A third-grade teacher gave the following example:

> What I don't get to participate in, which I think would be fabulous to participate in, is the kind of collaboration where you look at [the] unit-six assessment together with your colleagues, and you sit and you say, "Wow, look at this. Half of my kids don't know how to measure angles, but, look, all your kids can measure angles—how did you teach that, and would you show me? Would you reteach that with my kids?"

She then stated, "That would have never happened, though." Two teachers, Kim and Charlie [pseudonyms] went beyond describing possible alternatives to data use. Outside of grade-level meetings, the two teachers independently engaged with student-performance data to investigate disparities in students' learning environments. These were unique instances that they described in individual and group interviews, but not in grade-level meetings. Meaning that, outside of grade-level meetings, these teachers analyzed and made sense of data in unique ways. We describe these occurrences in more detail, in the next two sections.

Kim's Unique Uses of Data

Teachers and administrators often looked to Kim for support. She seemed to be a trusted source of knowledge on matters of instruction and student-performance data, as teachers and school leadership often asked for her perspective in grade-level meetings. Meaning that, in grade-level meetings, she was often vocal. At the same time, she did not question and/or attempt to change the matchmaking data use aim that occurred in grade-level meetings. Kim did, however, privately, and in meetings with school leadership, use data to investigate and respond to disparities in students' learning environments.

In an initial interview, Kim expressed frustration with the lack of supplemental math services at the school. She explained that a group of students in the third grade was on grade level in reading, yet below grade level in math. Due to school policy, these students received additional minutes on literacy, when the data indicated these students needed additional instructional time in math. Kim stated:

> I had a couple of students who were getting enrichment during our intervention block, but are failing math. Why are they getting extra reading, when they're already above grade level in reading, but are really struggling in math?

In a subsequent interview, Kim explained how she privately met with school leadership and successfully utilized a personal analysis of student data to secure supplemental math services for students during the RTI block. She stated, "This last time I basically just put the data out there and said, 'I have students who are in enrichment, but are failing math—why can't we give them the support?'" Kim identified student data as a critical tool for both identifying this gap in educational support and for convincing school leaders that the school needed supplemental math services and resources. She explained that, for the last two years, she advocated for supplemental math services, but, when she "put the data out there," she convinced the administration that this was a worthy investment.

In a rare occurrence, Kim also utilized student-performance data to more sufficiently target the instruction students received. Recognizing that, according to fluency data, a group of students were struggling readers, Kim again used these student data with school administrators to successfully secure additional reading resources for their instruction. Further, Kim paired up with the second-year teacher in her grade level and they co-taught a group of struggling readers together. She noted that this teacher was new and she believed he could use support when attempting to instruct struggling readers, a task that is quite complex and requires some experience. By examining students' data and the learning environment, Kim identified and responded to struggling readers who, due to her analysis, received both additional educational resources and access to two teachers. To ensure that the additional resources and the co-teaching were impacting students, Kim regularly collected and monitored student-performance data. She observed her students' scores go up and, at the end of the school year, many of these students tested at grade level, which was incredibly rare for African American students at this school. Overall, by aiming data use at investigating the learning environment, Kim made effective changes to students' opportunities to learn.

Charlie's Unique Uses of Data

Charlie had previously practiced DDDM in a different school district. In his previous district, there was a different data use aim, which was to identify school-wide strengths and weaknesses. With this background, Charlie engaged with data at Greenbrook in a novel way.

At Greenbrook, teachers collected behavior data in a systematic way, using an online behavior-management system that stored and analyzed data on students' behavior. In line with Charlie's experience in his previous district, he aimed to identify school-wide patterns in students' behavior data. Working with a team of teachers from multiple grade levels, Charlie and his colleagues identified a trend—teachers most frequently documented misbehavior on "Tuesdays at 10 o'clock" and struggling readers, according to fluency data, were typically the students documented as misbehaving. In an individual interview, Charlie explained that this time and day corresponded to silent reading, a learning activity that was prescribed to teachers as part of a mandated new curriculum. Using behavior and reading data, Charlie made the argument to school leadership that this spike in poor behavior on Tuesdays at 10 was related to the silent-reading time prescribed in the new mandated curriculum. He further argued that the behavior data offered evidence that the learning activity prescribed by the new curriculum did not meet struggling readers' needs.

In a different example, in what he deemed a "social experiment," Charlie conspired with the gifted teacher to move one of his general-education students into the gifted classroom. To be clear, this was not a data-driven decision, as students have to test into the gifted program. Yet, by experimenting, Charlie gained student-performance data to support his hypothesis that his general-education students might benefit from spending time in the gifted classroom. With access to the gifted program, his student's test scores rose significantly by the end of the school year. Further, as this student was African American, Charlie's experiment resulted in one of the very few instances of an African American student scoring above grade level at this school site.

In each of these examples, Charlie and Kim engaged with student-performance data to investigate disparities in students' learning environments. These teachers engaged with student-performance data both to advocate for changes in students' learning environments and to evaluate whether particular teaching strategies and learning environments would enhance students' educational outcomes. Further, these teachers had student data, which they interpreted as evidence, that their adjustments to students' learning environments were impactful, since students' scores increased.

The Promise of Investigating Over Matchmaking

The case of Greenbrook illustrates how data use aims can limit or expand the ways in which educators use data to inform instructional decisions. In grade-level meetings, the aim to match students to placements restricted data use to assigning students to a limited menu of instructional programs. This is in contrast to Kim and Charlie, who independently used student data to consider a variety of issues, such as correlations between students' behavior and particular instructional strategies, the need to support students who struggled in math, and the educational outcomes of a general-education student who gained access to the gifted program.

These different aims for data use raise questions about what or who should be the aim of data use. Is the aim of DDDM for teachers to investigate the root causes of students' poor performance, and critically consider students' learning environment? Or is the aim for teachers to "matchmake," and let data dictate students' placement, in an evidence-based treatment? In other words, is the aim of DDDM to support or restrain educators in making instructional decisions?

In educational research and policies related to evidenced-based teaching, the emphasis is often on curtailing educators' instructional options, to educational programs and curriculums that "work" (Fuchs & Fuchs, 2006; Kvernbekk, 2011; What Works Clearinghouse, 2015). Similarly, to the data use aim observed in grade-level team meetings at Greenbrook, teachers may be restricted to using student data for placing students into evidenced-based programs. A key criticism of this practice resides in the assumption that evidenced-based programs will work in diverse educational contexts (Biesta, 2007; Kvernbekk, 2011). Biesta (2007) and Kvernbekk (2011) argued that the notion that an educational program can work in the same way and produce the same positive educational outcomes across diverse contexts with completely different students is highly problematic. This is a particularly relevant concern for schools with too few resources and/or low-quality schools, which may not have the capacity to implement these programs with fidelity.

The case of Greenbrook illustrates how matching students to evidenced-based curriculums and programs may neglect context-specific challenges. As demonstrated in the case of Greenbrook, when using student data to "matchmake," teachers' insights into disparities in students' learning environments were not a part of the DDDM dialogue. Thus, although the data use aim of matchmaking has some empirical support, we suggest that the more promising practice for DDDM was the aim of investigating, which privileged teachers' knowledge of students and their learning environments. By aiming DDDM at resolving school-specific issues, teachers were able to identify and attempt to rectify disparities in the learning environments. Similar to the findings in previous studies, like Bernhardt (2009) and Park et al. (2013), data use aimed at investigating students' learning opportunities brought attention to specific structural inequities in the school.

Overall, educators' aim for DDDM is critically important. The data use aims educators hold shape the ways in which they engage with student-performance data and, therefore, shape the potential for this practice to foster reform in struggling schools. In contexts like Greenbrook, where schools or districts have large achievement gaps between African American students and their Caucasian peers, further research is needed on the ways in which specific data use aims promote or stifle inquiries into disparities in students' learning environments and their opportunities to learn.

Notes

1 We are grateful to the Spencer Foundation for funding this research, as part of their strategic initiative on Data Use and Educational Improvement.
2 All names of people and places are pseudonyms.

References

Barrett, T. (2009). *Teacher conversation and community: What matters in smaller learning communities and inquiry-based high school reform* (Doctoral Dissertation). Retrieved from New York University, Dissertations and Theses Global. (3390451).

Bernhardt, V. L. (2009). Data use: Data-driven decision making takes a big-picture view of the needs of teachers and students. *Journal of Staff Development, 30*(1), 24–27.

Biesta, G. (2007). Why "what works" won't work: Evidence-based practice and the democratic deficit in educational research. *Educational Theory, 57*(1), 1–22.

Booher-Jennings, J. (2005). Below the bubble: "Educational triage" and the Texas accountability system. *American Educational Research Journal, 42*(2), 231–268. doi:10.3102/00028312042002231

Coburn, C., & Turner, E. (2011). Research on data use: A framework and analysis. *Measurement, 9*(4), 173-206. doi: 10.1080/15366367.2011.626729

Coburn, C., & Turner, E. (2012). The practice of data use: An introduction. *American Journal of Education, 118*(2), 99–111.

Darling-Hammond, L. (1994). Performance-based assessment and educational equity. *Harvard Educational Review, 64*(1), 5–31.

Dillon, R. (2010). Data as a social justice tool. *Principal Leadership*, *11*(2), 32–35.
Earl, L. (2009). Leadership for evidence-informed conversations. In L. Earl & H. Timperley (Eds.), *Professional learning conversations: Challenges in using evidence for improvement* (Vol. 1, pp. 132). Netherlands: Springer.
Fuchs, D., & Fuchs, L. (2006). Introduction to response to intervention: What, why, and how valid is it? *Reading Research Quarterly*, *41*(1), 93–99.
Fuchs, D., Mock, D., Morgan, P., & Young, C. (2003). Responsiveness to intervention: Definitions, evidence, and implications for the learning disabilities construct. *Learning Disabilities Research & Practice*, *18*(3), 157–171.
Hargreaves, A., & Braun, H. (2013). *Data-driven improvement and accountability* (Report). National Education Policy Center. Retrieved from http://nepc.colorado/edu/publications/data-driven-improvement-accountability
Ingram, D., Louis, K. S., & Schroeder, R. G. (2004). Accountability policies and teacher decision making: Barriers to the use of data to improve practice. *Teachers College Record*, *106*(6), 1258–1287.
Johnson, R., & La Salle, R. (2010). *Data strategies to uncover and eliminate hidden inequities: The wallpaper effect*. Thousand Oaks, CA.: Corwin Press.
Kallemeyn, L. (2014). School-level organizational routines for learning: Supporting data use. *Journal of Educational Administration*, *52*(4), 529-548. doi:10.1108/JEA-02-2013-0025
Koschoreck, J., Skrla, L., & Scheurich, J. (2001). Accountability and educational equity in the transformation of an urban district. *Education and Urban Society*, *33*(3), 155-174.
Kvernbekk, T. (2011). The concept of evidence in evidence-based practice. *Educational Theory*, *61*(5), 515–532.
Lachat, M., & Smith, S. (2005). Practices that support data use in urban high schools. *Journal of Education for Students Placed at Risk*, *10*(3), 333–349.
Little, J. (2012). Understanding data use practice amongst teachers: The contribution of micro-process studies. *American Journal of Education*, *118*(2), 143–166.
Mandinach, E. (2012). A perfect time for data use: Using data-driven decision making to inform practice. *Educational Psychologist*, *47*(2), 71-85. doi: 10.1080/00461520.2012.667064
Marchand-Martella, N. E., Ruby, S. F., & Martella, R. C. (2007). Intensifying Reading Instruction for Students within a Three-Tier Model: Standard-Protocol and Problem Solving Approaches within a Response-to-Intervention (RTI) System. *Teaching Exceptional Children Plus*, *3*(5).
McMurray, S. (2013). An evaluation of the use of Lexia reading software with children in year 3, Northern Ireland (6- to 7-Year Olds). *Journal of Research in Special Educational Needs*, *13*(1), 15–25.
Moody, L., & Dede, C. (2008). Models of data-based decision making: A case study of the Milwaukee Public Schools. *Linking Data and Learning*, 233–254.
Oakes, J., & Guiton, G. (1995). Matchmaking: The dynamics of high school tracking decisions. *American Educational Research Journal*, *32*(1), 3–33.
Park, V., Daly, A., & Guerra, A. (2013). Strategic framing: How leaders craft the meaning of data use for equity and learning. *Educational Policy*, *27*(4), 645–675.
Simmons, W. (2012). Data as a lever for improving instruction and student achievement. *Teachers College Record*, *114*(11).
Stake, R. E. (1994). Case studies. In N. Denzin & Y. Lincoln (Eds.), *Handbook of qualitative research* (pp. 236–247). Thousand Oaks, CA.: Sage.
Stake, R. E. (1995). *The art of case study research*. Thousand Oaks, CA.: Sage.

Timperley, H., & Earl, L. (2009). Using conversations to make sense of evidence: Possibilities and pitfalls. In *Professional learning conversations: Challenges in using evidence for improvement* (pp. 121–126). The Netherlands: Springer.

What Works Clearinghouse [WWC]. (2013). *Reading recovery[R]: What works clearinghouse intervention report*. Updated. Retrieved from http://search.ebscohost.com/login.aspx?direct=true&db=eric&AN=ED544194&site=ehost-live

What Works Clearinghouse [WWC]. (2015). *Find what works*. Retrieved from http://ies.ed.gov/ncee/wwc/findwhatworks.aspx

9

MOVING BEYOND ACADEMIC ACHIEVEMENT

Using Nonacademic Data to Identify and Support Struggling Students

Tammy Kolbe, Katharine G. Shepherd, and Jonathan Sessions

In the past two decades, school-based decision-making teams have become nearly ubiquitous in elementary and middle schools nationwide (Dufour & Eaker, 1998; Kovaleski, 2007; Shepherd, 2006; Shepherd & Salembier, 2011). These teams are frequently charged with the task of evaluating academic-performance data to identify struggling students, and developing student-support interventions. The reasons students struggle in school, however, are often related to a broader range of factors that transcend students' academic performance. Teams that overlook these factors may fail to identify at-risk students and fall short of responding to a more diverse range of needs that impede student performance in school.

In this chapter, we describe how a school-wide decision-making team in one elementary school used academic and nonacademic data in its work to identify and support struggling students. In doing so, we show how teams can use other types of student data—including behavioral, socio-emotional, and health data—to better understand how and why students struggle in school, and to develop interventions that are better aligned with student needs. Specifically, we catalogue the types of data used by the team, describe ways in which these data were used by team members, and discuss how a problem-solving orientation to data use engenders a more integrated and holistic orientation toward data use by teams. We note that, in addition to incorporating both academic and nonacademic data in its decision-making, the team also drew upon formalized sources of data, as well as informal, yet information-rich, sources of input from a variety of individuals and groups. Additionally, we highlight three characteristics of the team's organization that both encouraged and supported the wide variety of data considered by the team in its decision-making: 1) the team's interdisciplinary membership, 2) the multiple pathways by which students were identified, and 3) a team infrastructure that supported collaborative decision-making practices. These elements were essential to how the team organized its work and contributed to the rich portfolio of data considered by the team in its work.

School-Based Decision-Making Teams

Teacher decision-making teams are key components of school-wide support systems for struggling students (Batsche et al., 2006; McCoun, 2006). Specifically, these teams: 1) are constituted to support classroom teachers' efforts to differentiate instruction for struggling students, 2) are comprised of multidisciplinary educational professionals, including general- and special-education teachers, instructional and support staff, and district and school leaders, and 3) digest a wide range of student-performance data, including achievement, diagnostic, and behavioral data (Shepherd & Salembier, 2011). Decision-making teams provide both the structure and processes through which many schools identify and provide support to struggling students and, when appropriate, refer a student for evaluation to determine special-education eligibility. Teams may be organized according to grade level or subject area, or as school-wide efforts. Alternatively, some schools employ nested models that involve both grade-level and school-wide teams. Schools utilizing multitiered systems of supports (MTSS) or other similar initiatives (e.g., Positive Behavior Interventions and Supports/PBIS) rely on teacher decision-making teams to identify and monitor the progress of students in need of early intervention and support.

Central to teams' functioning is their capacity to collaboratively digest and translate student-performance data into effective instructional interventions (Burns, Wiley, & Viglietta, 2008; Mandinach & Gummer, 2015). To do so, the team-based decision-making model presupposes that teams have access to and use data to develop interventions and supports that meet students' broader learning needs (Bender & Shores, 2007). Teams also must have the knowledge, expertise, skills, and capacity to collaboratively analyze and use data in their work. Not all teams approach their work in the same manner, however. Rather, two distinct decision-making processes have been used to characterize teams' orientations toward using data for problem solving: the *standard-treatment protocol* and the *problem-solving protocol* (Fuchs & Fuchs, 2011).

In the case of the standard-treatment protocol, teachers identify students performing below standards (e.g., individual students or groups of students not meeting benchmarks in literacy) and a research-based intervention (e.g., small-group instruction, specific remedial instruction) is implemented. Progress-monitoring data track the effectiveness of the intervention for students, and, after a period of time, data are reviewed, so that decisions can be made about whether or not to continue the intervention, increase the intensity of delivery of the intervention, or change the intervention.

Alternatively, teams that adopt a problem-solving protocol engage in a cycle of inquiry that is focused on collecting and analyzing data on an individual-student's situation, and understanding how this situation impacts learning (Deno, 2013). This approach features collective brainstorming around systems of support and interventions, and relies on a broad range of student data. For instance, rather than considering academic *or* behavioral data, to the exclusion of the other, or as isolated data points leading to distinct interventions or response, problem-solving teams view all data as related lenses on the factors that contribute to or impede student success and well-being, and collaboratively develop appropriate responses. The problem-solving approach generally adopts a cycle of inquiry that includes data gathering for the purpose of problem identification, generation of potential solutions, selection and implementation of an intervention, and evaluation of the intervention, to determine next steps.

It is this problem-solving model that Vermont has attempted to foster in its school-based decision-making teams. In 1990, the Vermont legislature mandated that all schools develop school-wide systems of support for children who require additional assistance to succeed in the general-educational environment. Within these systems, schools were required to put in place at least one Educational Support Team (EST). ESTs were to serve as a problem-solving resource where teachers and others could seek general input and support for meeting student needs, as well as refer students for additional evaluation and intervention. By design, ESTs are interdisciplinary, data-driven entities that serve as a hub for connecting children with a broad range of services, including instructional and behavioral interventions and accommodations, as well as community-based health and social-service resources. Over time, ESTs have become an established feature of Vermont's educational landscape, serving a critical coordinating function within schools where struggling students are identified and interventions for these students are developed and monitored. More recently, the role played by ESTs in schools has expanded, as the state embraced and implemented Multi-Tiered Systems of Support (MTSS), and Positive Behavioral Interventions and Supports (PBIS) as school-based student-support strategies.

In the sections that follow, we summarize our recent research on data use within Vermont ESTs and present a case study of the Tress River Elementary School. This school is one of three schools included in a larger study on data use in five teacher-decision-making teams; we highlight this particular case because of the team's promising practices for integrating a broad range of student data into its problem-solving process. Although these features were present to some extent across each of the schools in our study, the Tress River EST was an exemplar, given its holistic approach to using data and the team's organizational structures that supported its efforts to consider multiple sources of student data in its work.

Methods

This study utilized a case-study method (Yin, 2003) centered on weekly, in-depth observation of the Tress River Elementary School's[1] EST, as well as on interviews with individual team members. The application of a case-study methodology created opportunities for a deep reflection, and description of the patterns, nuances, and internal structures and processes utilized by the team.

Site Selection

Site selection for the larger study occurred through a three-step process. First, the research team contacted the Vermont Agency of Education to identify potential school districts, using a nomination process and selection criteria developed by the research team. Since the purpose of the study was to understand effective data use practices, these criteria articulated the need for participating schools and teams to have: 1) an established EST with regular meeting times and membership, 2) significant involvement by the principal, and 3) clearly articulated processes for identifying and monitoring student progress following the intervention. Second, we asked central-office administrators in identified districts to apply the same selection criteria, in order to identify potential schools and teams. Finally, we asked school principals to confirm that one or more teams within their schools aligned with these criteria.

The school-wide EST located in the Tress River Elementary School, a school serving a total of 455 students in grades prekindergarten to fourth from two towns, was one of the five teams included in the larger project, and is the subject of this case study. At the time of the study, the Tress River Elementary School employed 21 teachers, four of whom were full-time special educators. Approximately 9% of students were identified as eligible for special education, as compared to the state average of 15%, and approximately 21% of children received free or reduced lunch (FRL). This figure was consistent with other schools in the district and lower than the state average of 38%. The school's lower-than-average FRL does not, however, give a full picture of the significant socioeconomic diversity of students attending the Tress River Elementary School. The larger of the two sending towns is located near a year-round resort and tourist center, and the second, smaller town is a rural, mountainside community with no substantial economic base. Within the two towns, the reality is that some community members derive great benefit from the local tourist economy, whereas others derive little to no benefit, even if they also work in the tourist industry.

Participants

The eight standing members of the Tress River Elementary School EST participated in the study. These included: the school's co-principals, one special educator, one behavioral interventionist, the school librarian, the school nurse, a guidance counselor, and a school-based clinician, employed by the local community-health agency. Classroom teachers who referred students attended meetings when their students were scheduled for a review, and, as such, were included in the observations of team meetings they attended; they were not, however, included in the interviews.

Data Sources

Four research-team members conducted weekly observations during the EST's regularly scheduled 90-minute meeting, with the majority of observations conducted in pairs. Prior to data collection, the research team developed an observation protocol organized into three sections, and based upon an extensive review of the literature aimed at identifying effective team structures, data use, and collaborative practices. The first-section behaviors were associated with effective team structures and routines; examples include *use of public norms, consistent/punctual start and end times*, and *creation of clearly defined action steps*. The second section focused on data literacy and decision-making practices in three areas: *types of data being used, purpose of the data being used*, and *outcomes related to data use*. The final section was focused on three aspects of collaborative practices: *collaborative tasks, collaborative relationships*, and *monitoring and processing of team functioning*. During observations, research-team members recorded notes and reflections on the observation protocol; subsequently, these were loaded onto an online platform, accessible to research-team members only.

Researchers conducted interviews with team members using a 10-item semi-structured interview designed to elicit team-members' perceptions of their individual roles on the team, and the team's strengths and challenges, with respect to structure and routines, data use and decision-making, and use of collaborative practices. Additionally, we asked interviewees to comment on contextual and organizational factors that appeared to positively or negatively affect team decision-making, including the school's use of multi-tiered systems of support, staffing patterns, professional development, and school leadership. The co-principals were interviewed together for one hour, prior to the start of the observations, and separately for an hour each at the end of the school year. Their interviews provided additional contextual information, such as the formation and evolution of the team, the school's system of supports, and the school's connection to the community. All other team members were interviewed individually at the conclusion of the school year for 30–45 minutes each. Interviews were recorded and later transcribed.

Data Analysis

Throughout the school year, research-team members met at least twice monthly to discuss research procedures, researcher perceptions, and preliminary findings. We uploaded notes of these meetings to the online platform, as part of the field "memo-ing" process. Following completion of site observations and interviews, all transcripts and observation notes were coded and analyzed, using procedures associated with qualitative analysis (Glesne, 2015; Creswell, 2007). The team generated an initial set of codes based on the review of literature, and revised this coding scheme following a review of five sample observations and three selected interviews. The research team discussed variances in individual coding, after which a revised set of codes was identified and applied to the data. The research team continued to meet regularly to review coded fragments, compare the codes of respondents within and across cases, and document discussions about an emerging set of themes. The systematic and extensive cycles of coding and analysis of both the observation notes and interview transcripts led to a rich understanding of the types of data being utilized by the Tress River EST, the processes through which the EST's data use-and-inquiry cycle occurred, and the school- and team-level factors that appeared to enhance or work against effective and collaborative decision-making within the EST. The findings reported in this case study draw upon relevant portions of the coded data and emerging themes.

Historical Context of the Case

As a backdrop to the study's findings, it is important to note key contextual and historical features of the Tress River EST. In 2013 (two years prior to initiation of the study), the school's newly appointed co-principals reconstituted the EST to play a more central role in the school's educational support system. As an initial step, the team's membership was expanded to include its current eight-member, interdisciplinary composition. The principals also established new procedures for the team meetings and multiple pathways through which students might be identified as needing support. These pathways enabled the team to both respond to referrals as well as proactively identify struggling students. They also established a clear structure and process designed to promote the capacity of the EST to engage effectively and collaboratively with the data, including regular meeting times, coverage for participating teachers, and use of agendas and minutes.

Findings

Over the course of the year during which we conducted observations, we began to see how the Tress River EST's use of multiple sources of data—including student-performance data related to literacy and mathematics, as well as data focused on students' socio-emotional and behavioral health, and family circumstances—appeared to be beneficial for promoting positive student outcomes, coordinating services for students with complex needs, and addressing challenges facing families. In this section, we focus on three major findings that suggest a series of promising practices. First, we begin by describing the academic and nonacademic performance data considered by Tress River's EST in its work. Following this, we discuss the team's approach to integrating data across sources for the purpose of engaging in meaningful inquiry and problem-solving. Finally, we discuss key

Academic Performance Data

By design, decision-making teams frequently emphasize academic-performance data in their deliberations and, for teams at the elementary grades, the focus is most often on students' language, literacy, and mathematical skills. In these ways, Tress River's EST typified the work of many decision-making teams. That said, the team's orientation toward understanding student academic performance was somewhat different than that of national models. Rather than focusing on summative assessments that evaluate student learning and progress toward performance benchmarks, the team relied most heavily on data from formative assessments conducted by classroom teachers and school-based interventionists. Most important to the team's work were data derived from diagnostic tests that characterized not only in what areas students struggled but also the specific skills with which they met the most challenges.

Table 9.1 summarizes the range of skills and the diagnostic tools most frequently used by the team. For instance, to assess students' literacy skills, the team considered data on students' phonemic awareness, fluency, comprehension, vocabulary, sight-word reading, and written expression. There was no effort to distill student performance into a single metric; instead, the team considered more granular data

TABLE 9.1 Overview of Student Data Used to Understand Academic Performance

Academic Area	Skills Referenced	Diagnostic Tools Used
Literacy	Phonemic awareness Phonics Fluency Comprehension Vocabulary Sight-word recognition Written expression	Diagnostic Reading Assessment (DRA) Sight-word reading inventory (nonspecific) Student-writing samples
Mathematics	Forward/backward sequencing Operations Estimation Symbolic notation Grouping/place value	Primary Number and Operations Assessment (PNOA) Curriculum-based measures
Language	Articulation Oral expressions Receptive language Social language Oral motor Writing samples	Speech and language screeners (nonspecific)

(e.g., specific measures of fluency, accuracy, and comprehension) that described skill-based areas of strength and weakness, and then collaborated with classroom teachers and interventionists to develop and implement interventions targeted at more specific areas of weakness, as opposed to more generalized strategies.

The team's emphasis on understanding and interpreting students' strengths and challenges was consistent with its problem-solving orientation. When considering students struggling with acquiring basic literacy skills, for example, the team examined data from the Developmental Reading Assessment (DRA; a standardized reading assessment used to determine a student's instructional level in reading), sight-word reading inventories, and student-writing samples. Typically, teachers brought information from these assessments to the team when they referred struggling students for consultation. The team used these data to identify areas of student weakness, and work with teachers and reading specialists to develop intervention strategies to be applied during the following six weeks, at which time the student would be reevaluated for progress. The team reconsidered the updated data to determine next steps, if any.

Tress River's EST placed far less emphasis on summative assessments (e.g., performance on standardized-achievement measures) that identify students who fall short of performance benchmarks. When summative-assessment data were considered, it was typically for the purpose of identifying progress toward midyear milestones that signaled whether a student was on pace to meet end-of-year grade-level benchmarks. Not once during the school year did the team explicitly consider academic data that identified whether students had or had not met proficiency standards used by the state to track school performance for accountability.

Nonacademic Performance Data

School-level implementation of tiered systems of support allows for and, in fact, encourages ESTs to look beyond academic data for insights, acknowledging that students experience difficulties in a variety of areas that impact their performance in school. Consistent with this orientation, Tress River's EST sought to develop a more comprehensive picture of student experiences that contributed, both directly and indirectly, to performance in school. Table 9.2 summarizes the types of nonacademic data that we observed Tress River EST use in its deliberations, including additional information about student behavior and attendance in school, students' physical and mental health, and information about their families and circumstances outside of school.

Student Behavior

Tress River's school-wide system of support incorporated PBIS, a system that features proactive strategies for defining, teaching, and supporting appropriate student behaviors, and a tiered system of support for responding to student misbehavior. Necessarily data driven, Tress River's school-wide approach

TABLE 9.2 Overview of Student and Family Data Used to Understand Nonacademic Factors Affecting School Performance

Factors Considered	Indicators	Data Source
In-school Factors		
Student attendance	Number of absences Instances of tardiness	Classroom teachers enter data into school-wide attendance database
Student behavior	Number of behavioral referrals Teacher ratings of student-behavior challenges Specific behavior events	Behavior data entered in School-wide Information System (SWIS) by PBIS coordinator and behavior interventionists Student Data Questionnaire Student referrals by teachers or other instructional personnel for behavioral consultation
Student Health		
Physical health	Vision and hearing screenings Frequency, duration, and timing of visits to nurse's office Specific medical information provided to school by parents or outside medical providers	Health-office screeners Student Nutrition and Activity Program (SNAP) health data School-nurse logs Communications with outside providers and parents
Mental health	Student functioning Involvement with outside social-service agencies and protective services	School-counselor screening and logs Communications with outside providers and parents
Family Circumstances		
Physical/mental health conditions in family	Family health circumstances	Information shared with team by home-school liaison; collected by county social-services agency
Social services received	In-home interventions and supports	Information shared with team by home-school liaison; collected by county social-services agency
Legal circumstances	Custody standing Involvement with Child Protective Services Parental involvement with justice system	Information shared with team by home-school liaison; collected by county social-services agency Communication with outside providers and parents

to implementing PBIS included gathering data on individual-student behavior, referrals for interventions, and teachers' ratings of student behavioral performance. These data were captured by the school's PBIS coordinator and behavioral interventionists in a student-level database (Schoolwide Information System, SWIS). During the course of the school year, classroom teachers also completed a district-wide behavioral-performance survey for each student. Survey data were available to the team through a separate database showing teachers' responses.

Several circumstances prompted the team to consider student-behavior data. First, the team responded to referrals for students engaged in problematic behavior and in need of individualized responses and supports. The team also considered student-behavior data in the absence of a specific behavioral referral to the team, however. Student-behavior data from the SWIS and teacher survey were considered alongside student academic performance. In doing so, most often the team sought to further contextualize the challenges experienced by a student and, when necessary, develop more holistic systems of support beyond discrete academic interventions.

School Attendance

The team also considered student-attendance data, particularly the number of student absences and tardiness. Student-level attendance data were reported by classroom teachers and documented in the school's attendance database. As was the case with student-behavior data, the team frequently considered student attendance in the context of understanding student academic performance, with frequent absences and tardiness resulting in additional discussion about the factors outside of school that might be affecting students' academic performance. Oftentimes, this led the team to consider additional data about students' health and family circumstances.

Additionally, several times during the fall and spring terms, the team proactively culled student-attendance data, particularly student absences, to identify students who surpassed a threshold number of absences. In doing so, attendance data served as an early-warning indicator for circumstances that might impact student learning. For instance, approximately six weeks into the fall term, the team identified students who already had six or more absences for the school year. The team then reached out to classroom teachers for additional information on academic performance, as well as other information the teacher might provide on the circumstances for the absences. With these data in hand, the team then began a process of examining each student, to look for additional indicators of student need.

Student Physical and Mental Health

Tress River employed a school nurse who tracked the frequency, duration, and timing of student visits to the school's health center. She also kept records of why students sought attention. During team meetings, student health data were either volunteered by the nurse or sought by team members when discussing students who either had been referred to the team for consideration or were identified through other means. The school nurse also used these data to proactively identify students who were struggling with health issues that might impact academic performance. In many instances, team members were unaware of these circumstances and the nurse's presentation stimulated additional discussion and data requests, to better understand both the impact student health had on academic performance and other factors that might be contributing to student-health issues.

Similarly, the school counselor recorded her interactions with students, including the number and frequency of exchanges, and the types of support she provided to students. Like the school nurse, the counselor shared weekly observations about students with acute needs, and the team frequently considered these observations in light of other data, to develop more comprehensive systems of support. The school counselor served as a resource to the team, frequently volunteering information about her interactions with students and other observations from her work in classrooms.

Family Circumstances

Tress River's EST was unique in that one of its standing team members was a home-school clinician from the county's social-services office. This office is responsible not only for providing social services and case management for families in crisis but it also serves as a liaison, connecting the school to outside providers that receive student referrals. Each week, the home-school clinician reported to the team on the office's involvement with students (and their families). This information was considered alongside other data, including student academic performance, behavior, and attendance. The result was increased coordination between the school and the office on efforts to provide support and services to students and families.

Integrating Multiple Data Sources

As suggested previously, multiple sources of data were not considered in isolation, but, rather, Tress River's EST intentionally sought opportunities to triangulate among sources. Observations from one type of data oftentimes prompted the team to seek additional data about student needs. These efforts grew from collaborative exchanges among team members, during which they moved beyond a focus on what was observed to an interrogation of the data, that led to deeper understanding about why these patterns existed. These exchanges served two basic functions: 1) information sharing, whereby a broader range of school personnel were alerted to student issues they might not otherwise be aware of, and 2) an early-warning system through which students were identified for monitoring and sometimes additional follow up by EST team members.

For instance, on one occasion, the school nurse identified a student who had stopped by her office each day for the past few weeks, with no real health complaint. The nurse identified this pattern based on her log of students who visited the school clinic. Upon hearing this, another team member, the school's counselor, chimed in that the student had stopped by her office several times during the past few weeks. The home-school liaison shared that she had been contacted by the local family service bureau about the student's home situation, noting that the mother had recently been imprisoned and the child was being cared for by the father, who worked evenings. The team followed up with the student's teacher and found that there had been an uptick in missed homework and a decline in the student's academic performance. Through this data-based information exchange, the team developed a richer, shared understanding of the student's personal circumstances and how these circumstances were impacting her at school. In response, the team recommended a comprehensive support plan for the student that included one-on-one time with caring adults at the school (e.g., special lunch with the counselor) and academic support, including more time to complete assignments in school and frequent check-ins with the responsible parent.

At another meeting, the team proactively reviewed teacher-reported data on student behavior. The special educator on the team sorted the data by students who teachers reported were most likely to experience "difficulties with emotions, concentration, and behavior." The team identified 12 students where teachers reported significant concerns, but who had not been referred for additional behavioral supports. In doing so, the team found that most of the identified students were in the school's pre-kindergarten and kindergarten classrooms. The special-education teacher pointed out that the school did not have an early-intervention strategy for early-grades students. The school principal then observed that it might make sense to conduct 20-minute classroom observations for each student, to learn more about the behaviors in which the students engaged. This was accomplished prior to the next meeting. The observation data identified several areas of common concern. In response, the team embarked on a process of devising a new system for identifying and addressing emergent student behaviors among young children. It also alerted the school principals to the need for future positive behavioral supports for kindergarten students, including new curricular modules for young children that would be used during the next school year.

Team Organization

Two aspects of how the Tress River's EST was organized influenced the scope of data considered by the team: 1) the multiple perspectives and areas of expertise brought together by the team's diverse membership, and 2) the multiple pathways used by the team to identify students for consideration. In this section, we describe how these organizational strategies expanded the range of data considered by the team, as well as supported its efforts to both respond to and be proactive in identifying and supporting struggling students.

Multidisciplinary Team Membership

Tress River's EST reflected diverse membership and expertise, such that the team was able to approach data and problem-solving through a number of different lenses, including academic performance, behavioral indicators, family circumstances, and physical and mental health. Put simply, the breadth of data considered by the team was largely made possible by the fact that the team was comprised of a diverse group of education and social-service professionals with differing expertise and points of contact with students and families. In their roles outside the team, members collected and analyzed different types of data. They considered these data through the lens of their individual professional expertise and brought their individual perspectives to the table, as EST members.

Simply having a diverse team membership need not translate into collaborative data use, however. The school principals established a clear structure and set of routines designed to promote the team's ability to engage in effective collaboration and data-based decision-making. For example, team norms were developed and prominently displayed on the meeting-room wall. During meetings, agendas and minutes were projected, and roles such as timekeeper and recorder were assigned and adhered to by team members. The school principals provided coverage for teachers and other team members during weekly meetings, usually relying on an in-house floating substitute teacher. Problem-solving around individual students occurred through a typical process involving problem identification, clarification of the issues, additional data gathering and interpretation, restatement of the issues, and brainstorming for potential solutions (Friend & Cook, 2013). In facilitating these conversations, the school principals actively engaged all of the team members in the discussion. During interviews, individual team members described how this active facilitation and emphasis on collaborative decision-making bolstered the professional respect and trust among team members that led to more authentic discussions of student needs and problem-solving.

Multiple Pathways for Identifying Students

The types of data considered by Tress River's EST were influenced by the multiple pathways used to identify students for the team's consideration. Students for the team's consideration came from three sources: 1) referrals from classroom teachers seeking support and guidance from the broader school community in responding to the needs of struggling students, 2) ad hoc nominations by EST committee members, and 3) proactively reviewing student data for trends and outliers interpreted as early signals that individual or groups of students were struggling (see Figure 9.1).

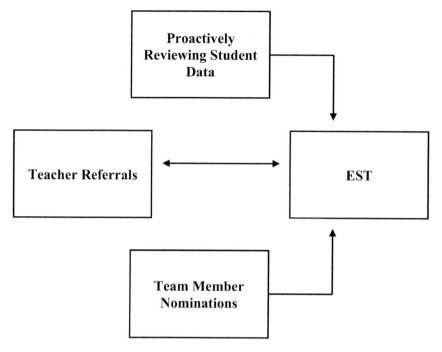

FIGURE 9.1 Student-Identification Pathways

In the first instance, classroom teachers referred students to the team, using an established process where they completed a referral form ahead of the meeting that described the challenges encountered by the student, the strategies already attempted or in place to address student needs, and relevant classroom-level student data. Typically, the data presented characterized a student's academic performance, using formative and summative assessments, as well as other artifacts exemplifying student work and behavior. The specific sources were grade- and subject-specific, and also reflected individual teachers' preferences for data that best informed their teaching; the school did not have a standardized protocol for the types of student-level academic data teachers provided to the team. Teacher-provided data also included classroom observations of student behavior. In the latter case, these types of student data were primarily descriptive, most often characterizing interactions and events with which the student was involved.

The team's weekly agenda also dedicated time at the beginning of the meeting for team members to nominate students identified as warranting discussion by the team. In many instances, the nominations were based on personal encounters with students in nonclassroom settings or, in the case of the representative from the community mental-health agency, her interactions with the family. One team member would bring up a student of concern, providing a description of their experience with the student and relevant evidence to support their observations.

Evidence was most often descriptive, and set the stage for a more general discussion by the team, where other team members chimed in with their observations and experiences.

Periodically, the team also reviewed school-wide student data, including information about student attendance, office referrals, student achievement on state and district assessments, and results of a school-based survey of teachers' qualitative assessments of each student's growth and development. These broader-based efforts occurred several times during the school year and served two purposes: 1) identifying trends within the school that needed to be addressed in the school's improvement plans or that required a more generalized intervention or change in policy, and 2) creating an early-warning system to identify students with emerging needs, who may not have yet been formally identified by school staff as struggling or needing support.

Conclusion and Considerations

The Tress River Elementary School's multidisciplinary school-based decision-making team takes a proactive and responsive approach to meeting the needs of all of its students. Three promising practices emerged from this case study that may provide guidance to similar teams: 1) the team's holistic approach to data use, 2) its attention to the integration of data across sources, and 3) the value of creating an interdisciplinary team, with an infrastructure that supports effective collaboration and data-based decision-making. The Tress River EST was intentional in its use of academic as well as nonacademic data, including in- and out-of-school factors that contributed, both directly and indirectly, to student experiences in school, including academic performance, student behavior, physical and mental health, and family circumstances. Beyond recognizing the value of multiple types of data, team members were skilled in integrating and drawing meaning from both academic and nonacademic student-level data. This integrated and holistic approach allowed them to define and address issues from multiple vantage points, with resulting plans focused on academic and behavioral interventions, as well as relevant family, health, and mental health circumstances. The team's simultaneous focus on school-level data (e.g., school-wide attendance, behavior and health data) and student-level data encouraged preventative and universal responses to potential challenges. Finally, the team's interdisciplinary membership and its structure and routines served to promote and sustain key features of collaborative teams, such as well-organized and regular face-to-face meetings, use of team norms, and effective problem-solving.

Implications

In consideration of these findings and emerging promising practices, we identify a number of implications and recommendations. At the practice level, the Tress River example underscores the need for similar teams to undertake data use and decision-making in a manner that is intentional, attends to multiple forms of data and pathways to identification of student needs, and draws on the expertise of its multidisciplinary team members. The case also points to the need for school leaders to play a major role in the design and sustainability of the team. The leaders of this team drew on their knowledge of effective teaming and collaboration in order to create a structure conducive to effective data use and problem-solving, and they nurtured the team's development through careful facilitation.

At the theoretical level, this case contributes to the body of literature emphasizing data use as a form of dialogue, inquiry, and sensemaking that develops over time, as a team works together (Spillane, 2012; Wheelan, 2016). The team went well beyond more transactional views of data use, in which student-level data are analyzed for the purpose of matching the student to a particular intervention or to improve student performance for the purposes of accountability; rather, the team drew on its varied expertise to push members to a deeper analysis and a more complex set of responses to both individual student needs and school-wide patterns indicating a need for improvement.

Future research might focus on data use as a form of sensemaking by examining multiple team "narratives" to identify patterns of inquiry that appear to contribute to this level of dialogue. The developmental aspect of data use and collaboration that we observed over time also warrants further research to determine what elements seem most likely to support teams in increasingly sophisticated approaches to data use and inquiry. A major limitation of the case presented here is the fact that it is just one case; we believe, however, that it points the way to what can happen when teams assume a more holistic focus and enact a commitment to creating a school culture that is proactive and responsive to student needs, as well as to the needs of families, teachers, and support staff.

Acknowledgement

We are grateful to Spencer Foundation for supporting our work.

Note

1 All names of people and places are pseudonyms.

References

Batsche, G., Elliot, J., Graden, Grimes, J., Kovaleski, J., Prasse, D., Reschly, D., Schrag, J., & Tilly, W. D. (2006). *Response to intervention: Policy considerations and implementation*. Alexandria, VA: National Association of State Directors of Special Education.

Bender, W. N., & Shores, C. (2007). *Response to intervention: A practical guide for every teacher*. Thousand Oaks, CA: Corwin Press.

Burns, M. K., Wiley, H. I., & Viglietta, E. (2008). Best practices in facilitating problem-solving teams. In A. Thomas & J. Grimes (Eds.), *Best practices in school psychology* (5th ed.). Bethesda, MD: National Association of School Psychologists.

Creswell, J. W. (2007). *Qualitative inquiry and research design: Choosing among five traditions.* Thousand Oaks, CA: Sage.

Deno, S. L. (2013). Problem-solving assessment. In R. Brown-Chidsey & K.J. Andren (Eds.), *Assessment for intervention* (2nd ed., pp. 10–36). New York, NY: Guilford Press.

DuFour, R., & Eaker, R. (1998). *Professional learning communities at work: Best practices for enhancing student achievement.* Alexandria, VA: Association for Supervision and Curriculum Development.

Friend, M., & Cook, L. (2013). *Interactions: Collaboration skills for school professionals (7th ed.).* Boston, MA: Pearson.

Fuchs, D., & Fuchs, L. S. (2011). Introduction to response to intervention: What, why, and how valid is it? *Reading Research Quarterly, 41*(1), 93–99.

Glesne, C. (2015). *Becoming qualitative researchers: An introduction* (5th ed,). Boston: Pearson MCC.

Kovaleski, J. F. (2007). Response to intervention: Considerations of research and systems change. *School Psychology Review*, 638–646.

Mandinach, E. B. (2012). A perfect time for data use: Using data-driven decision making to inform practice. *Educational Psychologist, 47*(2), 71–85. doi:10.1080/00461520.2012.667064

Mandinach, E., & Gummer, E. (2015). Data-driven decision-making: Components of the enculturation of data use in education. *Teachers College Record, 117*(4), 1–12.

McCoun, B. (2006). CASE in point: RTI as a general education initiative and the new role for educational support teams. *Journal of Special Education Leadership, 19*(2), 62–63.

Shepherd, K. (2006). Supporting all students: The role of principals in expanding general education capacity through the use of response to intervention teams. *Journal of Special Education Leadership, 19*(2), 30–38.

Shepherd, K., & Salembier, G. (Fall, 2011). Improving schools through a response to intervention approach: A cross-case analysis of three rural schools. *Rural Special Education Quarterly, 30*(3), 3–15.

Spillane, J. P. (2012). Data in practice: Conceptualizing the data-based decision-making phenomena. *American Journal of Education, 118*(2), 113–141. doi:10.1086/663283

Wheelan, S. A. (2016). *Creating effective teams: A guide for members and leaders* (5th ed.). Los Angeles, CA: Sage.

Yin, R. K. (2003). *Case study research: Design and methods.* Thousand Oaks, CA: Sage.

10

"EVERYONE'S RESPONSIBILITY[1]"

Effective Team Collaboration and Data Use

Amanda Datnow, Vicki Park, and Bailey Choi

Schools and districts promoting data-driven decision-making often have one thing in common: dedicated collaboration time for teachers. The teacher team is seen as a key unit in which data will be shared, analyzed, and used to inform instruction. The belief is that, by working together, teachers will support each other in developing shared knowledge for instructional improvement. Teacher teams face challenges in realizing these goals (Daly, 2012; Horn, Kane, & Wilson, 2015), yet we have little knowledge about the collaborative processes of teams that use data effectively.

Drawing on an in-depth, two-year qualitative case study of a teacher team at one school, this chapter addresses the question: How does data use play a role in the joint work of a highly collaborative teacher team? We analyzed the nature of the collegial relationships among teachers, highlighting the ways in which teachers' collaborative activities involved data-informed instruction, and identifying the contextual features that supported this work. As we will describe, the case we focus on is an exemplar, and we highlight promising practices. We situate our work within a framework informed by literature on data use and teacher collaboration.

Literature and Framework

Given the wide range of what constitutes data and its varied uses in school reform, it is important to define what we mean by "data" in this context. We see data, broadly speaking, as information that teachers use to inform instructional decision-making. Many schools and districts engage teachers in data use via the administration and analysis of benchmark-assessment data. In our prior work, we have found that using benchmark-assessment results can be an initial catalyst for teachers to use data (Datnow & Park, 2014). Even in these cases, however, the sources of data that teachers relied upon went beyond these measures and included teacher-created assessments, curriculum-embedded assessments, writing portfolios, results from student work with online instructional tools, and their own observations of student learning, among others. Thus, when we examined teachers' work with data for this study, we included both summative- and formative-assessment data sources.

Providing structured time for collaboration is one of the primary ways that many districts and schools attempt to build teachers' capacity to use data (Farley-Ripple & Buttram, 2015; Honig & Venkateswaran, 2012; Marsh, 2012; Means, Padilla, & Gallagher, 2010). Strong instructional communities organized to analyze data can assist teachers in using data in productive ways (Blanc et al., 2010; Cosner, 2011; Datnow, Park, & Kennedy-Lewis, 2013; White & Anderson, 2011). Various tools for supporting teachers' use of data, including district policies and protocols for analyzing and reflecting on data, assist in the process of data use, in some cases (Christman et al., 2009), but prove to be constraining in others (Datnow et al., 2013).

Although numerous studies have documented the benefits of collaboration, studies also find that grade-level agendas, cultural norms, and the level of expertise in the group all play into teacher collaboration around data use (Horn & Little, 2010; Young, 2006). Teacher teams with limited expertise can misinterpret or misuse data, or work together to perpetuate poor classroom practice (Daly, 2012). Teachers are sometimes also uncomfortable sharing data in collaboration meetings (Jimerson & Wayman, 2015). The variance in the quality of conversations can impact student learning (Horn et al., 2015; Timperley, 2009). For example, Horn et al.'s (2015) study found that teacher workgroups used different logics when interpreting the same district math-assessment data. One set of logics focused on instructional management, where the emphasis was on categorizing students according to achievement levels, whereas the other set focused on instructional improvement, such as diagnosing student mistakes. Leadership played a key role in framing these logics, and the logics had implications for teaching and learning.

Thus, even though collaboration is touted as a major vehicle for capacity building around data use, the work among teacher teams varies widely. In order to gain knowledge of how teacher collaboration for data use could be more productive, we need to better understand the intersection between data use and teacher-team cultures and structures. Although not focused on data use per se, earlier research on school change and teacher collaboration can help us conceptualize these dynamics. For example, Hargreaves (1994) and Little (1990) provided typologies of teaching cultures and collegiality. These scholars acknowledged that teacher cultures range from individualistic to collaborative, and reminded us that interactions can be contrived or focused on simple sharing, rather than joint work. Understanding how culture and structure are mutually reinforcing is also a critical insight from the educational change literature that we need to consider when we examine the conditions that allow a well-functioning data team to thrive (Stoll, 1998; Fullan, 2012).

In this chapter, we build upon this work to examine how data use plays a role in the functioning of a highly collaborative teacher team. We use Little's (1990) continuum of collegial relations to help define what constitutes a team in which teachers are interdependent. On one end of the continuum, teachers' relationships are characterized by a norm of independence, involving sharing, storytelling, and assistance. On the other end of the continuum, teachers' relationships are characterized by the norm of interdependence, leading to joint work. This type of collaboration:

1) anticipates collective action by teachers
2) requires interdependence in order for teachers to succeed in their own work
3) shifts teaching from a private to a public enterprise, and, in turn, teachers "are credited for their knowledge, skill, and judgment" (p. 521)
4) allows for deliberation of conflicting beliefs and practices

Little (1990) concludes by stating that "each one's teaching is everyone's business, and each one's success is everyone's responsibility" (p. 523).

Data use was not a prominent reform when Little's (1990) article was published, though she briefly notes that teacher deliberations in an interdependent arrangement involved a "greater reliance on verifiable information as a basis for preferred action" (p. 521). In general, teacher conversations about instructional improvement have not always relied on data and evidence for action planning; data use is now considered a key feature of contemporary school reform efforts, however, increasing its saliency in teachers' day-to-day work and collaboration. Thus, in considering the four elements previously described, we elevate the idea of anchoring decisions in data, in our chapter, as it is a focal point of the teacher collaboration in the school we studied.

Method

In this chapter, we draw upon data gathered from an in-depth, two-year qualitative case study of fourth- and fifth-grade teacher teams at Chavez Elementary school [pseudonym], located in a midsize school district in the U.S. We chose qualitative case-study methods due to our desire to understand educators' use of data as it unfolds in context (Yin, 2013). Employing qualitative methods also allowed us to interact with participants, observe behavior, and gain firsthand knowledge about the contexts of educators' work.

We studied Chavez Elementary as part of a larger, four-school research project.[2] Sites were purposely selected public schools in which teachers were expected to use data to inform differentiated instruction. During the period of our study, the racial/ethnic makeup of the school was 40% Caucasian, 30% Asian or Pacific Islander, 20% Latino, and 5% African American. Fifty percent of the students qualified for the free-or-reduced-price meal program, and 30% were English learners. We chose to profile Chavez for this chapter since their practices stood out in numerous ways.

The teacher team that we focused on included eight teachers from the fourth- and fifth-grade levels. Data collection took place during the 2014–2015 and 2015–2016 school years, and included 27 interviews with teachers and administrators, 37 hours of teacher-team-meeting observations, and 19 hours of classroom observations. Using a semi-structured protocol, most teachers were interviewed twice annually, with each interview lasting 45–90 minutes. The principal was interviewed twice and the school counselor was interviewed once. All interviews were audio recorded and transcribed verbatim. Interviews are identified in this chapter using numbered codes and the date of interview.

We focused primarily on observing teacher team meetings in which data were discussed. Using a semi-structured observation protocol, we noted the types of data used for discussion, uses of data-discussion tools, how data were analyzed, how data were talked about, and the types of decisions made on the basis of data. In addition, we collected school- and team-level documents that related to data use and instructional decision-making.

Data analysis included several rounds of content coding interview transcripts and teacher-team-meeting observation notes. Our first round of analysis involved writing a descriptive case report about the school, in order to get a holistic sense of the context and data use culture. Informed by theories in school change and research on teacher collaboration, we then coded interview and observational data using MAXQDA qualitative coding software, to identify the defining structural and cultural features of the team's work with data, as well as the nature of their collaboration.

Findings

Our findings are organized to highlight the promising practices that teachers engaged in that supported the tenets of interdependency, as described by Little (1990). As we will explain, the practice of jointly examining data on all students helped to make teaching a public activity and provided a venue in which teachers could support each other in meeting students' needs. The valuing of teachers' individual and collective expertise was also a key feature supporting both teacher collaboration and data use. Vertical and horizontal collaboration structures reinforced teacher interdependence. The culture of collaboration also anticipated collective action by teachers, through instructional planning informed by data use. In these discussions, teachers had a space for teachers to deliberate, disagree in a healthy manner, and, ultimately, come together to support data-informed instruction.

Jointly Examining Data on All Students

Teachers at Chavez shifted teaching from a private to a public enterprise through the joint sharing of data on their students. Educators at this school have long engaged in this comprehensive process of data analysis three times a year. This involved grade-level teams of teachers (e.g., fourth- and fifth- grade teams met together), two or three intervention teachers (including an English-learner support teacher), a school counselor, and the principal getting together for two hours to examine data on every student served by each team of teachers. Teachers were provided with substitute release time to attend.

The purpose of these meetings was to discuss student progress, assign students to interventions, or adjust flexible ability-group placements in English Language Arts (ELA). At the spring meeting, the group also discussed classroom placements for the following year. Although serving these goals, the meetings also served the purpose of teachers openly sharing data on all of their students, which allowed for a discussion of the strategies that would best meet students' needs, making teaching more public. Having teachers from two grade levels at these meetings helped to promote interdependence, as teachers were not only focused on students in their own class or even grade.

To prepare for the meetings, the school's data clerk (a position the school chose to fund) organized student data, enabling the team of educators to discuss each student and their performance on various assessments. Meeting participants were provided a spreadsheet that included data on every student in the grade level(s) being discussed. The team examined a wide variety of data on student achievement, including a range of assessments, interventions, or other designations (e.g., English learner), all of which appeared on a single sheet, listed by student. Data points included the student results from a statewide assessment, a benchmark-assessment test that the district administered three times a year in ELA and math, as well as spelling and writing assessments the teachers gave themselves. The meetings followed the administration of the benchmark assessment, even though the discussion of data was by no means limited to this measure.

In addition to the spreadsheets that were provided by the data clerk, the group also accessed other data on the district's data-management system. Occasionally, a member of the group would access the system to look up patterns of student attendance, assessment data dating back several years, to see if there was a trend over time, or even a student's birth date, to see if a student might be particularly young for the grade (i.e., a possible explanation for classroom behavior, etc.). As the principal explained, the goal is to figure out "what might be hindering the learning for students . . . and trying to get past those barriers" (Principal,

08/05/14). This problem-solving process required teachers to work in an interdependent manner.

In their analysis of data, the group paid particular attention to increases and decreases in student performance because, as the principal explained:

> We want to be sure that, if they scored high or low in one particular area and it seems to be a fluke, we have other assessments that we can, kind of, tease it out to see, was this just a bad day or is this where they really are?
>
> *(Principal, 08/05/14)*

Pulling together an array of data on each student in a single location was critical to this process. Even though many data points for each student were made available, teachers did not believe that numbers, especially achievement measures, were the sole or most important data worth discussing. Rather, educators engaged in a multidimensional evaluation of achievement, behavior, students' lives in and outside of school, and work habits, in order to meet the needs of each child. The meetings consistently reflected this holistic orientation to discussing students.

Little (1990) explains that interdependent relations among teachers focus on "the interests of a student clientele for whom they accept joint responsibility" (p. 523). This common purpose was abundantly clear at Chavez and was readily evident in team meetings. When educators at this school collaborated to examine student data, they held each other accountable for meeting the needs of all children. A teacher explained: "I think there has to be buy in that we're here to serve the whole community. I think when you have that common purpose, it really helps" (Teacher 111, 05/24/16). A teacher who was new to the school reiterated: "The team collaborates for literally everything. Talking about how we can help not just our own kids, but with each other's kids, is a whole other world for me. I came from a school where we just worked with our own kids, every teacher is to themselves. And it's just a different world, and I appreciate it" (Teacher 124, 05/20/16).

Teachers made it their business to know each other's students and their students' families. When one teacher shared a challenge with regards to meeting a particular-student's needs, others shared information or teaching strategies that might be useful. Their interdependence was readily evident during these moments. For example, in a collaborative meeting with teachers and administrators, one teacher expressed frustration regarding a student's drop in achievement, most likely due to poor homework scores. She explained that, when the student was at school, she was "fine," but she never turned in her homework. The principal suggested that the student stay after school to get her homework done, as she was consumed with family obligations at home. The group agreed that they would create an after-school homework club to help this student and other students in the same situation. This example was typical of the problem-solving approach we observed in team-collaboration meetings. Underlying the educators' shared sense of responsibility for meeting students' academic and socio-emotional needs were common beliefs about high expectations for students, and for themselves as professionals.

Valuing Teacher Expertise and Judgment

One of the main supportive features of collaboration at Chavez was the valuing of teacher expertise and judgment. Little (1990) explains that although interdependent relations among teachers make teaching more open to examination by others, it is built on the belief that teachers bring important professional wisdom and judgment to the table. Not only did the principal's actions communicate that she valued teachers' expertise but the teachers valued each other's expertise, as well.

The valuing of teacher expertise manifested in the fact that the principal allowed the teachers to use their collaboration time in ways that best suited their needs. There was early dismissal once a week to provide teachers paid collaboration time. One afternoon a month was dedicated to faculty meetings, but teachers used the other afternoons flexibly. Relying on faculty judgment to guide these meetings, the principal explained, "It depends on, really, the time of year, and the time of the month, as to what's going on. Sometimes they might be just teaming to plan, sometimes to assess. You know, it just depends" (Principal, 08/05/14). A teacher corroborated this point: "So, it really is very flexible and our administration gives us the flexibility of how we meet. There's just the expectation that you are meeting, you're talking about plans, you're talking about kids, but we do have the flexibility of what it is that we are meeting about" (Teacher 107, 10/15/14). The principal explained that, initially, teacher-collaboration time was "tighter" in structure, but they had made the move to less structured time because school administration wanted "collaboration time to be deeper, stronger, [and,] really, just take our collaboration, which is already amazing, to that next level" (Principal, 07/21/16).

The teachers jointly developed agendas for team meetings via email, and those included discussion topics such as the curriculum standards, report cards, or assessment. One teacher put together the agenda based on faculty input, and it was used as a guide for the meeting. A teacher explained:

> Every time we do sit down, we are always making sure that we're making progress in an area, so we, kind of, set a goal before we sit down, and then we make sure that we're hitting [it]. So, the [meetings] are always very productive.
>
> *(Teacher 110, 12/09/15)*

This time was viewed as extremely valuable. Another teacher explained, "We all crave that time to get together" (Teacher 108, 12/08/15).

The fact that the principal respected teachers as professionals contributed to a culture in which collaboration was not limited to the formal times when it was administratively organized. Rather, teachers also collaborated informally, and often. One teacher shared:

> A lot of it ends up being conversations on the fly, you know, in the hallway, in the lunchroom . . . particularly between partner teachers because we see each other so much that we kind of save what needs to happen just between our two classrooms for our own time. And we figure that out, so that it doesn't impact our scheduled time of being together with the four/five team.
>
> (Teacher 108, 05/23/16)

Teachers clearly valued each other's expertise. The high level of trust and respect allowed teachers to feel at ease in sharing challenges. One teacher elaborated:

> It's nice to have the stability and know each other's strengths. And to be able to, especially in all this change, be able to go and trust the people you work with, where you can say, "Look, I am messing up on this. I don't know. I need help in this area," or whatever, and to be comfortable to . . . do that. Because, [at] a lot of schools, you keep it within your four walls, you know, if you're struggling or something, and, here, that's not the case.
>
> (Teacher 112, 05/25/16).

Having an "open door" climate in which teachers felt comfortable accessing each other's expertise was critical. At times, data were connected to these help-seeking moments. A teacher explained, "I would go to [an intervention teacher] and I would say, 'Hey, I have Kelsey. Her fluency is 46 words per minute. I've tried everything; I don't know what else to do to help her. Do you have any suggestions?'" (Teacher 112, 11/03/14)

The teachers' valuing of each other's expertise was also evident in how they organized instruction at Chavez. Teachers rotated students for various subjects. Within and sometimes across grade-level teams, teachers departmentalized for math, science, and social studies. All teachers taught ELA, and students were grouped based on data, and, thus, were mixed across multiple classrooms. These groups were fluid and reevaluated throughout the year. This arrangement hinged on the fact that teachers were confident in each other's knowledge and skills. As one teacher explained:

> When I hand them off to [another teacher], I have to know that they're going to do the best that they can for that child, and vice versa. When they

give me their kids to teach math, or reading, or writing, or whatever it is, they have to trust that I'm going do the best I can for that child.

(Teacher 110, 05/16/16)

Not only did the teachers at Chavez feel comfortable sharing their students with each other, they also felt comfortable having their own children in each other's classes. All of the teachers we interviewed who had kids sent them to the school.

Strong informal and personal relationships supported the culture of collaboration. As one teacher said about their teammates:

We always go and eat lunch together. It's not like we're working through lunch. We make sure that we have that time to, to celebrate what's going on in our lives, and talk about your kids or . . . "what are you doing this weekend?" So, we're friends, I would say, as well, not just teammates.

(Teacher 110, 10/29/14)

However, the professional benefits of working together went well beyond positive interpersonal relations. This is relatively rare. As Little (1990) writes:

Case studies of "collaborative schools" often highlight the socio-emotional support that teachers offer one another, the generosity of spirit that prevails; they offer fewer examples of teachers who somehow balance personal support with hard-nosed deliberation about present practice and future direction.

(p. 520)

Vertical and Horizontal Collaboration Structures

Policies supporting teacher-collaboration time are one attempt to address the independence and, indeed, isolation that many teachers experience. Prior research reveals, however, that collaboration time alone is insufficient to produce the successful and meaningful joint work that reformers are aiming for (Little, 1990). Other structures must be in place to support joint productive work by teachers. Teacher-collaboration structures at Chavez supported teacher interdependence within and across grade levels. This was facilitated by the use of various horizontal and vertical collaboration structures. At times, they met as a full fourth/fifth-grade team. Other times, teachers met in subject areas. Sometimes they met in dyads or by grade level. The teachers felt that meeting in these different formations was critical to their work, but they acknowledged it was not always easy to do. As one teacher explained, "There's so many different configurations, and figuring out how to get to those configurations in a timely, efficient way is probably the biggest struggle" (Teacher 108, 12/8/15). Nonetheless, teachers felt it imperative to meet with each other frequently, both formally and informally.

Occasionally, the teachers engaged in vertical collaboration across a wider range of grade levels. A teacher explained how this worked, in relation to a district-wide math task:

> The first time we did it, we just, kind of, shared results informally. The second time we did it, we brought student work samples, and we got in vertical teams to, kind of, analyze what papers looked like at different grade levels, to, kind of, get that perspective, and really focusing on the positives of— What sort of math knowledge is the student demonstrating through their work?
> *(Teacher 111, 05/18/15)*

Teachers also worked with other grade levels to align expectations. A teacher explained:

> We decided, as a staff, at the end of the year that we need to bring back a time where fourth can meet with third grade, and talk about that transference . . . and, kind of, change those dynamics a little bit, just to make sure that . . . vertical alignment is still working.
> *(Teacher 111, 12/15/15)*

The cross-grade team structure allowed for the mentoring of newer teachers by teachers with more experience. The fourth- and fifth-grade teachers intentionally teamed together in order to foster mentoring and sharing of expertise, as the teams included both veteran and new teachers. Although the two newer teachers had an assigned district mentor for beginning teachers, one of them noted that they were much more likely to turn to their immediately available teammates for advice and problem-solving. She was struck by how different her experience was, in relation to teachers from other schools:

> It's amazing to get the perspective of some of my peers that are second-year teachers, and they're at more affluent schools. And I'm like, "Wait, what? You don't meet every day and talk about planning or talk about a kid or—.
> *(Teacher 110, 10/29/14)*

Reflecting on the relationships with senior teachers on the team, she perceived all of them as mentors and trusted colleagues. An experienced teacher who was new to the school shared the same sentiment. This teacher explained how the collaboration structures at Chavez allowed her to seek assistance and guidance from existing teachers, which, ultimately, helped her successfully acclimate to her new teaching assignment. She said:

> Compared to other schools I've worked at, this is the school to be, because the team collaborates for literally everything. So, when it comes to grouping

kids with reading groups, grouping kids for math, talking about how we can help not just our own kids but with each-others' kids, is a whole new world for me.... everybody's out to reach out and help each other.

(Teacher 124, 05/20/16)

Experienced teachers viewed mentoring more junior teachers within the team as an important part of their work:

We sit down and we spend a lot of time with new teachers and/or new team members, because, even as you [move from] grade to grade, . . . things change. And, so, we spend a lot of time helping new teachers figure out all that stuff.

(Teacher 112, 11/03/14)

Another teacher explained that the team shared resources, information on the state standards, and other helpful information to help get new teachers up to speed.

Bringing in a new member of the team was an occasion to articulate principles and practices, providing opportunity to make implicit practices and belief more explicit: "We've been on the same page for so long, so it's been nice to have those conversations" (Teacher 112, 05/26/16).

Collective Action in Instructional Planning, Informed by Data

Chavez's collaboration culture anticipated collective action by teachers through instructional planning as they examined and discussed student data. Little (1990) defines anticipated collective action as "teachers' decisions to pursue a single course of action in concert, or alternatively, to decide on a basic set of priorities that in turn guide the independent choices of individual teachers" (p. 519). Apart from the three-times-a-year comprehensive-data-analysis meetings, teachers at Chavez used other meeting times to examine data, to inform joint instructional planning. A teacher gave an example:

A few weeks ago, we met and looked at, how are we going to set up our [language-arts] goals. So, then, we brought in the data and looked at, how are we going to set up our goals within each classroom and design a paper for the students to have to set their goals. And, so, to make sure that each teacher was using the same form and it was consistent through[out] all the classes.

(Teacher 109, 11/03/14)

We saw this process in action, in a teacher team meeting. The field notes below capture how teachers used data to establish goals for student learning. This example also highlights the mentoring of newer teachers, which we discussed earlier.

> One teacher explains that one advantage of accessing the data through a website is that the student results are available immediately, whereas the district system doesn't load the data until several days later. She demonstrates how the teachers can create reports. For example, she says, "For reading, you can do it by strand, so, when we set goals and plan instruction, it's amazing." She clicks on "context clues" and shows the teachers how they can now see which students scored in each range, in this area. The teachers who are observing are impressed. "Cool!" says one teacher. Another teacher likens her enthusiasm to a ShamWow commercial.... The mood is collaborative and task oriented, but also light.
>
> The teacher demonstrates how she can set goals for the students: "I am setting goals, and that's what I am going to choose from." A newer teacher says, "I feel overwhelmed in what to choose from." The experienced teacher responds by saying, "As a teacher, it helps me see, I've hit this and this and this . . . but I have never taught this. . . . It takes something that feels overwhelming and breaks it down." A third teacher explains that students can help set their own goals: "You can give kids a few categories in kid language and ask them what they feel comfortable with and what they need help with." The new teacher grasps this quickly and says, "And that's something they can take back to [the online learning program]."
>
> *(Meeting field notes, 10/15/14)*

Teachers also relied on each other to manage district curriculum expectations, particularly when new expectations came along with the implementation of the Common Core Standards in math. They discussed adaptations that were needed, given that many of the students in their school were English learners and might need support in meeting the language demands of the new math problems. Teachers used the collaborative process to work through some other challenges. As one teacher explained:

> There was a lot of discussion. Every unit . . . what should be our emphasis, how are we going make the assessment worthwhile, so that it gives us information, gives the kids information, and assesses, actually, what and how we are teaching?
>
> *(Teacher 108, 05/13/15)*

Deliberation of Varied Beliefs and Practices, and the Use of Data

Little (1990) notes that an interdependent team does not require consensus on all matters. Rather, as part of the "de-privatization" of practice, competing views are made more public. She explains that, "Moderate levels of social conflict have been found to be essential to the development of integrative agreements" (p. 522). As we learned in our study of Chavez, data can play an interesting role in this process. When collaborative structures first began to develop at the school years ago, conflicting beliefs and practices were reportedly more prevalent. A teacher reflected on a team she had been part of years ago, before the strong norms of collaboration had developed at the school. She explained that teachers on this team had different approaches to teaching, but used the data as an impetus to come together. She explained:

> We had very different philosophies for teaching, and I like the people very much, they were very nice, but they were very worksheet oriented. They were very much, this is the test, this is the test, this is the test, this is what we're working toward, and it was very different. Their structure of management was very different from mine, but I knew the need to collaborate, so we did a baby step.
>
> *(Teacher 111, 11/06/14)*

The team examined benchmark-assessment results in reading and noted common language-arts skills across the grade level that numerous students in each class needed to work on, such as author's purpose, fact versus opinion, and cause and effect. The teachers planned lessons to address these areas and students rotated into classrooms, based on need, one hour per week. The teacher explained:

> That was our baby step, and it still gave us that common ground to discuss. And then, the rest of the week, everyone did what they were comfortable with. I think that was such an effective way to try and to look at your needs, as a whole, on the grade level.
>
> *(Teacher 111, 11/06/14)*

She added: "It gave us that area that we could have the conversations about, and do some planning, and, kind of, add in those elements of collaboration. So, that's something that helped" (Teacher 111, 11/06/14).

Years later, we witnessed a great deal of consensus among the teachers, and instructional planning across the grade level and rotating students were commonplace. Yet, although teachers at Chavez worked harmoniously, they were comfortable disagreeing with one another when needed. A teacher explained that they disagreed "respectfully" and that "it makes us all better teachers because we disagree, and we're comfortable disagreeing with each other" (Teacher 112, 05/25/15). Occasionally, teachers presented conflicting points of view about a student and, eventually, came to agreement about how best to characterize the student's achievement, as well as how to support them.

We also observed the team puzzle over the calibrated scoring of students' writing assessments, initially beginning with different ideas, and then reaching consensus. One teacher described the process:

> As a fourth/fifth-grade team, we'll meet and go over [the students' writing], pull a couple samples from our class, go over it together to look at the papers that we think are meeting those expectations, based on—for their grade level, based on the rubric.
>
> *(Teacher 111, 11/06/14)*

The following vignette from our field notes reveals how this process allowed teachers to work through various challenges and calibrate scoring of students' work:

> The team started their discussion by unpacking what is meant by "achieving standard," which is the score of three on the district rubric. They reviewed the standard to briefly discuss how they taught the concepts in their classes. The discussion moved to looking at the student exemplars—showing each other their students' writing: "Is this a two? Is this a three?" . . . They examined the language-arts standards, and decided how to prioritize, since there were so many of them. They decided on "errors do not interfere," because they thought that "demonstrates command of conventions" was "too vague."
>
> One teacher asked, "What about quoting from the text?" Another teacher said, "My kids are going to paraphrase, rather than direct quote." A third teacher replied, "Let's read and, when we get to those situations, we'll figure it out together." (Here we see an example of joint problem-solving). One teacher shared an essay. The team read the first paragraph. A teacher said, "That's a three." Another teacher added, "It's a strong three." A third teacher said, "It meets the needs, but it's not 'WOW!'" They read further into the paper and agreed that it was mainly providing facts, rather than providing an explanation.
>
> After reading the essay, they returned to the rubric and looked carefully at it to decide if the essay was a "two" or a "three." One teacher argued that it was a "two," but another teacher challenged this conclusion by asking, "But where is that on the rubric?" referring to the fact that the student does not explain the evidence chosen to support the main argument. After some deliberation, the team reached consensus on how to score the paper.
>
> *(Meeting notes, 03/03/15)*

These conversations, which sometimes included initial disagreements and questioning, provided this teacher team opportunities to collaboratively work through their own understandings of student work and data. This was one of several hallmarks of their productive collaborative activity.

Conclusion

Using data can be a powerful tool for school improvement, but a great deal depends on the substance of teacher collaboration and the team culture. Understanding data use for instructional decision-making requires close investigation into how teachers collaborate around data use, so that we can find out why it fosters positive outcomes in some places and not in others (Coburn & Turner, 2012). This study helps to fill this gap in the literature by "zooming in" on teachers' day-to-day collaborative activities around data (Little, 2012). We found that, in teachers' interdependent work, data was a tool for working through instructional challenges, developing common ground for instructional improvement, cultivating shared responsibility for students, and collectively supporting their needs. The ways in which teachers at Chavez collaborated—in general, and around data use, in particular—made their teaching more public, provided occasions for deliberation informed by evidence on student learning, and allowed them to draw on their professional judgment.

Implications

These findings have important implications for policy and practice. Transplanting the Chavez promising practices (e.g., comprehensive data-analysis meetings three times a year, horizontal and vertical structures for collaboration) may be useful, but these practices are not likely to be as productive in other sites, unless the principles and norms that undergird these practices are cultivated as well. Collectively examining data on each student would be far less effective if teachers did not have a sense that their job was to ensure the best education for all children, not just those in their classroom. This process also relies on valuing multiple forms of data as well as teacher judgment, rather than narrowly focusing data use around a single measure of student achievement.

The high level of teacher engagement that we saw at Chavez requires norms of professionalism and mutual respect, which often start with the principal modeling these behaviors. Principals need to strike a balance between providing scaffolds of support for teacher collaboration, but not being overly prescriptive in how teachers spend time together. Creating such a culture among teachers takes time and may involve small forays into joint lesson planning with data and creating opportunities in which it is safe for teachers to take risks, particularly if those risks are informed by evidence on student learning. Teachers must be encouraged to experiment with new methods of teaching and organizing instruction, and the examination of data can be a vehicle by which teachers notice patterns that suggest the need to do things differently.

Finally, this study reveals how closely documenting teachers' collaborative work with data can yield critical insights for practice and further investigation. There is a need for further research that takes a longitudinal approach to capture changes over time and documents the development of collaborative team relationships, whereby teachers shift from private, to public and shared practices. It is critical that such studies involve both observations and interviews, so that data can be triangulated across sources. The researcher's role is to use various data sources make visible the nuanced features of teacher collaboration around data use that cannot be captured with one method of data gathering. Ideally, this work also follows teachers into the classroom, so that connections can be made between teachers' instructional planning and data-informed instruction in practice.

Notes

1 Little (1990), p. 523.
2 We gratefully acknowledge the Spencer Foundation for funding this research.

References

Blanc, S., Christman, J. B., Liu, R., Mitchell, C., Travers, E., & Bulkley, K. E. (2010). Learning to learn from data: Benchmarks and instructional communities. *Peabody Journal of Education, 85*(2), 205–225.

Christman, J. B., Neild, R. C., Bulkley, K., Blanc, S., Liu, R., Mitchell, C., & Travers, E. (2009). *Making the most of interim assessment data: Lessons from Philadelphia.* Retrieved from www.researchforaction.org/wp-content/uploads/publication-photos/41/Christman_J_Making_the_Most_of_Interim_Assessment_Data.pdf

Coburn, C. E., & Turner, E. O. (2012). The practice of data use: An introduction. *American Journal of Education, 118*(2), 99–111.

Cosner, S. (2011). Teacher learning, instructional considerations and principal communication: Lessons from a longitudinal study of collaborative data use by teachers. *Educational Management Administration & Leadership, 39*(5), 568–589.

Daly, A. J. (2012). Data, dyads, and dynamics: Exploring data use and social networks in educational improvement. *Teachers College Record, 114*(11), 110305.

Datnow, A., & Park, V. (2014). *Data driven leadership.* San Francisco, CA: Jossey Bass.

Datnow, A., Park, V., & Kennedy-Lewis, B. (2013). Affordances and constraints in the context of teacher collaboration for the purpose of data use. *Journal of Educational Administration, 51*(3), 341–362.

Farley-Ripple, E., & Buttram, J. (2015). The development of capacity for data use: The role of teacher networks in an elementary school. *Teachers College Record, 117*(4), 1–34.

Fullan, M. (2012). *Change forces: Probing the depths of educational reform.* New York, NY: Routledge.

Hargreaves, A. (1994). *Changing teachers, changing times: Teachers' work and culture in the postmodern age.* London UK: Cassell.

Honig, M. I., & Venkateswaran, N. (2012). School—central office relationships in evidence use: Understanding evidence use as a systems problem. *American Journal of Education, 118*(2), 199–222.

Horn, I. S., Kane, B. D., & Wilson, J. (2015). Making sense of student performance data: Data use logics and mathematics teachers' learning opportunities. *American Educational Research Journal, 52*(2), 208–242.

Horn, I. S., & Little, J. W. (2010). Attending to problems of practice: Routines and resources for professional learning in teachers' workplace interactions. *American Educational Research Journal, 47*(1), 181–217.

Jimerson, J. B., & Wayman, J. C. (2015). Professional learning for using data: Examining teacher needs and supports. *Teachers College Record, 117*(4), 1–36.

Little, J. W. (1990). The persistence of privacy: Autonomy and initiative in teachers' professional relations. *Teachers College Record, 91*(4), 509–536.

Little, J. W. (2012). Understanding data use practices among teachers: The contribution of micro-process studies. *American Journal of Education, 118*(2).

Marsh, J. A. (2012). Interventions promoting educators' use of data: Research insights and gaps. *Teachers College Record, 114*(11), 1–48.

Means, B., Padilla, C., & Gallagher, L. (2010). *Use of education data at the local level: From accountability to instructional improvement.* Washington, DC: U.S. Department of Education, Office of Planning, Evaluation, and Policy Development.

Stoll, L. (1998). School culture. *School Improvement Network's Bulletin, 9,* 9–14.

Timperley, H. (2009). Evidence-informed conversations making a difference to student achievement. In L. Earl & H. Timperley (Eds.), *Professional learning conversations: Challenges in using evidence for improvement* (pp. 69–79). New York, NY: Springer.

White, P. A. U. L., & Anderson, J. U. D. Y. (2011). Teachers' use of national test data to focus numeracy instruction. *Mathematics: Traditions and [New] Practices,* 777–785.

Yin, R. (2013). *Case study research* (5th ed.). Beverly Hills, CA: Sage.

Young, V. M. (2006). Teachers' use of data: Loose coupling, agenda setting, and team Norms. *American Journal of Education, 112*(4), 521–548.

11

ADJUSTMENT IN PRACTICE

A Critical Response to Data-Driven Instruction

Nora M. Isacoff, Dana Karin, and Joseph P. McDonald

Background

Over the last 15 years, spurred by policy leaders, school-reform organizations, and state and federal laws, U.S. school districts have invested substantial financial and human capital in the pursuit of what is often called *data-driven instruction* (Bambrick-Santoyo, 2010; Boudett, City, & Murnane, 2014; Duncan, 2009; Supovitz & Klein, 2003). Data-driven instruction, as a theory of action, makes several assumptions:

1) Information about student learning that teachers garner from standardized testing (whether actual state tests or ones meant to mimic them) is the most valuable form of data, and is sufficient to guide ambitious teaching to improve learning for all children, especially those impacted by poverty.
2) Teachers are passive and willing subjects of the mandates around data use that come from the state, school administrators, and others, and they can easily infer curricula from standardized-test reports.
3) Teachers will effectively apply the influential pedagogical strategy of *backward planning*—devising curricula around learning objectives. Additionally, planning backward from *future* big data is equivalent to planning backward from rich images of learning.

Crucially, this innovation around data-driven instruction complicates the kind of data-informed instruction that has long been common in teaching: using tests, quizzes, journal writing, and reading-miscue notation, for example, as well as teacher intuition, to inform instructional choices. It may also introduce other kinds of assessment implicitly considered to be more valid—for example, interim standardized testing, test-preparation curricula, and individualized online-testing programs, all of which are meant to mimic state standardized testing—and new kinds of data-analysis tools and procedures available from an expanding educational marketplace.

In educational policy today, and in schools themselves, the call to tie these new sources of data and new analytical tools and procedures to teaching is pervasive. Studies of effective implementation are still rare, however. Our objective in this study was to understand the intersection of data-driven instruction, as an espoused innovation, with the day-to-day practices of schooling and teaching. To do so, we followed attempts to implement it in nine schools.

We knew that the path of implementation for complex innovations almost always involves adaptation—that an espoused theory of action is bound to morph when put into practice (Argyris & Schon, 1996). And, indeed, this is what we observed in our study. We call the phenomenon *adjustment in practice*, and, in this case, it challenges key assumptions embedded in the theory of action. Some innovators seek what they call *fidelity in implementation* (see Meyers & Brandt, 2015). They regard any transformation as a sign of degradation. We argue here, however, that adjustment in practice is desirable, so long as it is well-managed. That is, the innovation called data-driven instruction actually works best as a road map, rather than a driver—a tool to be used consultatively by teachers and support staff in negotiating the unique circumstances and needs of their school and classrooms. At the same time, adjustment in practice can expose flaws in an espoused theory of action, and practitioners can invent corrections on the spot for these flaws.

Teachers' and administrators' understanding of adjustment in practice, or their lack of understanding, can have far-reaching pedagogical consequences. In particular, we observed that rigid conceptions of the innovation we followed proved detrimental to genuine implementation, overlooked opportunities for greater professional learning, and exacerbated flaws in the theory of action. This was true whether the rigid conception resulted in a blind-faith following or in cool dismissal. Conversely, those who viewed the innovation as malleable were able to supply a fresh intentionality for the innovation that induced ownership among teachers and corrected for the theory's inherent flaws. This chapter explores data-driven instruction within the framework of adjustment in practice.

Methodology

Our qualitative research was designed as a collective case study to investigate what "data-driven instruction" means to teachers and administrators, and how these notions are constructed within several school cultures (Stake, 1995). In the broader company of colleagues from other parts of the U.S., with whom we met and shared findings over the last several years, and with the generous support of the Spencer Foundation and the assistance of the Research Alliance for New

York City Schools, we intimately explored this question, in the context of New York City.

Our team spent two years immersed in a total of nine New York City schools (five elementary and four middle). Schools were chosen on the basis of two factors. First, all schools were highly impacted by poverty. This choice was prompted by the fact that the policy push for data-driven instruction (most notably in the era of No Child Left Behind) has especially emphasized the use of data in teaching, as a tool for addressing the impact of poverty on student learning and achievement. Thus, our study presented an opportunity to investigate the efficacy of this tool. Second, since we hoped to illuminate a range of data use practices, including promising ones, we selected poverty-impacted schools with reputations within their networks for effective data use in teaching.

In each school, throughout the two years, we observed literacy lessons in one focal classroom (fourth or seventy grade), spending 30–90 minutes in each classroom, during each visit. We also conducted semi-structured interviews with teachers, principals, assistant principals, data specialists, and support staff, and attended meetings and professional-development sessions. Through these immersive methods, we studied not only teaching and learning practices but also the organizational structures supporting them (see Spillane, Parise, & Sherer, 2011). By engaging with multiple facets of school culture, we gained deep insights into the ways individuals' pedagogical beliefs interact with policy and organizational culture at national, state, local, school, and classroom levels. Our interviews and observations from all nine schools formed the basis of the analysis for this chapter.

We amassed a total of 90 observational and interview transcripts, with a median of 23,148 words across all transcripts. We used median, rather than mean, so that outliers would not skew our results. Each of these transcripts was blind coded by two or more members of our research team (the coauthors, plus one additional

TABLE 11.1 School Demographic Data (2013–2014)

School Code Name	Elementary or Middle School	Total Enrollment	% ELL	% SPED	% Asian	% Black	% Hispanic	% Free Lunch
ES. A	ES	251	13	22	3	54	39	82
ES. B	ES	379	32	16	1	8	89	92
ES. C	ES	999	15	13	88	1	5	66
ES. D	ES	355	6	23	0	24	75	83
ES. E	ES	792	32	14	93	1	3	88
MS. A	MS	324	11	25	3	29	65	87
MS. B	MS	487	42	24	6	2	87	89
MS. C	MS	450	35	24	2	11	85	78
MS. D	MS	100	24	28	4	17	75	89

researcher). At least two members of the team read each transcript and independently coded it for themes. We created the codes *a priori* (based on our review of the literature) and *post hoc* during the coding and analysis stages. Results were then analyzed in 302 research memos and eight successive analytic overviews of themes and other findings. The analysis was guided by several theoretical perspectives: extant and emerging research on data use in teaching, for example, on organizational routines in schooling, as these may affect data use (Spillane, 2012); research on deep dimensions of teaching (Cohen, 2011); theories of action in educational change (Argyris & Schön, 1996; McDonald, 2014); methodological guidelines for qualitative data analysis, for example, Reissman's (2008) guidelines for thematic and structural analysis that advise "keeping the story intact," and Lawrence-Lightfoot and Davis' (1997) guidelines for constructing accessible portraits of practice; and methods for studying practitioners, with attention to and respect for the complexity of their work (Argyris & Schön, 1996). We call this a collective case study because we conducted a systematic investigation into a particular phenomenon (data-driven instruction), with our unit of analysis being cases of adjustment in practice, rather than individual classrooms or schools.

Adjustment in Practice: Illustrations

In our introduction, we established the notion of adjustment in practice, with regard to implementation of the espoused theory of action for data-driven instruction in schools. We found adjustment in practice not only between external policy makers and schools but also within schools themselves—for example, among principals, assistant principals, data coaches, and teachers. This cascading transformation can play out like a game of telephone: a strategy emerges from some constellation of popular ideas, and an espoused theory of teaching and learning is articulated at various levels of policy making—in this case, federal, state, *and* district levels—with successive adaptations by policy makers at each level. The policy-embedded theory of action is then interpreted and implemented by school administrators; this implementation is further adjusted by data coaches, who work closely with teachers; and, finally, the teachers adjust it still further in putting it into practice. Argyris and Schön (1996) posit that this transformation is natural, as organizations move from espoused theories of action to theories in use.

In the following table, we illustrate this phenomenon by demonstrating one instance of transformation that occurred, as a principal, an assistant principal, and a teacher in the same school differently interpreted the theory of action for data-driven instruction. The quotes in the table reveal how the espoused theory of action, with regard to data use, is diffused and distorted as it moves down the line from principal to teacher.

In this particular example, we see how the principal's espoused theory of action, in response to policy mandates for data use in teaching, was attenuated as it moved across personnel in the school. What began as an intact, detailed,

TABLE 11.2 An Illustration of Adjustment in Practice Within a School

Principal	Assistant Principal	Teacher
Every teacher gives a diagnostic.... The teachers take that information and enter it into a tracking system that we've devised.... Then, it's rated on a system of 1–4. Then, the teacher can see, where is the weakest overall area in the class.... The teachers fill this out.... This is something that guides them.... The state came out with these shifts ... in the curriculum. Teachers take the ... Common Core Learning Standards.... They also take trends that we've seen in our school.... You look at what the standards are.... You look at how the child did on the state exam.... You look at how the child did on your diagnostic, which is much more valid, because we know that this diagnostic covers what has to be taught during that exam. Then, you look at reality—what is the kid able to do and not able to do—and, then, you make your decisions about what you're going to teach (MS. C, 08/10/15).	The teachers meet and they look at the data.... Then, they think about their curriculum and if any modifications need to be made, on that, kind of, global level, adding things in, or maybe they have kids who're advanced, so they want to adjust it that way.... Then, each department meets: the whole literacy team, every grade, etc. Then, each grade-team department meets.... They might give the teachers some sort of graphic organizer ... and lead them through some data-analysis protocol ... just some guiding questions to help prompt them, through looking at the enormous amount of data.... They're going to look at their curriculum, [and] make any adjustments.... They're also looking at students who need more intensive support, and then creating lab groups (MS. C, 11/17/14).	We come together, as a department, after we've done the diagnostic, and talk about, like, "What are the trends that you see in your classes? What are some strengths throughout? What are some weaknesses throughout?" It's never discussed after that. I think the point is to keep it in the back of our minds as we're designing our lesson plans and having instruction (MS. C, 11/03/14).

theory-driven approach, through adjustment in practice, ended as an unintentional and ill-defined residue of the original.

This, however, is not always the pattern of adjustment in practice. For example, in other selections from our data set, the whole school managed to engage in adjustment in practice. This pattern is illustrated in the next table, where both the principal and the teacher critiqued implicit assumptions in the espoused theory, as they received it from the state and district.

Data use in teaching is much more complicated than policy makers presume, these practitioners say, with the principal emphasizing the limitations of standardized-testing data and instructional systems that mimic it, and the teacher emphasizing superficial applications of the district's school-inspection regime. Both complaints contributed to some significant adjustments of practice in this school—ones that made the *implemented* innovation there more beneficial for students (McDonald, Isacoff, & Karin, in press). In the majority of the schools in which we immersed ourselves, however, adjustment in practice was not particularly well managed, leading to negative consequences. In the following section, we explore highlights of this poor management, then turn to one model of good management.

TABLE 11.3 An Illustration of Adjustment in Practice, as a Critique of an Espoused Theory of Action

Principal	*Teacher*
You're inundated with so much data—which way do you turn? You have data from online programs, you have data from testing. But does the testing actually, truly identify anything other than: they got the question wrong? . . . You need a lot more in-depth knowledge and analyzing, to be able to get a true picture. I mean, the item analysis from the testing is only good at the beginning of the year, to set things up. . . . We did the citywide assessments for baseline, and the kids did horribly. It didn't tell us much (MS. B, 11/24/14).	How do they want to see all this data presented? And that's the question that I feel gets asked over and over again, but nobody has an answer, and that's a problem. I think a lot of my colleagues and I are in the same boat, when it comes to that. . . . Like, we had a state review come in a few weeks ago, and they said they didn't see x, y, and z. But I had it, and nobody asked for it. So, I don't know what systems are in place that, if your teachers do have it, why is it not being presented? . . . They [the administration] want us to . . . figure out how those kids can track their progress. But, then, it's like, what's the next step after that? I think, isn't that enough? It's, like, constantly wanting more and more. When does it stop? Like, when is this ok, that they're doing this? Why does there have to be a step beyond that? . . . I don't know what steps go beyond that, but I'm being told that you still need to go beyond that. I'm getting very frustrated (MS. B, 12/16/14).

Managing Adjustment Poorly and Well

Exacerbating Adjustment

As we outlined in the introduction to this chapter, several assumptions are typically embedded in the policy making around data-driven teaching. In this section, we focus on one of these assumptions: that backward planning is an essential element of effective teaching and is relatively easy for individual teachers to achieve. Our purpose here is to use this specific assumption to demonstrate more generally how the flaws inherent in a theory of action can be exacerbated in practice. We chose this example because backward planning was referred to by teachers, administrators, and support staff across the schools we studied, either with references to specific instantiations of it (e.g., *Understanding by Design*, by Wiggins & McTighe, 1998) or more generally, and often in ways that illustrated exacerbating adjustment in practice.

We concur with many of the teachers and administrators we spoke to that backward planning—beginning with a learning goal in mind (as captured, for example, in a state learning standard) and then planning steps toward it—is a desirable condition for cultivating data use in teaching, although doing so demands deep content knowledge and is best conducted within a supportive community of teachers (Wiggins & McTighe, 1998). But crucial to backward planning is that teachers begin with an objective, then move to an assessment of that objective, and, finally, move to specific instruction. Truncating backward planning—suggesting, as some champions of data use in teaching do, that the learning goal one plans toward can be good results on a standardized test, rather than the standard itself—fundamentally undermines its impact. For example, one such champion, a principal we interviewed, told us, "Assessments are the primary driving force for how you instruct" (ES. A[1], 03/02/15).

This truncated version of backward planning is problematic because no assessment has perfect validity; that is, no assessment perfectly measures satisfaction of an instructional goal (Ravitch, 2010). Therefore, by aiming for success on assessments, rather than mastery of educational goals, teachers are following a skewed instructional road map. Viewed within this framework, we argue that "teaching to the test" is ultimately the result of exacerbating adjustment in practice.

Indeed, in many of our interviews, teachers and principals cited test content, rather than learning objectives, as the motivation for their instructional choices. For example, one teacher explained, "I don't tell [the students] it's for the exam, but I have to use these [academic] words, like 'integrity'" (ES. B, 09/25/15). Crucially, the teacher did not say that academic vocabulary would elevate students' ability to engage with difficult texts, or scaffold their learning in a variety of academic disciplines, or prepare them for successful careers, all of which are valid learning objectives, from the perspective of teaching for genuine learning. Similarly, when a teacher was asked whether she finds support from her school's data team helpful, she responded, "They can be very useful... especially when it comes to test prep and things like that. [They tell us], 'This is how you build in that type of question to your everyday instruction, so that they're ready. Here's the language'" (ES. C, 01/20/15). She did not say that the data team is helpful in meeting instructional goals, but, rather, that they provide information about introducing students to assessment-specific language. Still another teacher explained that she has students practice reading in different fonts, in preparation for doing so on the state test, even though she does not think this is the best use of instructional time. In our observations of several classrooms, we heard teachers caution their students about the importance of working quickly and monitoring their time, explaining the importance of time management on exams. We did not observe these same teachers telling their students that working quickly is important for non-exam-related reasons.

Focusing on assessment is problematic because it can lead to ignoring educational goals. One teacher lamented, "I have a student who is so bright, but he can't read. So, I would hate to see him do poorly on a writing assignment just because he can't read" (ES. B, 09/28/15). The teacher elaborated that she was investigating ways for the student to perform well, despite not being able to read. The teacher's instructional motivation appeared to be the student's performance on the assignment, not helping the student meet an educational goal. Another teacher said that there is a "disincentive" to choosing a "rigorous" curriculum because students will likely perform poorly on a difficult curriculum's benchmark assessments, which will negatively impact Measures of Student Learning scores, on which schools themselves are evaluated by the New York City Department of Education. The teacher also said that schools must choose between academically "rigorous" curricula and "less rigorous" curricula that use the language of standardized exams (ES. C, 11/14/14).

One principal was replacing her school's current baseline-mathematics assessment because it was "merely computational," which, she believed, is a poor indicator of success on the state "reading math" assessment. She explained: "When I give you a word problem about fractions, it's not the same thing as me telling you to add two fractions." The principal did not offer an opinion about whether students should be able to both answer word problems about fractions and add fractions. Instead, she offered, "Creating an assessment that's aligned to what the state test looks like ... makes all the sense in the world" (ES. B, 11/06/14). Similarly, one teacher explained that she prefers multiple-choice to written exams because the former are less affected by students' moods and "how their day is going" (MS. A, 12/15/14). The teacher did not say whether writing skills are important beyond the skills demonstrated on a multiple-choice exam.

In another school, a teacher and principal explained that they were using data from their Quality Review to improve instruction. They elaborated that they were increasing the number of school-wide assessments because they received a "proficient" score, and they wanted to be rated as "well developed." Neither individual said that collecting this extra data would benefit teachers in improving instruction (ES. E, 10/06/15).

And even more generous learning targets may end up cheating students of the academic press that backward planning, at its best, can achieve. For example, one consultant hired to assist with lesson planning at one school told us, "Teachers used to plan on the fly, so the goal is to have them plan in advance and look at what they are trying to achieve with each unit" (ES. B, 09/28/15). We argue that that is, actually, an unhelpful adjustment. The goal should be more specific and more learning centered than this. In our study, we coded for what we called LCDU (learner-centered data use). We used the code only nine times, and for only two teachers. One of these teachers seemed to strive for LCDU. For example, she told us, at one point:

> The data I create is cocreated by the students. They are responsible for keeping track of certain data . . . and [for] being able to talk about their learning and their growth, and [for] being able to set goals for themselves.
> (MS. D, 12/07/15)

The other teacher became our model for what we thought of as the antithesis of LCDU, namely the planting of right answers. Here is a short example:

> Teacher asks students what they need to look for when they are reading. He says, it begins with an "E." Several students wave their hands in the air. One of these is called on, and says, "Evidence."
> (ES. B, 09/25/15)

Cajoling students to recite a predetermined answer on cue minimizes opportunities for critical thinking or authentic learning.

Corrective Adjustment

All of this, we would argue, is adjustment in practice, although in the wrong direction. Yet, we also found the contrary: adjustment in the right direction, that is, in a direction likely to enhance deep and content-rich learning. At one school, we found deliberate tailoring of policy-compliance efforts to foster opportunities for reflective practice and for the invention of local innovations to meet specific student needs. For example, the district requires an annual School Comprehensive Educational Plan (SCEP) with data-based yearlong goals. One of the school's teachers recalled for us the process of his school's SCEP development. He explained, "Last year, we did our SCEP. We had to justify our decisions using data. We looked at all our students' [English Language Arts] scores. We identified four reading standards. Too big!" Just as in the previous-year's experience of SCEP, he told us this SCEP might have inundated the faculty with data. Instead, he told us,

"This year we're smarter. We just pulled it back, and we're just doing one reading standard" (MS. D, 12/7/15). This was enough, he implied, to ensure useful adjustments in practice. With respect to the unavoidable incursion on practice of the "material world"—our term for the ever-encroaching educational marketplace on many schools—the school also introduced efforts to regulate the incursion internally. The teacher told us that he saw a data use "protocol" or routine for engaging stakeholders in the exploration of a data set, and, as he put it, he just tweaked it for his school's use. Rather than perceiving the protocol as doctrine, the teacher took it as a guideline, a recommendation for practice that, with some modification, could help facilitate his school's student learning.

Discussion: Conclusions, Implications, and Promising Practices

Conclusions

Adjustment in practice is necessary to thoughtful translation between policy and practice. The idea that it is, on its face, evidence of weakness in either policy or practice needs to be reconceptualized. What is wanted is an iterative process through which policy and practice continuously inform and improve each other.

Schön (1983) has argued that policy making and implementation often suffer from a hierarchical separation of research and practice. This approach is hierarchical, both in terms of order—with research driving policy and policy driving practice—and, also, in terms of prestige, with "experts" superseding practitioners. It is problematic because the path from teaching policy to teaching practice requires a mapping of general pedagogical principles onto specific problems, despite the fact that a defined one-to-one mapping will never exist. Therefore, it is the job of the teacher to artfully frame a practical problem in terms of a given set of theories. By doing so, for better or worse, adjustment in practice ensues. In order for adjustment in practice to be corrective, practitioners need training in mapping theory to practice in a positive way, and they need the freedom to carry this out. They also need a clear understanding of the derived ends of a theory, rather than about the theoretical process itself. In close keeping with Schön's insights, one teacher described a distinct lack of hierarchy in his school:

> Our school is . . . really lateral, in terms of authority and in terms of our ability to make decisions. Since it's so devolved and it's so not centralized, we're not really told what to do. We're given the opportunity to create our own systems . . . [which] eventually cross-pollinate.
>
> (MS. D, 12/07/15)

This devolution of a strict hierarchy leads to teachers feeling empowered, which, in turn, allows them to alter policies in ways that promote, rather than constrain, learning, as seen in the examples of corrective adjustment in practice outlined previously.

This nonhierarchical structure seems possible in light of two other related, supportive structures we observed at this school: 1) a culture of professional learning, and 2) sites for information dissemination. The same teacher told us, "I think that there's still a core-level belief that we read and we learn.... As teachers, we're open to things, we try things, we want to get better" (MS. D, 09/12/14). For example, an English teacher told us he was reading a book about the neuroscience of storytelling. According to the teacher, one result of this culture of learning, including out-of-the-box learning, is that, "Everyone's been really innovative" (MS. D, 09/12/14). Professional learning both encourages and is encouraged by another organizational system—ample opportunities for information dissemination. At this school, teachers meet regularly with their departmental teams, benefit from regular informal visits and debriefings from the principal, and have *intervisitation partnerships*, involving weekly visits by other teachers, who get to know the class intimately, and can provide feedback and share innovations. Crucially, teachers and administrators who recognize the inevitability of adjustment in practice can foster organizational systems, such as nonhierarchical relationships, professional learning, and information dissemination, to reconnect policy with practice and develop corrective, rather than exacerbating, instances of pedagogical change.

In many cases, a hindrance to corrective adjustment in practice seems to be teachers' and principals' anxiety associated with the culture of accountability. A principal shared:

> Sometimes, data's being used to judge teachers or schools. What gets done with [data] publically is the piece that would concern me. It's being used to grade schools. They were giving a report card to the school. It's also being used, in some cases, to give grant money to schools, extra grant money to administrators, and, in some cases, it's also being used to close schools down.
> (ES. B, 11/06/14)

This principal also called it "unfair" that English-Language Learners are required to take the state exam after being in the United States for only a year. This policy is "unfair," not for instructional reasons, but because the performance of ELLs "still affects our school's scores" (ES. B, 11/06/14). Yet another principal explained that she "violates" the Department of Education's social-studies curriculum in order to prepare students better for standardized assessments, because these determine her "rating" (MS. C, 10/09/14).

A starting point for addressing exacerbating adjustment around backward planning is to separate the objective from the assessment, and separately evaluate how to improve each of these components. To begin, policy makers need to determine which set of skills and knowledge all children should develop and which can be left to the discretion of principals and teachers. For example, most educators and education-policy makers agree that all children should have the opportunity to learn to read. It is probably less important that all children read *Charlotte's Web*, however. Clarification on the part of policy makers, in terms of the scope and specificity of a particular policy, is one way to empower practitioners to avoid exacerbating adjustment in practice.

Second, assessments (whether designed by external vendors or by teachers themselves) need to be developed with subsequent action in mind. That is, it needs to be clear whether the purpose of an assessment is to inform a teacher's instructional methods, to encourage teaching accountability, or something else. Depending on the purpose, there needs to be a clear path from the test results to an action: how a teacher's instruction will change, or the consequences of test results for a teacher's job security.

Our research data suggest that adjustment in practice is an inevitable byproduct of educational-policy implementation. Recognizing this inevitability and taking comfort in examples of corrective adjustment in practice can encourage policy makers, administrators, and teachers to find flexibility in policies and in the strictest readings of their espoused theories of action. Doing so can empower teachers and school leaders to implement policies' true intentions more faithfully, but also in ways compatible with the realities of teaching practice.

Implications

The most important implications of our findings concern the probability of adjustment in practice, with respect to implementing the complex innovation we call "data use in teaching" and the need to manage it, rather than fight it or ignore it. We propose several methods for managing this innovation. The first is to make its steps explicit to the champions and users of the innovation. These steps include, first, defining the theory of action and its expected path, then, noticing some practical designs that emerge and alter this path, and, finally, observing how actual use of the theory further alters the path.

A second management method is engaging in reframing of the innovation at predictable joints in its evolution—for example, as a law becomes a policy, then a district practice, then a school-wide practice, then an actual factor in teaching and learning. In this sense, reframing means anticipating the challenges of new contexts and the demands these challenges will make on the innovation. A final management method is tracking the adjustments in practice over time and across contexts, and determining for each whether it is beneficial or detrimental, and whether it should be embraced or abandoned (Argyris & Schön, 1996; Schön & McDonald, 1998; McDonald, 2014).

Promising Practices

Finally, we found several promising practices in our study of nine schools working hard to implement an innovation that many hope will make a beneficial difference in the education of all students, including those impacted by poverty. Here is our short list:

- Building a school-wide community of practice, capable of managing the innovation and the adjustments in practice that it demands (Little, 2006; Panero & Talbert, 2013)
- Ensuring that everybody in the school who works with data is knowledgeable about the strengths and limitations of standardized assessment (Boudette et al., 2014)
- Developing well-facilitated internal teams and organizational routines to manage data and its use in teaching (Spillane, 2012)
- Taking the innovation deeper than teaching, by ensuring that students become data users, too (Berger, Rugen, & Woodfin, 2014; McDonald, Isacoff, & Karin, in press)

Acknowledgements

We thank the Research Alliance for New York City Schools (RANYCS) for its encouragement and support in pursuing the research we report here, in particular Executive Director, James Kemple. We also thank Susan Neuman, who helped enormously in fashioning the research design, data collection, and analyses. Thank you also to the Spencer Foundation for its support, and to our Spencer Foundation colleagues for helping us shape this project. Finally, we thank the schools and teachers who invited us into their classrooms and collaborated with us throughout this endeavor.

Note

1 All names of people and places are pseudonyms.

References

Argyris, C., & Schön, D. A. (1996). *Organizational learning II: Theory, method, and practice*. Reading, MA: Addison-Wesley.

Bambrick-Santoyo, P. (2010). *Driven by data: A practical guide to improve instruction*. San Francisco, CA: Jossey-Bass.

Berger, R., Rugen, L., & Woodfin, L. (2014). *Leaders of their own learning: Transforming schools through student-engaged assessment*. San Francisco, CA: John Wiley & Sons, Inc.

Boudett, K. P., City, E. A., & Murnane, R. J. (Eds.) (2014). *Data wise: A step-by-step guide to using assessment results to improve teaching and learning*. Cambridge, MA: Harvard Education Press.

Cohen, D. K. (2011). *Teaching and its predicaments*. Cambridge, MA: Harvard University Press.

Duncan, A. (2009). *Robust data gives us the roadmap to reform*. Speech presented at the Fourth Annual IES Research Conference. Washington, DC.

Lawrence-Lightfoot, S., & Davis, J. H. (1997). *The art and science of portraiture*. San Francisco, CA: Jossey-Bass.

Little, J. W. (2006). *Professional community and professional development in the learning-centered school*. Arlington, VA: National Education Association.

McDonald, J. M. (2014). *American school reform: What works, what fails, and why*. Chicago: University of Chicago Press.

McDonald, J. M., Isacoff, N. M., & Karin, D. (In press). *Data and teaching: Moving beyond magical thinking to effective practice*. New York, NY: Teachers College Press.

Meyers, C., & Brandt, C. (2015). *Implementation fidelity in education research*. New York, NY: Routledge.

Panero, N. S., & Talbert, J. E. (2013). *Strategic inquiry: Starting small for big results in education*. Cambridge, MA: Harvard Education Press.

Ravitch, D. (2010). *The death and life of the great American school system: how testing and choice are undermining education*. New York, NY: Basic Books.

Riessman, C. K. (2008). *Narrative methods for the human sciences*. Los Angeles, CA: Sage.

Schön, D., & McDonald, J. (1998). *Doing what you mean to do in school reform*. Providence: Brown University Press.

Schön, D. A. (1983). *The reflective practitioner: How professionals think in action*. New York: Basic Books.

School/Comprehensive Educational Plans (S/CEP). New York City Department of Education. Retrieved from http://schools.nyc.gov/community/OSFEP/CEP/CEP.htm

Spillane, J. P. (2012). Data in practice: Conceptualizing the data-based decision-making phenomena. *American Journal of Education, 118*(2), 113–141.

Spillane, J. P., Parise, L. M., & Sherer, J. Z. (2011). Organizational routines as coupling mechanisms: Policy, school administration, and the technical core. *American Educational Research Journal, 48*(3), 586–620.

Stake, Robert E. (1995). *The art of case study research*. Thousand Oak, CA: Sage.

Supovitz, J. A., & Klein, V. (2003). *Mapping a course for improved student learning: How innovative schools systematically use student performance data to guide improvement*. Philadelphia, PA: Consortium for Policy Research in Education.

Wiggins, G., & McTighe, J. (1998). *Understanding by design*. Alexandria, VA: Association for Supervision and Curriculum Development.

12

PROMISING PRACTICES OF DATA USE FOR LITERACY AND LANGUAGE DEVELOPMENT OF KINDERGARTEN STUDENTS

Tonya R. Moon, Catherine M. Brighton, Jordan M. Buckrop, Kerrigan Mahoney, and Marcia A. Invernizzi

Introduction

An ever-expanding body of empirical work on data use in an educational setting has occurred over the past 15 years, with a number of factors being shown to facilitate data use at the classroom level (e.g., Datnow, Park, & Wohlstetter, 2007). The bulk of this research has been conducted in contexts supportive of data use. What is less known is the role that the larger organizational level—the school district—plays in school- and classroom-level practices of data use. Secondarily, less is known about contexts not specifically known for excellence in data use. Therefore, the purpose of this chapter is to report on a study that focused specifically on the ways in which school districts facilitated, at all levels or not, systematic use of data for making instructional decisions.

Conceptual Lens and Study Assumptions

Research suggests that classroom, school, and district contexts shape data use in important ways. Districts play a central role in providing school administrators with the leadership and support to effectively engage in data use (Englert, Fries, Goodwin, Martin-Glenn, & Michael, 2004). For example, districts having strong central-office leadership committed to collecting and using data for continuous school improvement is an essential characteristic, as are providing training for school leadership in data literacy and a management information system for timely data access, for both school- and classroom-level decision-making (e.g., Armstrong & Anthes, 2001; Datnow et al., 2007).

Research has also indicated that school leaders are foundational in encouraging teacher buy in to successful data use. Without specific time set aside for collaborative planning, time for sharing effective assessments and teaching strategies, it is unlikely that the practices of using data for instructional decisions will happen (Thornton & Pereault, 2002). Also important to a data-friendly school culture is an atmosphere of trust and data-informed inquiry (Goldring & Berends, 2009; Knapp, Coplan, & Talbert, 2003; Sutherland, 2004). The degree of trust teachers and instructional staff have in the school leader will determine the degree of progress made with data use (Jazzar & Algozzine, 2006; Knapp, Swinnerton, Copland, & Monpas-Huber, 2006).

Another key element to successful data use is teacher buy in—the value of data increases when teachers participate in collaborative discussions that use data to focus on teaching and learning (Goldring & Berends, 2009). The school leader must offer resources and support to motivate teachers to use data on a regular basis (Supovitz & Klein, 2003).

Study Assumptions

A number of assumptions helped frame this study and its findings. We approached data collection and analysis with the assumption that there are a variety of types of data that teachers have access to on a daily basis in their classrooms. These types of data range from "on-the-fly" informal data that a teacher collects as a part of interactions with students, to more formal data that are collected on a routine basis and are mandated by the school and/or the district (e.g., benchmark assessments, weekly classroom assessments). We further acknowledged that there are conditions that influence the use of data by a teacher, some of which are internal to the teacher (e.g., beliefs) and others that are external to the teacher (e.g., database systems). Furthermore, we realize that there are processes for analyzing and interpreting the data that have implications for its use. For example, the use of professional learning communities (PLCs) is one avenue for aiding teachers in analyzing and interpreting data for the purpose of making instructional decisions. Furthermore, decisions can be made at the classroom level and/or at the individual-student level by the teacher when using data for instructional purposes.

Available Sources of Data

The data available to teachers and school-level administrators vary, in terms of where the data originate from (e.g., student assessments, other sources for reporting purposes), the timeframe when data collection occurs (e.g., interim, yearly over time), and level of student confidentiality (e.g., individual versus aggregate).

The data that teachers have access to, in theory, range from data collected by the teacher directly from the students and tied to specific classroom activities (e.g., teacher-developed assessments, classroom-embedded assessments), to data collected as part of record keeping and reported by school administration (e.g., attendance records, grades, discipline reports, graduation rates), to mandated data collected for accountability purposes at the district and/or state level (e.g., interim data, benchmark data).

Methods

Context of the Study

The promising practices reported here are based on a study investigating kindergarten teachers' data practices for instructional decisions in the areas of literacy and language arts. Each of the two participating school districts resided within a state that has an emphasis on oral language and reading within its curriculum framework at the kindergarten level. State-approved documents indicate that students should be immersed in a print-rich environment and engage in a variety of activities (e.g., drama, retelling, drawing, writing, listening, speaking, and discussions) to further understanding of language and literacy. In the following sections, we present the two cases, Wayne Hills[1] School District and Cornerstone School District, and highlight promising practices in the areas of data use messaging, in terms of consistency, provision of spaces and structures for data use, use of literacy coaches, and data-system infrastructure. Additionally, we outline ways that these promising practices could be further enhanced for more precise data usage, to guide programmatic effectiveness and instructional decision-making.

Wayne Hills School District

Wayne Hills School District's central mission was to provide high-quality education for all students, through a process of evaluation, continual improvement, strategic planning, analysis of data, and consensus-based decision-making. At the time of the study, fall membership was 3,230 K–12 students, with 254 students enrolled in kindergarten. One of the participating schools had not met its accreditation benchmark in the area of reading since the 2012 school year, but was accredited in all other content domains; the second school was fully accredited in all content domains, with all yearly and three-year accreditation benchmarks being achieved.

Cornerstone School District

Cornerstone School District's mission was to provide a world-class education that enabled every student to choose and pursue any post-K–12 endeavor. Fall membership for the district, at the time of the study, was 8,138 students K–12, with 526 students enrolled in kindergarten. Of the two schools participating in the study, both schools were fully accredited in all content domains, with all yearly and three-year accreditation benchmarks obtained.

Table 12.1 provides each district's kindergarten demographic data and Table 12.2 provides the same data by school.

TABLE 12.1 District Kindergarten Demographics

District	Racial/Ethnic Breakdown					Other Student Demographics			
	White, Non-Hispanic	Black	Hispanic	Multi-racial	Other	Disabilities	Econ. Disadv.	ESL	Migrant
Wayne Hills (N = 254)	63%	11%	14%	11%	1%	5%	62%	7%	–
Cornerstone (N = 526)	74%	13%	4%	75%	2%	10%	47%	4%	2%

TABLE 12.2 School Kindergarten Demographics

School	Racial/Ethnic Breakdown					Other Student Demographics			
	White, Non-Hispanic	Black	Hispanic	Multi-racial	Other	Disabilities	Econ. Disadv.	ESL	Migrant
Wayne Hills District									
Perkins (N = 99)	59%	17%	11%	12%	2%	9%	36%	8%	–
Westhaven (N = 76)	72%	7%	9%	10%	3%	8%	43%	5%	–
Cornerstone District									
Campbell (N = 70)	82%	11%	1%	7%	4%	10%	44%	<1%	–
Lewis Avenue (N = 92)	72%	12%	8%	6%	2%	10%	44%	6%	2%

Participants and Data Sources

Across the two school districts, two central-office administrators, four principals, 16 teachers, and four instructional-support staff (e.g., reading specialists) participated in the study. The data corpus included documents (e.g., lesson plans, district-planning documents), student test scores, observations, and interviews with school and district personnel. A subset of teachers' observations and interviews representing each school, all principals, reading specialists, and central-office personnel was considered most germane and, thus, was considered as the primary data source for this chapter.

Data Cycle

Across all four schools, there was a common cycle for the collection of formal literacy data (see Table 12.3). In both districts, a state-approved early-literacy assessment (SELA) was regularly administered as part of each district's accountability program, which was not mandated by the state.

180 Moon et al.

TABLE 12.3 Schools' Data Sources

Type of Assessment Data	Purpose of Assessment
Prekindergarten SELA	Used to create kindergarten classes in the fall; for those students that did not have a prekindergarten SELA, a modified version (letters and sounds) was administered during summer registration
SELA (fall)	Administered during weeks 3–4 of the kindergarten year (September), to form student groupings, set reading-specialist schedule, and establish teacher SMART goals in Wayne Hills District
Developmental Spelling Analysis (DSA)	Given if students topped out on the SELA spelling component
Quick Checks	Typically done every Friday within teacher-led group, by individual student
Formal Four-Week Assessment	Formal running records administered every 4–6 weeks, to report on student progress and teacher SMART goals
SELA (midyear)	Administered in January to only those students who were identified in the fall SELA administration, to assess their growth status; school-based decision to administer
SELA (spring)	Administered in April to every kindergarten student, as part of yearly-growth documentation; also used in assigning first-grade classrooms for the fall

Data Collection

Observation of formal teacher meetings (e.g., data meetings), formal meetings with school leaders (e.g., SMART[2] goal setting), classroom reading instruction, and semi-structured Think Aloud interviews formed the centerpieces of data collection. In addition, relevant documents were collected (e.g., lesson plans). Over the course of the study across all four schools, 132 classroom observations were conducted, ranging from 30 minutes to three hours, and 63 Think Aloud interviews (10–30 minutes each) were conducted, with five formal-data-team meetings observed. Each building principal was also interviewed twice, for an average of 25 minutes per interview, and each central-office staff member responsible for the district curriculum and instruction was interviewed for an average of 30 minutes each. On occasion, observations were also conducted outside of the structured reading-instruction time.

Data Analysis

Data analysis occurred throughout the study period, using the analytic techniques of Strauss and Corbin (1997), with the teacher or administrator being the key analytic unit. With the classroom observations and the Think Aloud interviews, open-coding was done, initially anchoring the codes in the existing literature. Following this open-coding round, axial coding was carried out, looking for connections among the initial codes, for identifying themes. During this second round of coding, data were read for the context in which the code was embedded (e.g., formal or informal processes), the ways in which the code was used (e.g., grouping of students, differentiation of instruction), and the conditions that facilitated, or not, the use of the code (e.g., SMART goal record keeping, team meetings).

This iterative process of coding involved two analysts independently coding the data, followed by a final coding of all the data by one of the lead researchers. Throughout the final stage of analysis, areas of divergence or convergence were sought across all of the data sources. In instances where data divergence appeared to exist, clarifying conversations were undertaken with other research-team members who had participated in data collection and the initial round of coding.

In the following section, we identify promising practices related to data use in kindergarten-level literacy contexts. Since data use practices can always be further refined, we also offer discussion of how these practices could be strengthened with some additional considerations in place. In both cases, what we learned directly from these cases, as well as our recommendations for future practice, we situate into the larger literature base related to best data use.

Promising Practices around Data Use

Promising Practice #1: Administrators Serve as Facilitators of Best Data Use Practice

The two district-level administrators in this study spoke about the importance of data use to guide curriculum and instruction in classrooms, schools, and districts.

Wayne Hills District Administrator (Ms. White)

Ms. White was the Director of Instruction for Wayne Hills School District, and was responsible for overseeing the development and implementation of the district's curricula as well as all staff development related to curriculum and instruction. She explained that assessment data served multiple levels and multiple purposes for the school system—from classroom and school levels to district level. She indicated that the district held the expectation that classroom-level data were to be used in two ways: 1) formative and instructive, to impact daily, in-the-moment instruction, and 2) district/state-mandated assessments (interim, benchmark, state), to structure the year, regarding student grouping, as well as other data to make it [student groupings] more fluid. Data at the school level were used for resource allotment (e.g., placement-reading specialists), to monitor student growth from fall to spring, and to ensure that each "teacher is aligned and

[she] is getting the same results, sometimes as an evaluation tool and sometimes just as a staff development tool" (#1, p. 2). Although the state early-literacy assessment (SELA) was given twice annually, in fall and spring, the administration of the assessment was voluntary, on the part of the school and district, and not mandated by the state. District-level data were used to guide decisions regarding educator effectiveness, curriculum and pacing guides, and resource allotment across schools, so as to support schools whose data indicated need for additional support.

Cornerstone District Administrator (Ms. Williams)

As part of her responsibility, Ms. Williams spent a large amount of time focusing on improving the elementary-literacy program through in-house professional development of literacy coaches, teachers, and principals. On a weekly basis, Ms. Williams and the literacy coaches had a standing meeting where time was spent talking about "kids and data, and how we're moving forward on that" (#1, p. 12). When asked about the district's philosophy regarding teachers' practice of data use, Ms. Williams indicated:

> Using data to drive instruction on a minute-by-minute, hour-by-hour, day-by-day basis, to ensure students are progressing. Those students that are not on level are actually being caught up. So, that data needs to be used. I wouldn't say even [on] a daily basis, but[, rather,] a minute-by-minute basis because, in a lesson, you need to be reacting to that.... We're really pushing teachers, now, to also identify what is the clear criteria, what is the clear outcome for what you're doing.
>
> (#1, p. 9)

Ms. Williams indicated that she had concerns about the teachers lacking clarity on clear learning goals. "I don't think our teachers clearly understand the need to have clarity on intended instructional outcomes" (#1, p. 9). She supported this statement by sharing a conversation she had with one of the teachers:

> When I'm [the teacher] doing the activity, words, and text for the word-bank activity, I don't know what my outcome is, or I don't even know what I'm expecting from my students. So, to have good data, I need to know what I am expecting? So, data on a day-by-day basis, on a lesson-by-lesson basis, with clear criteria?
>
> (#1, p. 9)

We met district-level administrators with knowledge about data use, including how using data takes a variety of shapes, depending on the context for the data use, from daily instructional modifications at the classroom level, to school-level distribution of limited human and material resources, to investment in professional-development experiences. Further, these district administrators established norms for communication systems that ranged from standing meetings between the district administrator and the building-level literacy coaches (e.g., "They report to me and I've given them the directive to focus on the 'why,' rather than just the 'do'" [#1, p. 7]), to weekly data-team meetings and the use of PLCs (e.g., "I have them, hold it [data meeting] an hour, hour and a half, once a month," with "PLCs occurring weekly" [#1, p. 10]). District-level administrators employed their own informal assessments of the school-level personnel, related to their readiness for data use (e.g., "My coaches vary knowledge-wise. I have one very strong coach, one coach that is learning more and more and getting stronger, and, then, I have three coaches that I'm trying to monitor" [#1, p. 8]). One district administrator indicated that she had been "trying to move principals in leading [asking]: 'What students have made no progress? What students have made below-average progress? What students have made average progress? And what student have made above [-average progress]?" (#1, p. 4). Where administrators seemed to stop, however, was in responding to the teachers' novice assessment literacy with in-the-moment coaching support. One administrator reflected on the lack of coaches building teacher capacity and, instead of simply relying on an "I'll tell you" approach, when responding to a teacher question, said, "Teachers ask a question, they want a tell, and, so, coaches will tell. Or they'll say, 'Let's think about that,' but not give them guidance, not scaffold their thinking" (#1, p. 8). This lack of support for teacher learning around data use limits teachers' ability to use data for informed pedagogical actions.

Practices Supportive of Administrators as Facilitators of Effective Data Use

The district-level support described by administrators in the two participating districts transferred to school leaders, in establishing goals for data use (Engler et al., 2004; Datnow et al., 2007). For example, Ms. Williams talked about looking at "data at least three times a year" and that she had specifically "worked with the principal there to use data" (#1, p. 4).

School-Leader Practices Supportive of Data Use by Teachers

One principal arranged the schedule so that there was a "common planning time every day, except one" (Rogers, #1, p. 14) for the teachers. On the one day, the team engaged in a PLC meeting. Furthermore, the principal acknowledged that she "looks at the data before" planning the PLC meeting. Although the principal acknowledged that she had to decide "what battle we choose right now" (#2, p. 6), she felt progress was being made: "They are meeting as a PLC on a weekly basis, they are coming with data, [and] they are making a common assessment, either in math or reading" (#2, p. 6).

Although teachers were required to create and maintain data notebooks that were also used for their end-of-year evaluation, teachers felt that the school leadership encouraged them to use their professional judgment in the types of data that were housed in the notebooks. For example, Ms. Biggers recalled, "We have our own way of collecting data. We can show, okay, this is the progress my kids have made. And they're [school leadership] fine with that" (#2, p. 3).

Teacher Buy In to Data Use for Instructional Decision-Making

Data notebooks were used in one school district, which housed both formal (e.g., SELA) and informal data (e.g., teacher reflections on class status, teacher communication with parents). These notebooks were required by the principals and were used in monthly meetings with each teacher. As one teacher commented "This is just something our principal asks us to do, which I think is a really good idea" (T. Bean, #3, p. 5).

Maximizing the Full Potential of the Promising Practice of Administrators as Facilitators of Data Use

Although each district and school participating in the study emphasized data use at varying levels for instructional decision-making, there remains room for growth to support more systematic use of data at all levels of the system. Districts, schools, and classrooms swim in a sea of data and, as such, need assistance and support in maximizing the benefits of data use for decision-making. Although the use of data is social in nature (Means, Chen, DeBarger, & Padilla, 2010), the extent to which data are utilized (i.e., interpreted and acted upon) is dependent upon individuals involved in the process. Building a system to increase administrators' and teachers' data-literacy knowledge and skills, and to demonstrate how data connect to pedagogy is one step towards facilitating data use at all levels.

Administrators can focus their own data use on a larger context than simply state or district data. For example, district administrators can not only communicate expectations that go beyond accountability measures for data but can also demonstrate how other types of data influence district-level decisions. Although student achievement and growth are critical for districts, schools, and teachers, research indicates that teachers find use in data that focuses on the whole child (Anderson, Leithwood, & Strauss, 2010). Setting the expectation to go beyond student achievement, by district administrators, sends the message that, although achievement is important, understanding the causes of such achievement or strategies to help in raising achievement are critical.

Promising Practice #2: Consistent Messages Sent by Administrators Regarding Spaces and Structures

There was an expectation from the district leadership that principals would lead teachers in conversations around essential literacy knowledge and skills that students were to have acquired. An example of this expectation was communicated in the district-developed pacing guides: "By the end of January, we would like our students to have an understanding of concept of word" (Cornerstone District pacing guide). In order to achieve these identified goals, building leaders sent consistent and aligned messages regarding literacy development, as it related to the use of data: 1) teachers should use data to describe where their students are in their literacy development, 2) teachers should consider each student's development, in comparison to prescribed benchmarks, and 3) based on the teacher descriptions, teachers should make intentional instructional decisions, so that students continue to progress toward the targeted goal(s).

Alongside stated expectations, principals attempted to further operationalize the use of data to guide conversations about students' literacy development, through the establishment of *spaces* set aside for collaborative meetings (e.g., Professional Learning Communities [PLCs]) and *structures*, such as progress-monitoring templates, to guide teachers' thinking, in terms of how students performed in relation to the essential literacy skills, and what instructional next steps they might take to further students' literacy development.

Spaces

In both districts, school-level data meetings occurred outside of typical PLC meetings. At Westhaven (Wayne Hills District), the data meetings were conducted by grade level and included the building principal leading the establishment of individual-teacher SMART goals. In the Cornerstone School District, the data meetings were also known as School Improvement Meetings and represented members across the school. The principals led the meeting, with the assistant principal, one teacher per grade level, one Title I teacher, one special educator, and the building literacy coach in attendance. The purpose of this monthly meeting was to look at school-level data from a broad perspective. One principal explained:

> I try to have them hold those data meetings once a month for 60–90 minutes, focusing on big-picture things, so they are different from PLC meetings, which are held weekly. They are talking about kids, and they should be talking about formative assessments they are using to measure progress for a specific essential skill or understanding.
>
> *(Ms. Williams, #1, p. 10)*

Structures

The two districts differed in how they approached the structures related to progress monitoring and the degree of formality of the structures. In the Wayne Hills District, teachers employed the use of SMART goals to document targeted students' identified areas of academic struggle in literacy, and to establish companion strategies designed to remediate the students' weaknesses. At Westhaven, SMART goals were set in collaboration with the principal, whereas, in Perkins, the goals were set by the teachers themselves. In both instances, SMART goals focused exclusively on struggling students, as identified by the SELA scores.

> Basically, we just write up, kind of, a plan, and show where they are and what we're going to do to help them improve in that area. I would say, "I'm responsible for this," or "I'm going to give so-and-so this to work on." Then, we give them a certain amount of time to reach that goal, and, then, we reevaluate and see if we can stop with that goal or if we need to just continue with it until they improve. So, it can be different things, different strategies to get them where they need to be.
>
> *(Warren, #1, p. 5)*

Data notebooks were used in the Cornerstone District only for Title I students, to chronicle targeted students' growth toward formal goals. The students experienced formal assessments every three weeks in the relevant subject area (primarily literacy, for the purposes of this study, although the system was also used in math, as well). During the intervening weeks, following the initial formal assessments, the reading specialists or literacy coaches conducted two separate interventions with the students, followed by the post-intervention formal assessment after three weeks, to determine the students' progress toward the targeted goals. Additionally, the notebooks were home to regularly scheduled less-formal assessments, such as Quick Checks and weekly assessments. These three-ring data notebooks included entries chronicling the artifacts of the formal assessments, and anecdotal notes on Post-its or in teachers' handwriting, tied to the interventions. These data notebooks served numerous purposes: they were used to document targeted-students' growth over the course of the school year, during parent/teacher conferences, and for a portion of the teachers' performance evaluation, related to meeting students' needs. Reading specialists were expected to also keep data notebooks, as well as the kindergarten teachers.

> I took this data notebook and showed [the principal] things I'm doing in the classroom, running records I've taken, all of my data, and everything you see in this notebook. She [the principal] just goes over it with us and discusses if she has any concerns for us, that we can then take back and work

on. At the end of the year, we have our formal evaluation, and its included as part of that.

(Bryan #2, p. 6)

One reading teacher commented on the notebook and her use of it for documentation: "What we do is keep a record [for] each of the three weeks with what we are working on and what their scores are" (Baring #2, p. 1).

In both districts, progress monitoring focused exclusively on the lowest-performing students, rather than considering students across the full academic spectrum. These were limited targeted-growth opportunities for only those most-struggling students. Although the structures between the SMART goal setting and the data notebooks shared several commonalities, the primary focus of the former (SMART goals) was on achieving the intended outcome. By contrast, the data notebooks, which included artifacts and evidence from over an instructional and assessment cycle, permitted teachers the opportunity to reflect on more than just the outcome; teachers were able to also focus on the processes leading to the student outcomes.

Maximizing the Full Potential of the Promising Practice of Spaces and Structures

It was noted in the study data that, although there was the clear and unwavering expectation of collaborative meetings through PLC-like meetings, there were also limited understandings of how to engage in such gatherings to leverage their full potential. For example, one district administrator indicated that all the principals were on board with the PLC meetings, but that they were unsure of what to do (e.g., "They're still trying to figure out how, when, [and] where" [Ms. Williams #1, p. 9]). Common obstacles known to deter the successful implementation of PLCs included the lack of team norms, a lack of trust among participating members, a lack of team goals, leading to a lack of purpose, communication barriers between meetings, and a lack of identified essential student-learning outcomes (Fullan, 2005; Reichstetter, 2006).

Furthermore, because of the limited understandings that teachers held regarding early-literacy development, the structures (e.g., data notebooks) designed to facilitate data use, in terms of instructional decision-making, often were used in a procedural or rule-driven manner.

Promising Practice #3: Literacy Coaches Connect Literacy Data Directly with Instructional Practice

In the Cornerstone School District, literacy coaches, under the supervision of Ms. Williams, played multiple roles focused on improving teachers' growth and refining their practices for serving students, in the context of literacy. These coaches rotated between schools, serving each elementary school for a minimum of a full day per week or more, depending on the size of the school. This additional resource was designed to help teachers improve their practice through connecting literacy data to the creation of lesson plans.

> [Literacy coaches] do trainings, they co-teach with teachers, they help plan with teachers, [and] they do some modified lesson studies with teachers as we implement the SELA plans. They've gone in and taught lessons for teachers, so they can model. They look at the data with teachers after [the] beginning of the year, midyear with all [the] teachers, and throughout, as teachers ask for them.
>
> *(Ms. Williams #1, p. 3)*

Although teachers did not elaborate specifically on changes that were made as a result of looking at data with the literacy coach, there was the opportunity for teachers to meet either individually or as a team twice a week with the coach. One principal commented, "I encourage them. A lot of times, what's good for one is good for all, so, if it's a planning time where they all can sit with [a literacy coach], that they can do that, as well" (p. 1, #14). One teacher commented further about meeting with the literacy coach: "We also keep a school-wide spreadsheet that any kindergarten teacher and [the literacy coach] can look at, as we meet for our PLC [time. We look at those children . . . and what they need for their intervention-enrichment section of the day" (B. Tallent, #1, p. 5).

Maximizing the Full Potential of the Promising Practice of Literacy Coaches

Three areas of challenge seemed to impact the ability of the coaches to fully actualize the potential strength of the literacy-coaching model. The first area was the limited knowledge on both the part of the coaches and teachers regarding data use and lesson planning. Although some coaches held a reading-specialist endorsement and were familiar with the development of early literacy, none of the coaches had expertise or familiarity with how to translate the literacy data directly into lesson planning. Compounding this incomplete knowledge regarding data use and lesson planning were several other practical challenges. In all instances, coaches rotated among schools, and, then, further, rotated among grade levels within each school. This rotation schedule limited the amount of work time with individual teachers on collecting relevant assessment data, and on how those data could be turned into information for lesson planning.

Although the districts faced challenges in the ways in which literacy coaches helped teachers, there are strategies that could be utilized to ensure a successful coaching model, regardless of the particular coaching approach implemented. For the most part, the literacy coaches in the study had had success as classroom teachers and had more content knowledge in the area of literacy development than the teachers they were coaching. The lack of a professional-development program specifically targeting coaches, to assist them in better carrying out their responsibilities, was a noted weakness, however. Ongoing professional development in the areas of understanding how to coach/teach adult learners, bettering communication skills, and expanding expertise in innovative instructional and assessment practices are all areas that would have increased the power of the coaching model implemented. Furthermore, having a system for better allocating coaches' responsibilities and time would have also increased the power of the coaching model. Although each coach was assigned to schools on designated days, what occurred on those days tended to be more of a reactive approach to coaching, rather a proactive approach to coaching teachers. Coaches, teachers, and others' (e.g., reading specialists, principals) responsibilities should be clearly outlined on a regular basis, to maximize the time spent directly working with teachers.

Promising Practice #4: Districts Developed and Utilized Electronic Systems for Managing Data

In these cases, we observed how educators at the classroom, school, and district levels utilized an electronic system for assessing interim data on student literacy knowledge and skills, which was firmly established in the state "culture" and easily accessed by teachers and school leaders.

Research (Means et al., 2010) indicates that teachers and school leaders need one-stop integrated access to data that can be used for decision-making. The data can provide guidance in several areas: 1) monitoring individual student needs to ensure appropriate placement in groups, interventions, classrooms, and programs (e.g., programs for gifted and talented students), 2) informing needed modification of curriculum materials, 3) shaping needed support for teachers and other instructional personnel, 4) aiding in the decision to adopt, adapt, and evaluate programs, and 5) bolstering communications with external audiences.

The SELA assessments used in the two districts' case studies were accompanied by an online entry-and-reporting system that was accessible from within the schools by the school leadership and teachers. The system was designed to allow school personnel to easily manage the formal literacy-screening data from the SELA assessments. As part of the assessment system, students were identified as needing additional support if they did not meet the established benchmarks. Furthermore, there were planning resources complementing the reporting system, which included access to electronic lesson plans aligned with key literacy areas.

Maximizing the Promising Practice of an Electronic System

Although there was a robust electronic system associated with the SELA assessments, several areas warrant additional considerations, in order to actualize the full potential of an electronic system for storing data that are easily accessible by educators.

First, the electronic system was external to the study sites, housed in the office of the testing service, which was unaffiliated with the state department of education or the individual school districts, thus limiting the warehousing of data to only the SELA assessments. For educators to use data in an ongoing manner to support student learning, there should be an internal data infrastructure to warehouse the data, available to the right users at the right time. The first step toward this infrastructure is identifying users' information needs. For example, tracking individual-students' attendance patterns is different than tracking individual-students' achievement patterns on weekly common formative assessments. Yet, having access to both types of data may help teachers and support staff identify relationships between students' absenteeism and their literacy growth over time. It is important that internal systems allow the linking of data from different assessments, as well as the linking to non-assessment data, in order to monitor student progress over time.

Teachers' limited understanding of literacy and its associated data, and how those data map onto the development of literacy and language in young children, led to total reliance on the SELA system's suggested groupings, which, in most instances, became static over time. Furthermore, with limited knowledge and understanding of children's literacy and language development, allowing teachers to develop a lesson plan by self-selecting from a database of literacy strategies may not align with what would be instructionally appropriate for any given student.

Finally, both external data systems, like the SELA assessment system, and internal data systems should enhance teachers' implementation of differentiated instruction, in support of all learners, from struggling to advanced. For example, if the assessment system for the formal literacy assessments interfaced with locally developed common formative assessments, teachers could triangulate the information to get a more complete picture of students and their needs, and, then, correspond with appropriate instructional plans.

Conclusions

These cases, each comprised of two districts and two elementary schools each within them, paint the picture of coordinated efforts related to data use, for the purposes of improving student learning. Both school divisions signaled that commitment in their stated mission statements and both central-office administrators spoke about the importance of data use for numerous reasons, ranging from resource allocation to adjusting classroom instruction. Principals spoke about their expectations for teachers' practices related to data use, such as setting and monitoring learning goals for students, and their expectations for chronicling the learners' progress using notebooks or other structures. Further, teachers partnered with literacy coaches to provide more literacy support to students, especially those students who struggled to meet expected thresholds. Finally, the districts represented in these cases demonstrated their commitment to data use by utilizing electronic resources for capturing and warehousing formal data. There was an evident system for data use. The story of coordinated data use in schools is far more complex, however. Although the school districts signaled commitment in mission statements and investments in electronic resources, and despite central-office and building-level administrators insisting that routines and practices occur, literacy coaches and teachers were often unclear about exactly how to proceed. The messages were being sent that these practices were important, and all participants complied with the expectations to the best of their ability. Absent from these cases, at all levels of the system, however, was evidence of a deep understanding (and confidence about that understanding) about how to harness the power of data for strategic purposes.

Recommendations

Increasing the use of data for decision-making, from the district to the classroom level, can increase effectiveness for educators and the students for whom they hold responsibility. To improve data use by teachers and school leaders, district leaders can ensure that there is a robust infrastructure that houses both internal and external student data, inclusive of both academic and nonacademic data, while, at the same time, protecting student privacy; ensure that all individuals with access to the data system can interpret and use the data in informative ways, from instructional planning, to resource allotment, to evaluation of programs and decisions; and establish structures and expectations district wide for collaboration among educators engaging in data-based decision-making.

For their part, school leaders can support the district's message of data use, as well as ensure that each teacher has access to and understands the implementation of a content-rich curriculum that has embedded in it the use of data for making instructional decisions. Furthermore, school leaders can ensure that there are staff-development opportunities specifically focused on data use training, inclusive of all educators responsible for student learning (e.g., classroom teachers, literacy coaches, reading specialists, gifted teachers, special-education teachers, Title I teachers, and ESL teachers). Staff development should specifically focus on helping educators ask relevant instructional questions that can be addressed by available data, organize and analyze data for information to address the identified questions, and create constructive conversations around data and instruction among colleagues (e.g., teacher to teacher; teacher to literacy coach).

Acknowledgements

The authors would like to thank the Spencer Foundation for their generous grant support of this work.

Notes

1 Pseudonyms used to protect the identity of the school districts and study participants.
2 SMART is an acronym standing for Specific, Measurable, Achievable, Realistic, and Time-bound.

References

Anderson, S., Leithwood, K., & Strauss, T. (2010). Leading data use in schools: Organizational conditions and practices at the school and district level. *Leadership and Policy in Schools, 9*, 292–327. doi:10.1080/15700761003731492

Armstrong, J., & Anthes, K. (2001). How data can help. *American School Board Journal, 188*(11), 38–47.

Datnow, A., Park, V., & Wohlstetter, P. (2007). *Achieving with data: How high-performing school systems use data to improve instruction for elementary students*. Los Angeles, CA: University of Southern California, Rossier School of Education, Center on Educational Governance. Retrieved from www.newschools.org/news

Englert, K., Fries, D., Goodwin, B., Martin-Glenn, M., & Michael, S. (2004). *Understanding how principals use data in a new environment of accountability*. Aurora, CO: Mid-Continent Research for Education and Learning. Retrieved from https://ericed.gov/?id+ED484396

Fullan, M. (2005). Learning communities writ large. In R. DuFour, R. Eaker, & R. DuFour (Eds.), *On common ground: The power of professional learning communities* (pp. 209–223). Bloomington, IN: Solution Tree.

Goldring, E., & Berends, M. (2009). *Leading with data: Pathways to improve your school*. Thousand Oaks, CA: Corwin Press.

Jazzar, M., & Algozzine, B. (2006). *Critical issues in educational leadership*. Boston, MA: Pearson.

Knapp, M. S., Copland, M., & Talbert, J. E. (2003). *Leading for learning: Reflective tools for school and district leaders*. Seattle, WA: University of Washington Center for the Study of Teaching and Policy. Retrieved from www.wallacefoundation.org

Knapp, M. S., Swinnerton, J. A., Copland, M. A., & Monpas-Huber, J. (2006). *Data-informed leadership in education*. Seattle, WA: Center for the Study of Teaching and Policy, University of Washington. Retrieved from www.wallacefoundation.org

Means, B., Padilla, C., & Gallagher, L. (2010). *Use of education data at the local level: From accountability to instructional improvement*. Washington, DC: U.S. Department of Education, Office of Planning, Evaluation, and Policy Development.

Reichstetter, R. (2006). Defining a professional learning community. E & R Research Alert, Report No. 06.05. Retrieved from www.brokersofexpertise.com/cognoti/content/file/resources/docments/33/338ea0d4/338ea0d4aae30061442847e6afcd0991753a8f63/DefiningaProfessionalLearningCommunity.pdf

Strauss, A., & Corbin, J. M. (1997). *Grounded theory in practice*. Thousand Oaks, CA: Sage.

Supovitz, J. A., & Klein, V. (2003). *Mapping a course for improved student learning: How innovative schools systematically use student performance data to guide improvement*. Philadelphia, PA: Consortium for Policy Research in Education. Retrieved from www.cpre.org

Sutherland, S. (2004). Creating a culture of data use for continuous improvement: A case study of an Edison project school. *American Journal of Evaluation, 25*(3), 277–293. DOI: 10.1177/109821400402500302

Thornton, B., & Perreault, G. (2002). Becoming a data-based leader: An introduction. *NASSP Bulletin, 86*(630), 86–96.

INDEX

Note: Page numbers in *italic* indicate a figure and page numbers in **bold** indicate a table on the corresponding page.

academic performance data **134**, 134–135
accountability 1, 37, 63, 80–81, 96, 109–110, 135, 143; culture of 172; data collection for purposes of 177–178; data-driven decision-making (DDDM) 112–113, 116; state-approved early-literacy assessment (SELA) 179; in team collaboration 150
adaptation 163, 165
Adding It Up (NRC) 99
adjustment in practice: corrective adjustment 170–171; exacerbating adjustment 168–170; illustrations 165–167, **166–167**; managing adjustment 168–171
administrators: as facilitators of best data use practices 181–184; message consistency regarding spaces and structures 185–187
aggregated data *102*, 102–104, **103**, *104*
aims for teacher data use 112–125; findings 117–124; implications 124–125; matchmaking as data use aim 118–121, 125; methods 115–116; picking the right bullseye 113–115
ambitious science teaching 82, 92
assessment literacy 15, 16
assessments: asset-based interpretations of student work 91–92; curriculum-embedded 41; developed with subsequent action in mind 173; double-dipping practice 19–21, 25; focusing as problematic 169; frequency of 69–70; multiple-choice 26, 69, 71–72, 74, 76, 102, 109, 169; restricted response quizzes and tests 66; in school district data use case study **180**; of school-level personnel and readiness for data use 183; state-approved early-literacy assessment (SELA) 179, **180**, 182, 186, 188–190; using for instructional change 70–71; validity of 168; varying 70; *see also specific assessments*
at-risk students 128

backward planning 162, 168, 172
behavior, student 135, **136**, 137, 139
Bloom's Taxonomy 71–72
buy-in, teacher 177, 184

case study: aims for teacher data use 113–125; collective 19; data-driven decision-making (DDDM) practice 113–125; learning trajectory 47–61; meaningful data use to teach for understanding in middle-school science 80–93; middle-school-mathematics-teacher workgroup 97–109; school-based decision-making teams 128–143; school district data use 176–191; science

teachers' assessment practices case study 63–77; sensemaking 33–41; value of 64
climate, teaching 153; see also collegiality; teaching cultures and collegiality
coding of data 47–48, 68, 132–133, 148, 165, 170, 181
cognition 71–73, 76
collaboration: decision-making 128, 133, 140; instructional planning 155–156; providing structured time for 146; teaching cultures and collegiality 146–147, 148, 153–154; team collaboration 145–160; vertical and horizontal collaborative structures 148, 153–155
collegiality 146–147; see also climate; teaching cultures and collegiality
compliance: over commitment 114; thoughtful 99, 109
conflicting beliefs and practices 156–158
contextualization 22–25, 26; to curriculum goals and sequencing plan 24; to school and community events 24–25; to students 22–24
continuous improvement 5
conversations: data-centered 91; teacher workgroup 96–109; variance in quality 146
co-teaching 34–37, 41
culture: of accountability 172; data-friendly school 177; teaching 146–147, 148, 153–155, 159
curriculum-embedded assessments 41
cycle of inquiry 129–130

data: concept of 4–5; context of 6; meaningful 90–93; meaning of 81, 145–146; nonacademic 128–143
data-driven decision-making (DDDM) 6, 30, 96, 112–125, 191; as activity trap 113; bus route narrative and 112; effective team collaboration and 145
data-driven initiatives 80–81
data-driven instruction: adjustments in practice 163–174; assumptions of 162, 168; conclusions from 171–173; corrective adjustment 170–171; critical response to 162–174; exacerbating adjustment 168–170; illustrations 165–167, **166–167**; implications 173; managing adjustment 168–171; promising practices 173–174; theory of action 162–163, 165, **167**, 167–168, 173
data for sensemaking 31, 32

data-informed instruction 162
data management, electronic systems for 189–190; system, school district 149
data notebooks 184, 186–187 data portfolio 37
data uniformity 37
data use: aims for teacher 112–125; concept of 5; as contested sensemaking 81–82; definitions of 15; effective team collaboration and 145–160; learner-centered 170; meaningful 90–93, 100–109; meaning of 81; productive practices 96
"Data Use and Educational Improvement" initiative 5–6
data use strategy 48, 51–53, *52*, 58, 60, **60**
Data Wise framework 66
DDDM see data-driven decision-making
decision-making teams, school-based 128–143
de-privatization of practice 156
Developmental Reading Assessment (DRA) 135
double dipping 19–21, 25

early-warning system 142
educational improvement: better schooling, differing ideas of 3; concept of 5; continuous 5
Educational Support Team (EST) 130–135, 138–142
electronic systems for managing data 189–190; see also data management
embedded checks for understanding 41
English Language Arts (ELA): ability-group placements in 149; assessments, teachers' use of data gathered from 18–27; contextualization 22–25, 26; data collection 19; double dipping 19–21, 25; findings 19–25; practical considerations 26–27; student performance data 19; tracking systems 21–22, 25–26
English-Language Learner (ELL): assessment of 172; matchmaking and 117
Episodes of Pedagogical Reasoning (EPR) 99–100
evidence-based explanatory models 92
Evidence for the Classroom initiative 7–10
experts/expertise: expertise on teacher teams 146; manufactured expertise 89; methods for identifying 17–18; teacher expertise 16–18; valuing teacher expertise and judgment 151–153

Index

family circumstances, performance and **136**, 138
feedback to students 75
fidelity in implementation 163
formative assessments: enhancement with learning trajectories 45; in school-based decision-making teams case study 134–135; in science education 68–71, 75–76; standardized testing 63

gifted program, matchmaking and 117

health, student **136**, 137–138
holistic orientation to discussing students 150

implementation, fidelity in 163
Individualized Education Programs (IEPs) 37
inquiry teams, formalized teacher-led 30
instruction, data-driven *see* data-driven instruction; data informed instruction
instructional change, using assessment for 70–71
instructional decision-making, using data for 70–71
instructional inquiry, whole-school models of 30
instructional planning, collective action in 155–156
instructional practice, linking interpretations to 105–109, **106–109**
Instructional Quality Assessment (IQA) 99
interpretations, linking to instructional practice 105–109, **106–109**
interviews: in aims for teacher data use case study 121–124; data-driven instruction case study 164, 168; in science teachers' assessment practices case study 66–68; in team collaboration case study 148; Think Aloud 19, 21–26, 180

kindergarten students, promising practices for data use for literacy and language development of 176–191

language development of kindergarten students 176–191
learning community 10–12
learning targets 84–85, 170
learning trajectory 44–61; case study 47–61; conceptual framework 45, 47; implications for use 60–61; positive impact on instructional decision-making 45; as promising practice 59–60; reflections on use of 58–59; sensemaking 45, 47; visual models 45, 50–51, 54–55, 58–59, **60**
linking interpretations to instructional practice 105–109, **106–109**
literacy coaches 182–183, 187–191
literacy of kindergarten students 176–191

manufactured expertise 89
mapping theory to practice 171
matchmaking: case study 117–121; as data use aim 118–121, 125; investigating *versus* 114–115, 124–125; meaning of term 114; teachers' alternatives to 121–124
mathematics: curriculum prepackaged assessments in 18–19; learning trajectory 44–61; middle-school teacher workgroup 97–109; open-area model 45, *46*, 49–50, *50*, *54*, 54–56, 58, **60**; open array 53, 55–56, **60**; visual models 45, 50–51, 54–55, 58–59, **60**
MAXQDA qualitative coding software 148
MDL (Model of Domain Learning) 17–18, 27
meaning, making of *see* sensemaking
meaningful data 90–93
meaningful data use 90–93, 100–109
Measures of Student Learning 169
mentoring of new teachers 154–155
Middle-School Mathematics in the Institutional Setting of Teaching (MIST) project 97
modeling-based-inquiry in science teaching 84, 92
Model of Domain Learning (MDL) 17–18, 27
MTSS (multitiered systems of supports) 129, 130, 132, 135
multiple-choice assessment 26, 69, 71–72, 74, 76, 102, 109, 169
multiplicative reasoning, learning trajectory for 45, *46*
multitiered systems of supports (MTSS) 129, 130, 132, 135

National Research Council 64
Next Generation Science Standards (NGSS) 63, 68, 73–75
No Child Left Behind 1, 98, 164
nonacademic data, use to identify and support struggling students 128–143

nonacademic performance data: family circumstances **136**, 138; school attendance **136**, 137; in school-based decision-making teams case study 135–138, **136**; student behavior 135, **136**, 137, 139; student health **136**, 137–138
notebooks: data 184, 186–187; Quality Assessment in Science (QAS) Notebook 65–68

organizational conditions of data use 8
organizational learning 5–6

PBIS (Positive Behavior Interventions and Supports) 129, 130, 135, 137
performance data: academic, in school-based decision-making teams case study **134**, 134–135; nonacademic 135–138, **136**; sensemaking and 40
planning: backward 162, 168, 172; collective action in instructional 155–156
PLC *see* professional learning community
Positive Behavior Interventions and Supports (PBIS) 129, 130, 135, 137
poverty, impact on student learning of 164, 174
principals: district leadership expectations of 185; expectations for teachers' data use practices 190; role in teacher collaboration 159
Principles to Actions (NCTM) 99
problem-solving protocol, for school-based decision-making teams 129–130
professional development: collaborative workgroups 97; features of effective 65; investment in 183; literacy coaches 189; in science education 63–68, 76–77
professional learning community (PLC): learning trajectory research and 44, 47–49, 51–56, 59; school district 177, 183, 185, 187; science teachers' assessment practices 65–71, 75, 77; spaces set aside for 185
promising practices 16, 17, 19–21; administrators as facilitators of best data use practices 181–184; collective action in instructional planning 155–156; contextualization 22–25, 26; curriculum-embedded assessments 41; data-driven instruction 173–174; for data use for literacy and language development of kindergarten students 176–191; deliberation of varied beliefs and practices 156–158; double dipping 19–21, 25; for instructionally meaningful data use 100–109; jointly examining data on all students 149–151; learning trajectory 59–60; linking interpretations to instructional practice 105–109, **106–109**; literacy coaches 182–183, 187–191; looking beyond aggregated data to consider student thinking *102*, 102–104, **103**, *104*; for meaningful data use when teaching science for understanding 80, 82, 90–93; message consistency of administrators regarding spaces and structures 185–187; opportunities for teachers to develop new assessments 76; practical considerations 26–27; quality over quantity 100–101; in school district data use case study 181–190; sensemaking 41–42; in team collaboration 145, 148, 159; tracking systems 21–22, 25–26; vertical and horizontal collaborative structures 148, 153–155

Quality Assessment in Science (QAS) Notebook 65–68

reframing 173
release time 149
Research Alliance for New York City Schools 163–164
research on data use by Spencer Foundation 1–12; background and rationale 2–4; concepts of focus 4–6; early efforts in "Data Use and Educational Improvement" 6–7; Evidence for the Classroom 7–10; framework for "Data Use and Educational Improvement" initiative 5–6; learning stance 8–9; request for proposals (RFP) 7–10
running records 19–20

scaffolding 76–77
SCEP (School Comprehensive Educational Plan) 170
school-based decision-making teams 128–143; academic performance data **134**, 134–135; integration of multiple

data sources 138–139; nonacademic performance data 135–138, 136; organization 139–142, *141*; participants 131–132; problem-solving protocol 129–130; ; site selection 131; standard-treatment protocol 129; team organization 139–142, *141*
School Comprehensive Educational Plan (SCEP) 170
school district data use 176–191; conceptual lens for 176–178; conclusions for 190–191; context of study 178, **179**; data analysis 180–181; data collection 180; data cycle 179; data sources 177–179, **180**; electronic systems for managing data 189–190; message consistency of administrators regarding spaces and structures 185–187; methods 178–181; participants 179; promising practices 181–190; recommendations from 191; study assumptions 177
School Improvement Meetings 185
Schoolwide Information System (SWIS) 137
science assessment: dimensions of effective 64, **65**, 66, 69–77; practices 63–77
science education: ambitious science teaching 82; meaningful data use to teach for understanding in middle school 80–93; Next Generation Science Standards (NGSS) 63, 68, 73–75; professional development 63–68, 76–77
science education in middle school 80–93; study method 83–84; theoretical perspective 81–82
science teachers' assessment practices 63–77; analysis 68; data sources 66–68; dimensions of effective assessment 64, **65**, 66, 69–77; interviews 66–68; methods 65–68; notebooks 66–68; project description and participants 65–66; Quality Assessment in Science (QAS) Notebook 65–68; summer institutes and PLC sessions 67–68
SELA (state-approved early-literacy assessment) 179, **180**, 182, 186, 188–190
sense-givers 31–32
sensemaking 31–42; case studies, cross-case comparison of 40–41; case study (Ms. Apple) 33, 34–37, 40; case study (Ms. Edwards) 33–34, 37–40; data for 31, 32; data use as contested 81–82;

data use as form of 143; definition of 82; description of 31–32; learning trajectories and 45, 47; promising practices 41–42; research study methods 32–34
separation of research and practice 171
SMART goals 180–181, 185–187
special education (SPED) 117, 121
Specific, Measurable, Achievable, Realistic, and Time-bound (SMART) goals 180–181, 185–187
Spencer Foundation 1–2, 163
standardized testing: data-driven instruction 162, 168; data used as starting point for inquiry 96–110; emphasis on 63; interim 163
state-approved early-literacy assessment (SELA) 179, **180**, 182, 186, 188–190
struggling students 128–143
student behavior 135, **136**, 137, 139
student health **136**, 137–138
student thinking *102*, 102–104, **103**, *104*
summative assessments 134–135
SWIS (Schoolwide Information System) 137

teacher expertise 16–18
teaching cultures and collegiality 146–147; see also climate, teaching
teaching for understanding 80–93
teaching to the test 112
team collaboration 145–160; collective action in instructional planning 155–156; deliberation of varied beliefs and practices 156–158; findings 148–158; implications 159–160; jointly examining data on all students 149–151; literature and framework for 145–147; methods 147–148; problem-solving process 150; valuing teacher expertise and judgment 151–153; vertical and horizontal collaborative structures 148, 153–155
team meetings, data use 16
teams: grade-level 41; school-based decision-making 128–143; team of teachers, in middle-school science education 80–93
theory of action 7, 162–163, 165, **167**, 167–168, 173
Think Aloud interviews 19, 21–26, 180
tracking systems 21–22, 25–26

understanding, embedded checks for 41
Understanding by Design (Wiggins and McTighe) 168

vertical and horizontal collaborative structures 148, 153–155

video recordings, of teacher workgroups 98–99
visual models 45, 50–51, 54–55, 58–59, **60**

workgroup conversations 96–109

PGMO 04/27/2018